Automatic
Keyword Classification
for Information Retrieval

Automatic
Keyword Classification
for Information Retrieval

KAREN SPARCK JONES
Computer Laboratory
University of Cambridge

ARCHON BOOKS

Published in the United States of America by
Archon Books, The Shoe String Press, Inc.,
995 Sherman Avenue, Connecticut 06514

© Butterworth & Co (Publishers) Ltd, London 1971

ISBN 0-208-01201-X

Filmset and Printed in England

Contents

Introduction

This book is primarily a research monograph, in which the discussion of the main topics has been broadened so that they are related to their surrounding context in information retrieval as a whole; it is not a textbook, and no attempt has therefore been made to justify the choice of topic, or account for the use of certain concepts, or to provide an elementary description of either. For instance, in Chapter 1, it is assumed that the reader is familiar with the idea of using keywords in information retrieval: I have not considered the relation between this kind of retrieval device and a controlled thesaurus or descriptor set, or that between the use of simple class lists as document descriptions and the use of descriptions with a syntactic structure, for example. Equally, in Chapter 2, I have made use of recall/precision ratios as a means of characterising retrieval performance, without justification or argument; but this does not mean that I am unaware of the difficulties of doing this, or of the attention which has been devoted to, and controversy which has raged round, this subject; it is simply that from the point of view of my main purpose it is reasonable to use these ratios, if only as expository devices, and I have again assumed that the reader is acquainted with the ideas and problems which are involved.

In general plan, the book is divided into three sections. The first, comprising Chapters 1 to 4, deals with the problems which arise if we want to use a keyword classification for retrieval, and if we attempt to construct one automatically, and presents the approaches we have adopted in trying to solve these problems, or at least in examining them in detail. The second section, which consists of Chapters 5 to 8, is devoted to an account of the actual experiments we have carried out, which are presented on the one hand as of interest in their own right, since they represent the most extended investigation which has been carried out in this area to date, and on the other as an example of the kind of research which is required if the questions posed in Section I are to be answered. In the third section, Chapters 9 and 10, the conclusions to be drawn from these experiments are presented, and an analysis of the reasons for our results is attempted. The relations between these results and those of other projects, and between the approach to the construction and use of automatic keyword classifications presented in the body of the book and some which have been proposed elsewhere, are also considered, and some lines of work which require investigation in the future are noted.

I am grateful to the Office for Scientific and Technical Information of the Department of Education and Science for funding most of the experimental work on which this book is based; to the Royal Society for supporting me during its writing; to Professor M. V. Wilkes for permitting me to use the Cambridge University Computer Titan, and to the staff of the Computer Laboratory for enabling me to do so.

I would particularly like to thank Mr. C. W. Cleverdon for providing our test collection, and for general advice and encouragement; Dr. David Jackson for developing most of the programs, and for his overall collaboration during the project; and Dr. Roger Needham for being an ever-ready and stimulating consultant.

SECTION I

Theory

Chapter 1

Problem and Approach

SUMMARY

This chapter discusses the background to our project, that is the reasons why we began work on the construction of automatic keyword classifications, and the approach to classification we adopted as a result. We became interested in the use of a classification as a means of simplifying a keyword network, and in automatic procedures for obtaining such a classification, on the grounds that automatic grouping techniques would be less laborious, and more objective, than manual ones. The object of the classification was to obtain sets of intersubstitutible keywords which would extend the range of request-document matches using keywords alone, and the assumption was that such classes could be derived from co-occurrence information: the more two keywords or terms tend to co-occur, the more likely they are to be substitutible. We were thus thinking of a keyword classification as a recall-promoting device, rather than as a precision device; and as a consequence of the way we thought of it as a replacement for a network which could be derived from co-occurrence information, we believed that the classi-

fication we would try to construct should have certain properties: from the linguistic point of view we should accept a classification without any marked semantic properties, consisting of word groups based on shared contextual or topic references, and not necessarily on any stronger relations; from the classificatory point of view, we would want a classification which permitted loosely organised sets of words, rather than tightly connected ones; and from the retrieval point of view we would want a classification which was comprehensive, rather than selective. We have in fact found that some of these assumptions about the properties which are desirable in a keyword thesaurus were mistaken; the object of the chapter is to make the position from which we started clear, as a preliminary to the more detailed discussion of the different aspects of keyword thesauri and automatic classification procedures which follow.

The problems of automatic thesaurus construction

The idea of using a vocabulary classification, or thesaurus, for information retrieval is an old one, but automatic methods of obtaining this kind of classification have only recently been considered, for obvious reasons. Research in this area is therefore concerned with three problems, namely

(1) whether a keyword classification is really of value in retrieval;
(2) what kind of classification is of most value; and
(3) whether this kind of classification can be obtained automatically.

Work on automatic thesaurus construction is thus concerned with the problem of classification which is the librarian's traditional interest, but any attempt to use a computer to form classifications poses new problems as well; it forces us, in particular, to examine the whole question of the use and character of a retrieval thesaurus with a fresh eye. The general assumption is that a thesaurus classification is needed for retrieval because it extends or normalises the descriptions of documents which are provided by

3

any actual words which may be extracted from the documents: this should permit matches between requests and documents which are really about the same thing, though this happens to be expressed in different words. A thesaurus classification, therefore, consists of connected words which are intersubstitutible in retrieval. These words need not be synonyms or even near-synonyms, and they need not be generically related either; for retrieval purposes two words which are collocationally related, like 'boundary' and 'layer', may be acceptable substitutes for one another because they refer to the same (aerodynamic) topic. In practice, the suggestion that groups of intersubstitutible words should be used for retrieval often follows experiments with an associative word network, or semantic map, which is used for travelling from one word to other related ones, again to enlarge the scope of request document matches. The difference between a thesaurus and a map is, however, as important as their obvious relationship: for the distinctive property of a classification is that it is a simplification of, and generalisation from, detailed information about word relationships of the kind represented by a map; it is just the ability to infer that two words are related from the fact that they are class-mates, though they are not clearly marked as such in a map, that a classification gives us.

The first problem which arises in thesaurus construction is thus that of finding a suitable base for these classes of intersubstitutible words; we want both appropriate information, and information of the kind which leads to automatic processing. But it has been argued that this information is given by notes of the occurrences and co-occurrences of keywords in documents (or abstracts or titles), because the more words tend to co-occur, the more likely it is that they are related, and can be treated as substitutible for one another in the required way. At the same time, this is only a general argument, and it has to be made more precise before we can actually exploit it to obtain a classification; and at this stage, many interesting questions arise, because the attempt to make the general argument more precise tends to involve assumptions about the nature of a retrieval thesaurus, assumptions, that is, about its linguistic, classificatory and retrieval properties, where these assumptions in turn depend on assumptions about the purpose of the classification. These assumptions naturally influence the approach to automatic classification which is adopted, and as they may not be made explicit, and may indeed not be well founded, any experiments may be misdirected, or their results misinterpreted.

In what follows, these questions are discussed at greater length, in the context of the project on automatic classification for which I have been responsible. The book is based on this project, and the experiments carried out under it, and the results obtained from them, will be described in some detail, on the one hand because they are of interest in their own right, since the project represents the most intensive study to date of automatic thesaurus construction for retrieval purposes, and on the other, because they form a convenient vehicle for a discussion of the questions as a whole. So without further ado, I shall turn to the origin of our project, as a natural way of introducing the kind of argument on which work in this area is based: the particular approach we adopted can be taken as an illustrative example which provides the material for a discussion of the questions we can ask about the object and character of a retrieval thesaurus.

One approach to automatic keyword classification

We thought, when we began work on our project, that we had only one problem to investigate, namely that of constructing 'clump'-type keyword classifications on a large scale. We thought that we knew what we wanted a classification to do for us in retrieval, and so what it should be like; and we thought that we could obtain this kind of classification automatically by applying the theory of clumps[1]. Previous experiments had shown that clump classifications could be constructed for sample sets of keywords, and they looked sensible enough, though they were never seriously tested in retrieval. The object of our project was therefore to set up classifications of this kind for a real keyword vocabulary, and to test them in a controlled way by carrying out searches with requests for which lists of relevant documents were available. We thought that our difficulties would be mainly techno-logical ones; we did not think that the idea of using clumps for retrieval would present any problems of principle in connection with the use of keyword classifications in retrieval. But we found that we were mis-taken, and our project became much more ambitious as a result. Our first experiments did not turn out very well; and we found ourselves asking the fundamental questions about the use of keyword classifications we failed to ask when we began: first, what do we in fact want a keyword classification to do for us in retrieval that we cannot achieve with unclassified keywords; and second, what should it be like if it is to do this properly?

These questions are very important, but they have not really been answered by anyone working in this area. This is partly because information retrieval systems are very complicated, and this makes controlled experi-ments difficult to design and carry out. But it is mainly because some answers look so obvious that they do not appear to need any justification. Some of the arguments for keyword classifications are very convincing, and there is no doubt that they contribute something to retrieval. But Cleverdon's experiments have shown, for example, that many of the assumptions which have been made about the value of various retrieval devices do not stand up to investigation, and this is confirmed by the experiments which have been carried out under the SMART project[2]. This research shows, in par-ticular, that a much better understanding of the effects of keyword classi-fications is needed before we can say that we want a classification of such and such a kind because it will do so and so for us. The consequences for

5

automatic classifications are obvious; we cannot evaluate an automatic classification unless we know what to expect of a classification, however it is constructed. Most of the work that has been done on automatic classification suffers from the absence of solid enough foundations, largely because it is based on assumptions about the use of keyword classifications in retrieval which have not been properly investigated because they look so plausible. We started in this way ourselves; but our first experimental results showed us that some of the assumptions on which the use of clumps was based were wrong. We realised that a much more comprehensive approach to keyword classification, and to automatic classification in particular, was needed; and the object of our project has therefore been that of investigating the two fundamental questions that can be asked about the purpose and character of keyword classifications, from the point of view of automatic classifications. The natural way of doing this is by comparative experiments, and our research has therefore been based on a whole series of controlled tests which have been designed to provide some of the information we need to answer the two questions. We cannot claim to have answered them completely; but we can claim that we have gone some way towards answering them.

Given, then, that we have these fundamental problems to consider, what do they involve in detail? What answers could we give to our questions? The best way of introducing this detailed discussion is by looking at the historical background to our research. We began work on our project by thinking that we wanted a clump-type classification, that is a classification with particular linguistic, classificatory and retrieval properties, because this would enable us to extend the range of request-document keyword matches; and we were obliged to think more carefully about what we wanted when we found that the retrieval performance of the classifications we constructed on this basis was very poor. Quite different approaches to classification are possible, and we could not be certain that we had the right one for our purpose. We also realised that classifications can be used for different purposes in retrieval, and that different retrieval requirements can lead to quite different kinds of classification. We then found that the characteristics of the vocabulary which is being classified are very important, that these too have to be taken into account in the construction of a classification. The particular way in which the classification is used to index the documents in a collection also matters. The situation as a whole is in fact very much more complicated than we thought it was, and we were therefore obliged to make a much more careful analysis of the relation between a keyword classification and the retrieval system of which it forms a part than we were prepared for, and indeed than is usual in research on keyword classifications. In what follows, therefore, I shall start by describing the work on which our project was originally based, and the particular assumptions about the purpose and character of a classification that we derived from it[3]. This is needed for an understanding of the work we have done; it also leads naturally to the subsequent discussion of the general problems underlying the use of keyword classifications we have to examine.

The idea that we needed a clump classification was ultimately derived from some early work on the use of a lattice-type keyword network in retrieval. We wanted to replace the lattice by a classification, and the assumption 'that a clump classification was the right kind of classification appeared to follow from the argument we used to proceed from the lattice to a classification. This argument is therefore the foundation of our work on automatic classification, and it is worth looking at in some detail for this reason.

The aim of the lattice was to promote matches between requests and documents not containing identical words, given lists of extracted keywords, or rather 'terms', since morphological variations in the keywords were disregarded, for each*. The arrangement of the terms in the lattice was therefore based on the principle that term *a* should be placed above term *b* if we would accept a document containing *b* in response to a request containing *a*. An individual term could therefore have many terms under it, either immediately or at successively lower levels; it could also be placed itself under any number of higher terms, according to its different senses or different subject or topic affiliations. This was the important feature of the lattice, and the one which distinguished it from a hierarchy. The result was an irregular structure without clearly defined levels which had something in common with association networks, but differed from them in being ordered from top to bottom. The general idea can be illustrated by an example, as

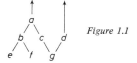

Figure 1.1

in Figure 1.1. The structure was exploited in searching with a 'scale of relevance' procedure: an initial match on a given keyword would produce any documents containing either this term, or any terms below it; a move upwards would then bring out any further documents containing not only the higher term itself, but any terms subsumed under it, which were presumably related to the term we started with. If we begin with *b* in the example just given, for instance, we get documents containing *b*, or *e* or *f*; if we now move up to *a*, we get documents containing *a*, and also documents containing *c* or *g*. If we start with *g*, on the other hand, we move up to either *c* or *d*.

The lattice was successful in that it pulled out relevant documents which

---

* 'Keyword' and 'term' will be used interchangeably in general discussions to refer to extracted descriptive items as opposed to, for example, ones selected from a controlled vocabulary, though they are explicitly distinguished in detail in the later chapters dealing with our experiments.

could not be obtained by straight keyword matches alone. The search procedure was also mechanisable in principle; but the lattice itself had to be
set up by hand, and this was a great effort. We found, in fact, that it involved
more work, when the number of keywords topped 1 000, than we were
prepared to put into it. We wanted, therefore, to find some way of organising
extracted keywords which would have the same effect in retrieval, but which
could be mechanised; and the natural line to follow was suggested by what
happened when we used the lattice, particularly in following the scale of
relevance procedure. This was that we were treating a given term and those
underneath it as if they were substitutible for one another in a request or
document. A request containing b could be satisfied by a document containing b or e or f, indifferently, on the assumption that documents which
contained any of these words would be about the same thing. When we
applied the scale of relevance procedure, we enlarged the set of alternatives.
Moving from b to a meant that a and b and c and e and f and g were treated
as substitutible. We were really using the lattice as a classification, because
we were exploiting the fact that terms were close enough to one another to
be regarded as substitutible for one another, without looking at the individual connections between them. The effect of searching with b, for instance, would be the same whether e and f were directly subsumed under
it, or e was subsumed under b with f below e. The procedure only worked,
however, because the connections were there, and even more, because there
were parts of the lattice which contained a number of closely connected
terms. The lattice as a whole, that is, clearly constituted a classification
containing groups of mutually substitutible terms. These groups were, moreover, overlapping ones, because individual terms, like g in the example, were
subsumed under different terms and so occurred in different substitution
sets. In looking at our lattice as a whole, therefore, we could say that the
terms in it fell into groups in the natural way that the different items in the
lattice of Figure 1.2 fall into five overlapping classes.

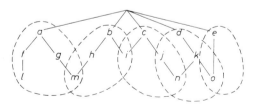

Figure 1.2

This suggested the idea of a keyword classification. The next problem
was that of constructing the classification using only the document keyword
lists from which we obtained the lattice, and not the lattice itself. But the
fact that we were interested in sets of mutually substitutible, or intersubstitutible, terms gave us the clue. If a and b are substitutible for one another

8

in the sense that we are prepared to accept a document containing one in response to a request containing the other, this will be because they have the same meaning, or refer to a common subject or topic; and one way of finding out whether two terms are related in this way is by looking at the documents in which they occur. If they tend to occur in the same documents, the chances are that they have to do with the same subject, and so can be substituted for one another. If two terms always co-occur in the same documents, in other words, we can clearly treat them as intersubstitutible because it does not matter which we use to ask for the documents; and while we cannot expect terms to co-occur in this regular way, they may tend to co-occur if we have several documents dealing with the same or similar subjects. We may then be justified in treating these terms as mutually substitutible on the grounds that any document in which one occurs could probably be described by the other, though it was not actually used by the author in question. We can proceed, therefore, from the indubitable fact that two terms which always co-occur in a given set of documents are necessarily substitutible for one another in the sense that each retrieves exactly the same documents as the other, to the assumption that we can legitimately treat two terms which tend to co-occur as if they were equally substitutible for one another; and this is what we need to build up our classification. We do not know much about our keyword vocabulary; but the document word lists we start with give us the occurrence information we need. We can use the lists to find pairs of terms which tend to co-occur, and we can then proceed to sets of keywords which tend to co-occur. We can clearly conclude that a and b and c and d form a class of substitutible terms, for example, if we know that a tends to occur with b, and with c, and with d, that b occurs with c and with d, and c with d. This whole approach is, just simply, a more systematic version of the approach we adopted in constructing the lattice: terms were related in the lattice by the fact that they were connected with the same documents.

The argument, then, is that if we want to obtain the classes of terms we need to match requests and documents which do not contain the request terms themselves, we can do this by looking for classes of terms which tend to co-occur in documents. These can be substituted for one another not only in the trivial cases where they actually co-occur, but in the important ones where they do not. This method of obtaining a classification is, moreover, mechanisable in principle: all we have to do is note the co-occurrences of pairs of terms, and then look for sets of co-occurring pairs. The result should be a classification which is like the lattice in all material respects. We should in particular be able to obtain the overlapping groups which were an important feature of the lattice: if we have a term with different meanings or topic affiliations, it will presumably tend to co-occur with distinct sets of terms, and so fall in different classes which reflect the distinction represented by different routes up from the term in the lattice. The classification is at the same time based on the simple lists of extracted keywords we used to set up the lattice. This is an advantage not only because these lists are easily obtained, which makes them cheap, but because they characterise documents quite well if they are long enough. They contain valuable information, which is preserved in the lattice as a vocabulary normalising device for connecting different words with similar meanings or shared references.

The argument I have just outlined will be familiar to anyone who has attempted automatic classification for retrieval purposes. Research in this area has been based on the assumption that a classification is required to iron out vocabulary differences and to pick up connections between different words; and on the belief that a suitable classification can be obtained automatically from occurrence information about keywords. It must in fact be obtained in this way, because we cannot ask direct questions about the meanings of words if we are using automatic techniques. We came to this conclusion because we started with the lattice, and it is a natural one for anyone wanting to summarise the information contained in a keyword network or association map; but it is also the obvious approach to automatic classification as such, for anyone interested in substituting a mechanised thesaurus for the expensive manual ones which are frequently used in retrieval.

It must nevertheless be recognised that any attempt to construct an automatic classification on this basis must depend on some specific assumptions about the character of the classification. These assumptions are, as we have seen, not always made explicit, though they are very important; and they are not always supported by argument, even when they are more explicit. The argument I have just outlined led us to base our own work on automatic classification techniques on some assumptions about the sort of classification we would need which were not really well founded, though they looked plausible enough at the time. It is true that we could hardly show that they were right until we had carried out a reasonable number of experiments; but we should have looked at them more carefully before we began. In the section which follows, therefore, I shall consider these assumptions in some detail, not only because they explain the approach we adopted when we began our project, but because they are typical of the assumptions on which research on automatic classification for retrieval is based. The discussion as a whole can therefore be used to bring out the fundamental questions about the use of automatic classifications that any project in this area should attempt to answer, and for which we ourselves have provided some provisional answers.

Assumptions about the character of a keyword thesaurus

I have so far shown that the idea of a keyword lattice leads us to that of a classification based on term co-occurrences in documents. The important point about this argument, however, is that we drew some more specific conclusions about the kind of classification we wanted for our retrieval purpose from it. We concluded, first, that word classes based on document co-occurrences of the kind envisaged may be semantically ill defined, rather than well defined; second, that these classes can be loose, rather than tight, so that the classification as a whole is irregular and not schematic; and third, that they may be comprehensive rather than restricted, because the classification is intended as a recall device for enlarging the scope of request document matches, so that more relevant documents are obtained, as opposed to a precision device for restricting matches to exclude irrelevant documents. We went further than this, in fact: we said that any classification we constructed should have these linguistic, classificatory and retrieval properties. We should, therefore, concentrate on grouping techniques which would allow us to obtain semantically unobvious, weakly connected, widely extended classes.

The reasons for these conclusions are obvious enough, given our starting point; but other approaches to classification involving quite different property specifications can look equally convincing. The important point is that these properties are in principle independent of one another, though they may be connected in practice; the choice depends on the purpose for which the classification is required, and on the nature of the vocabulary which is being classified. Thus we may say that we want weakly connected classes because we want widely extended ones; or we may say that there is no point in looking for weakly connected classes because we have a very small vocabulary: it would probably simply give us the whole vocabulary as a class. We therefore have a range of choices, from which we select particular combinations, depending on our purpose and the material with which we are dealing. These relationships make it very difficult to discuss these aspects of the use of a keyword classification separately, but I shall attempt it in the hope that the implications of particular choices at particular points will be fairly clear. I shall start by considering the purpose for which a classification may be required; I shall then discuss the characteristics that it may be required to have, and finally the effect of different properties of the keyword vocabulary. The discussion will be kept short because many of the points are taken up in more detail in the chapters which deal with our own work: the object of the section which follows is to provide the background for the description of our research.

The purpose for which a thesaurus is required

At first sight, the purpose for which we require a classification does not appear to present any problems. If indexing devices can be described either as recall devices for increasing the chances of obtaining relevant documents, or as precision devices for avoiding irrelevant documents, a classification is presumably a recall device. It is customary to think of a classification as a recall device, and we thought that we wanted an automatic classification for this purpose; we wanted a classification, that is, to obtain relevant documents which were not pulled out by direct matches on the request keywords alone. This followed naturally from the idea that we wanted a classification to have the same effect in retrieval as the scale of relevance procedure we used with the lattice; but there is no doubt that keyword classifications are normally regarded as recall devices: the common belief that a retrieval thesaurus should consist of groups of synonyms shows this quite clearly. Various consequences then follow for the classification itself: we presumably want bigger classes rather than smaller ones, for example, because these allow more matches, and so on.

Though it may be convenient to say that a given indexing device is either a recall device or a precision device, however, it is not always easy to maintain the distinction in practice. In Cleverdon's analysis, recall devices like keyword groups are supposed to be quite independent of precision devices like coordination[4]. We imagine, rather arbitrarily, that we start, in characterising a request or document, with a mere heap of words; and we then process this heap in various ways to obtain a specification designed to promote the best retrieval performance in terms of recall and precision. Thus when we derive a class description for a request or document from its initial keyword description, in the usual way, we are in principle doing quite separate things: we are replacing individual words by word classes, to promote recall; and we are coordinating these classes, to promote precision. Or if we think of ourselves as starting with a list of coordinated keywords, so that we can say that we have a specification in an indexing language which is characterised by the null recall device, so to speak, and a particular precision device, we are substituting classes for words to promote recall. In this case, the recall device is associated with the individual units of the description, and the precision device with their combination; but it could be the case that we sought to promote precision by modifying the units themselves, and recall by combining them in a particular way. We might, for instance, think that we could improve precision by replacing keywords, which are often ambiguous, by keywords with sense descriptions, so that the different meanings of natural language words are distinguished; and we might try to promote recall by 'or-ing' words together instead of 'and-ing' them.

A given device may, of course, fail to work in the intended way in practice. It may also be the case that a device works in more than one way. This seems to be true of some classifications. The idea that a classification should function as a recall device is obvious enough, and there is no doubt that classifications do promote recall in practice. But suppose that we have an overlapping or non-exclusive classification, of the kind we described earlier. If a word occurs in more than one class, this should be because it has different meanings, or because it appears in different topical contexts. An overlapping keyword classification distinguishes the senses of the words in it, that is, in a way that can presumably be exploited to obtain more precision in retrieval than we would naturally obtain with the unclassified keywords alone. The classification is at the same time still a recall device, because each word is associated with others in a class. The point is that each word is associated with a different set of words for its different senses.

An overlapping classification is therefore a potential precision device. The question is, how do we exploit the information it contains in retrieval, to obtain the actual sense distinctions we need? The natural way of doing this in fact follows automatically from the use of coordination. This is best shown by an example, as follows. Imagine that we have one classification, I, in which a occurs only in one class, along with b, c, d and e, say; and that we also have a second classification, II, in which a occurs in two classes, with b and c, and with d and e, respectively. Now suppose that we take a request containing the word a and replace this by the class specification of a in classification I; when we match the request with all our document specifications, we will pull out any documents characterised by this class, that is any documents which contain a or b or c or d or e; or, if we imagine, with the object of showing specifically how the classification works, that a itself does not occur in any documents, any documents containing b or c or d or e. Now if we use classification II instead, we will in this case obtain the same result, although we are matching two classes for a: we will simply select documents characterised by either class, because we have no reason for preferring documents characterised by one to documents containing words from the other. In this case we get no discrimination, though the fact that a occurs in two classes suggests that we might be happier with only some of the documents in which a occurs, than with all of them.

Consider now what may happen when we have more than one request keyword, say a and f. We will again assume that a and f do not themselves occur in any documents. We may in this case find that some documents match the class specifications for a and f, but in such a way that we are exploiting the distinction between the two classes containing a. We may find, that is, that those documents which share classes with a and f in fact contain words which occur in only one of the classes for a, so that we are effectively obtaining a subset of the documents containing class-mates of a. This is easily seen diagrammatically, if we imagine we have the distribution of terms shown in Figure 1.3.

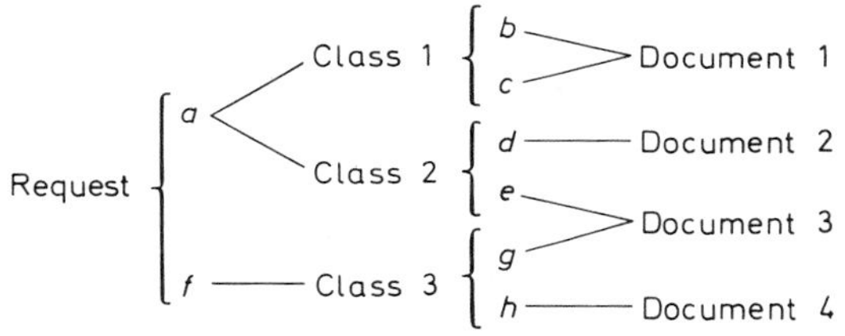

Figure 1.3

Document 3 here, is clearly a better match with the request than documents 1, 2 or 4; and it is also the case that we are selecting one class for *a*, which presumably represents the correct meaning or topic affiliation of *a*. Document 2 is also characterised by this class, but we cannot see that it may be more appropriate than document 1, in the way that we can clearly see that document 3 is what we want. We are using the classification as a recall device, because we are pulling out documents which do not contain our request terms, but we are doing this in a discriminating way.

In this example we imagined that *a* itself did not occur in any documents. Now suppose that we have some documents containing *a*. These will clearly be pulled out for any request containing *a*. It may, however, be the case that the class specifications for other request terms which do not occur in any documents are satisfied by documents containing either *a* or class-mates of *a*. These documents match the class specification of the request more fully than the documents containing *a* alone, and they should therefore be preferred. This is apparent if we look at an example which differs from the

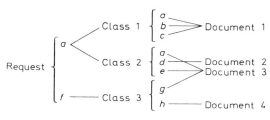

Figure 1.4

previous one only in the occurrence of *a* in some documents, as in Figure 1.4. In this case we are making a more direct attack on the different uses of *a*, by preferring one of the documents containing it, namely document 3, to the others. We are, that is, clearly treating our classification as a precision device. Of course the recall element must enter in as well, if we permit one word to replace another to obtain a match; but we want this: if we have a document containing *a* and *f* themselves, we gain nothing by using a classification; we simply obtain the result we would obtain with keywords. But if we can gain from a classification because we can obtain documents which are not retrieved by keywords alone, we can also do this in a more discriminating way than is apparent at first sight.

The example shows how a classification can work as a precision device in terms of request document matches. But the device itself is of course really a feature of the indexing language. When we say, that is, that we prefer document 3 because it matches one of the classes for *a* and the class for *f*, we are really saying that we are searching with a request specification consisting of one class for *a* and a class for *f*. Unfortunately, we have no means of setting this specification up directly; we are as it were assuming that this is the right specification of the request because it is the fullest of the possible specifications which is satisfied by a document. This shows how difficult it is to sort out the different parts of a retrieval system; we have what is in principle a precision device of the indexing language, but it is used in the matching operation rather than in the construction of the request and document specification. We can, however, say that the classification is acting as a precision device, because this is much more convenient, and it is not really misleading.

The fact that we initially wanted an overlapping classification, to represent the different affiliations of words, meant that we were interested in precision, though we thought of a classification primarily as a recall device, and the actual results we have obtained in some of our experiments show that classifications can act as precision devices as well as recall devices. Similar results have been obtained by Lesk[5]. This means that we have a choice if we are setting up a classification of the kind we were considering when we began: we can say that we want to treat a classification of this kind primarily as a recall device rather than as a precision device, or as a precision device rather than a recall one, so that we design our classification accordingly. We may, for example, say that we are more interested in a classification as a recall device than as a precision one, so that we opt for large classes rather than small ones, given that they are overlapping, because this should stimulate recall more than precision. The choice must, as we shall see, depend on the sort of retrieval performance we can obtain with our unclassified keywords, because this is what we want to improve on.

The fact that a classification may work both as a recall and as a precision device, if it is used in the way described in the examples, must not, however, be allowed to obscure the much more important fact that a keyword classification can be used simply as a recall device, or as a precision device; we can say that we want it for either of these purposes. If we replace the terms in a request or document by their classes in an exclusive classification, we are using the classification purely as a recall device; and if we use their class membership in an overlapping classification to tag the terms in a request with sense descriptions in some way, without replacing the terms by the classes, we are using the classification purely as a precision device. We in fact have an open choice: a keyword classification of some kind can be used in either way; and we can therefore say that we want a classification for recall purposes, or for precision purposes. Some of the consequences of the choice for the kind of classification we set up will already be evident; and others should become apparent in the discussion of the actual properties a classification may have which follows.

The properties of a keyword classification can be described under the three headings listed earlier; it can, that is, have, or be intended to have, certain linguistic properties, certain classificatory properties, and certain retrieval properties. We can, for instance, say that we want a classification to consist of sets of synonyms: this defines its linguistic character; that

15

these sets should be small, which defines its classificatory character; and that the sets should be restricted or selective, in the sense that they do not pull out many documents, which defines its retrieval character. We in fact argued when we began that we wanted classes which were semantically vague, loosely connected, and comprehensive, because we thought that this would give us a classification which would promote recall. It will be clear that a large number of alternatives exist under the three heads, and therefore that many classifications representing different combinations of alternatives can in principle be constructed. We may, nevertheless, find it very difficult to say which combination is suited to our purpose, whichever this is, and equally, because the properties are related to one another in practice, to attribute the performance of a given classification to its having the particular linguistic, classificatory or retrieval properties that it has. Our choice is bound to be affected, too, by the vocabulary we are classifying: it is no good saying that we want synonym classes, for example, if the vocabulary does not contain any synonyms. The nature of keyword classifications in general is really too large a subject to fully examine here; and it is in any case not clear that this would be appropriate. I shall concentrate instead on the characteristics of the kind of automatic classification we are interested in, in the hope that this will throw some light on the problem of keyword classification as a whole. First, what kind of linguistic properties can a co-occurrence-based keyword classification have?

The linguistic character of a retrieval thesaurus

The best way of approaching this question is by considering the assumption we originally made about the semantic character we wanted our clump classification to have. We said that we did not expect it to have a semantically well-defined or obvious character, or, to put the requirements in a positive, though rather misleading way, that we wanted it to be semantically unobvious. The reason for this is evident: it follows naturally from the way we were proposing to obtain the classification. It is easy, that is, to see that word classes based on distributional information need not have a well-defined or obvious semantic character, in the sense in which a set of synonyms has a well-defined character. If we have a collection of documents on the history of transport, for instance, we may find that the terms '18th century', 'turnpike' and 'speed' tend to co-occur, so that we obtain them as a class. They are not, however, related to one another in meaning in the straightforward way that synonyms are. Adjoining terms in our lattice were often not related in meaning in any obvious way, and the co-occurrence lists we have for the keywords characterising our test documents show that individual words, like 'boundary', may be very closely connected with other words, like 'layer' and 'flow', to which they are not directly related in meaning. And we have found that the classes we obtain from this information,

16

whatever grouping procedure we adopt, are often very heterogeneous in character. We may, for instance, obtain 'ablating', 'capacity', 'combustion', 'shield' and 'teflon' as a class. We can indeed see that this class has a rationale: the words in it are all used in the context of a particular topic, namely rocket noses. We can, moreover, call this a semantic rationale. It is also true that the class does not have the clearcut semantic character of a synonym class; the words concerned are not related to one another in the way that synonyms and near-synonyms are, by their meanings having anything in common.

The question is, does this matter from the retrieval point of view? It is an empirical fact that manual thesauri usually consist of groups of words which are semantically obvious in the sense that they are based on a comparatively straightforward meaning relation like synonymy, or the generic relation which connects, for example, the names of different vegetables; and if manual thesauri are like this, we may well imagine that the automatic classifications which are designed to replace them should be the same, particularly if we have any reason to think that the manual thesauri are of value in retrieval. This means that we can test any automatic classification procedures we propose by applying them to a vocabulary for which we already have a manual thesaurus, to see whether it gives us similar word groups. We cannot expect the two classifications to be identical; but we may expect them to be very like one another.

But have we any real reason for thinking that classifications like these manual ones can be obtained automatically from distributional information? Can we, for example, obtain the synonym and near-synonym groups which are frequently found in manual thesauri. Lesk points out[6] that it is often assumed that this is what automatic classification techniques should give us, just because it is what we have already; and it has been suggested that groups of this kind can be obtained from keyword lists if we look, not at words which are directly related to each other because they co-occur, but at words which are indirectly related because they co-occur with other common words. It is a reasonable assumption, if a and b tend to co-occur, not with each other, but with c, and also d, that they are likely to resemble one another in meaning more than they resemble c or d. But Lesk found that this was not a reliable way of obtaining sets consisting only of synonyms, given simple lists of keywords. It is true that classes of words with similar meanings were obtained, along with sets of generically related words, in some experiments carried out at the Rand Corporation[7]. But these were based on word co-occurrences in specific syntactic frames, and they are therefore not strictly comparable with Lesk's experiments, which were restricted to the information about words which is normally available in retrieval applications. It is in fact a moot point among linguists whether really well-defined semantic classes, that is classes based on a single clearcut meaning relation, can be derived from distributional information of any kind. But it is unlikely that very good classes could be obtained from the

17

keyword lists for the average document collection, which are not full enough for the purpose. It is also doubtful whether what is really a fundamental problem in linguistics has anything to do with document retrieval. The question we really have to ask ourselves is not whether semantically obvious word classes can be derived from keyword lists, but whether these are in fact the classes we want for retrieval purposes.

This is not certain. It is true that groups of synonyms or near-synonyms can be of value in retrieval, and that groups based on other relations of an obvious kind, like the generic or part-whole relations, can be very useful. But the belief that classes based on these relations are all that we need seems to be based on a somewhat dubious inference, namely that as human beings are very good at classification, generally speaking, any classification they may construct should be what we want. But it is also a fact that human beings tend to stick to obvious principles of classification, if they are simply invited to divide a set of objects into convenient groups, however much they may recognise that other classifications based on less obvious principles are quite acceptable if they are presented with them. This means that they are likely to group words by their direct connections in meaning, if they are asked to construct a thesaurus, rather than by the indirect connections between them which follow from their uses. Manual thesauri are usually based simply on the meanings of the words concerned, and not on their uses: two words are regarded as related if their meanings have something in common, to put the point rather crudely. We can, however, also say that two words are related if they are brought together in the context of a topic or subject of discourse: they are related by their shared reference. 'Boundary', 'layer' and 'flow', for example, are related by their combined use in aerodynamic contexts, though their meanings have nothing in common.

These are the relations that human beings tend to miss. But it is arguable that they are the relations we really want to pick up for retrieval purposes, whether we are interested in recall or precision. If we are interested in recall we want, in retrieval, to be able to approach a topic from any angle, which means that we must be able to use any of the words which refer to it; and if we are interested in precision we still want topic classes, because these distinguish the different meanings of words. The objection to classifications based only on the obvious relations like synonymy is not that they are the wrong sort of classification, but that they do not help us enough. They are inadequate because they are too limited. We want to be able to exploit other relations between words, and in particular those collocational relations which hold between words which are brought together by being used in the same context; we want indirect relations as well as direct ones. And this will naturally mean that we may get classes which look unobvious because they are not held together only by the meanings of the words concerned; we should, however, be able to see that they are quite straightforward if we look at them from another angle, because they are held together by the use of the words in the document texts from which they are derived. The members of such a class may indeed be related in meaning, so that we do, for instance, find some synonyms in a class; but the class is not based on these relations. The words concerned are brought together because they are related in another way.

We can, therefore, say that we really have a positive semantic requirement: we want classes which are topic classes, that is classes which are based on one semantic relation, namely collocation, rather than on the others, like synonymy, on which retrieval thesauri are more often based. When we started by saying that we did not want classes with a well-defined semantic character, we were saying that we were not interested in the usual kind of classification which is based on direct relations in meaning between words; what we do in fact want are classes with a rather different, but no less genuine semantic character.

The important point which follows, however, is that a classification based on collocations is necessarily specific to a given document collection. The words are grouped together precisely because they are used together in the documents in question. This is not to say that classifications based on other relations cannot be document specific in this way: we could perfectly well attempt to find sets of words which were synonymous for a given collection. But it is an empirical fact that classifications which are based on direct relations in meaning are often not specific in this sense, though they may be subject specific rather than wholly general. We can, however, say that retrieval from a particular collection should be very much more effective if the classification we use is tied to the collection: a retrieval classification should be document specific. Lesk comments on this point in comparing the manual thesaurus and automatic 'semi-classification' consisting of association lists he set up for a test collection. The associative classification was not a simple synonym classification like the manual one, to start with; and Lesk also found that only just over 16 per cent of the associated pairs of terms were judged to be significantly related, from a general point of view. But when the character of the collection from which they were derived was taken into account, just over 73 per cent were judged significant. The automatic classification itself gave quite good results, which suggests that we can profit from the specific relations between words that are established in texts. This of course does not mean that we are not interested in the general relations between words at all; the point is that we are only interested in those which are relevant to the documents we are working with, that is in those general relations that are also specific to our collection. We may therefore obtain groups of words which, though they are based on the collection, contain some items which are generally related, like regular synonyms; but this fact about these words is irrelevant.

The argument I have just outlined is, of course, an argument about retrieval classifications in general, and not about automatic classifications in particular: it simply arises naturally in connection with automatic classification because automatic methods tend to produce these topical classifica-

19

tions, whereas human beings tend to produce rather different ones. But this fact should not be allowed to obscure the general point. It does not mean, either, that collocational classifications cannot be constructed manually, though it may be doubted whether the other kinds of classification can be constructed automatically. But classifications of this kind are very difficult to construct manually, and we can therefore hope to gain something positive from the use of automatic methods; we can, that is, hope to obtain the kind of classification it can be asserted we need for retrieval more easily and more effectively than we can obtain it without a machine.

The classificatory character of a thesaurus

Turning now to the classificatory properties of our thesaurus, the assumptions that we made about these again followed naturally from the fact that we started with the lattice. This led us to choose a particular approach to the definition of a class. Quite different approaches to the definition of a class are possible, under the general heading of classification; we can choose different criteria for a class, so that we have different ways of assigning an object to a class, and have different ways of distributing objects among classes. This gives us different kinds of classification; and we can then choose specific class definitions, and specific class-finding procedures, to obtain particular classifications of this kind. Our initial starting point led us to one kind of classification, and we thought that our experiments would be chiefly concerned with identifying the most satisfactory classification of this kind.

The general character of the kind of classification we thought would be appropriate for our retrieval purpose can be summarised by saying that a set of objects are regarded as a class if they are relatively well connected. This gives us overlapping classes rather than exclusive ones, and, generally speaking, allows us to treat sets of objects which are not very strongly connected as classes. A classification of this kind is clearly unlike a hierarchical one; it also differs from some non-hierarchical classifications in not being exclusive; and it differs from other multiple classifications in not being based on single key objects. We can also distinguish it from very similar classifications in which a set of objects is selected as a class on the basis of the connections between them, rather than, as in this case, on the basis of difference between the internal and external connections of the set.

I shall not attempt a full-scale discussion of classification and classification theory here, partly because this is a very large subject, but mainly for the more important reason that it is not clear how much of what has been said on the subject is relevant to information retrieval or information retrieval research. All kinds of ways of sorting objects can be used to produce all kinds of classifications, but some of these seem to be quite inappropriate if we are interested in obtaining keyword classifications for retrieval purposes. Thus if we broadly divide classifications into ordered and unordered classifications, a great deal of work has been done on hierarchical and ordered classifications in general, but this type of classification does not appear to be at all suited to multifariously used words; and there is no well-founded theory of unordered classification that we can exploit. A rather different but more significant point is that in information retrieval we are not interested in classification solely as a means of describing a set of objects: we want a keyword classification for a specific purpose, namely as a device for maximising our chances of retrieving relevant documents in response to a query, and minimising our chances of getting non-relevant ones as well; and in principle we need to know what our classification should be like if it is to be satisfactory for this purpose before we can attempt to choose a classification procedure which will give us a classification of the required kind, for a given set of keywords. But we are unfortunately not yet in a position to be at all precise about what we want; and since there are no really solid techniques for constructing unordered, multiple classifications to hand, the most straightforward course is to adopt a relatively crude approach to grouping keywords, in the hope that the results obtained from any retrieval experiments with our classes will throw some light on the properties a good retrieval classification should possess, so that an attempt can then be made to set up theoretically acceptable procedures for obtaining classifications with these properties. Clearly there is some danger that any such simple methods may be objectionable in some respect, so that the resulting classifications may be suspect and their behaviour in retrieval unreliable. But hopefully, if enough experiments are carried out, we may be able to draw sufficiently sound conclusions from them to act as guides for future research. This at any rate is the approach we have adopted, and which will be described in what follows: the relatively restricted comparison between it and other approaches to classification in the retrieval context, which should be made, will be deferred to Chapter 10.

Adopting a crude approach to the treatment of classification, therefore, we can say that we can characterise classifications according to whether they are hierarchical or non-hierarchical, overlapping or exclusive, and object-based or set-based, that is according to whether a class is generated by a single object or not. We can in principle have any combination of these properties, though the idea of a non-exclusive hierarchy is perhaps rather odd. We in fact, in our research, opted to start with non-hierarchical, overlapping, set-based classifications; and from the kinds of classification covered by this specification, we selected one kind as apparently suited to our needs, namely the kind of classification depending on a balance between the internal and external connections of a set, rather than on its internal connections only. This then led to the research on clumping techniques which immediately preceded our project.

The reasons for our choice of this particular approach to classification will be clear. An exclusive hierarchical classification is quite unlike the

21

lattice, and hierarchical classifications do not seem to be really suited to collections of keywords anyway, just because natural language words are usually related to one another in all kinds of ways, as they were related in the lattice: a hierarchical classification is much too systematic for objects of this sort. Exclusive classifications, even if they are not hierarchic, are unsuitable for the same reason. The occurrence of a term under several higher terms was a characteristic feature of the lattice, and this could only be represented in a classification if a term was permitted to appear in several classes. Particular terms were linked with as many different areas of the lattice as seemed appropriate, and this meant that we wanted a classification which permitted any degree of overlap, depending on the co-occurrence relationships of the terms being classified. We were therefore interested in classification techniques which lead to what may be described as essentially overlapping, rather than accidentally overlapping, groupings, that is to groups for which overlap is normal rather than pathological, and free rather than controlled.

It is hard to believe that an overlapping, or multiple, classification is not what is wanted for retrieval purposes, given the indubitable fact that even in very specialised collections individual words are ambiguous, or at least are used in different contexts. Even if we are interested in recall rather than precision, we presumably want to eliminate irrelevant documents as much as possible; and one way of doing this is by avoiding matches on the wrong senses or uses of words.

The character of the lattice also suggested that classifications which consist of classes which are necessarily based on individual elements would be inappropriate: the relatively denser parts of the lattice network, which is what we were hoping to replace by classes, were often not dependent on any specific terms; and it is in fact the case that a classification based on individual items can cut right across a classification which is obtained by picking out sets of connected terms. In particular, it may not reflect the existence of relatively dense sets of connections; and the latter are what we thought we wanted. It can, however, be argued, if we forget about the lattice, that classes based on individual items may be appropriate for retrieval purposes, given that requests and documents are initially described by particular words: we want to replace these specifically by sets of words which are directly related to them. If we substitute a clump for a term, we may bring in a term which is not directly related to a given term; and while we may say that the two are as good as related, because they are both connected with other common members of the clump, this may be a mistake from the retrieval point of view, because the substitution brings out an irrelevant document.

The need for what may be described as a weak class definition rather than a strong one, that is for a definition which does not impose very strong requirements on the membership of a class, is also a natural consequence of starting with the lattice: we could see that some terms in the lattice were relatively well connected to one another, but they were often not fully connected; and when we consider the distributional information from which we have to obtain our classification, we can hardly suppose that words will tend to co-occur with each other in a very consistent or complete way. This is, on the contrary, very unlikely; we are much more likely to find that *a* tends to co-occur with *b*, and with *c*, and with *d*, say, and *b* with *c* and *c* with *d*, so that we may want to say that *a* and *b* and *c* and *d* really form a class, though *b* does not tend to co-occur with *d*, or even, perhaps, does not co-occur with *d* at all. The irregular relationships in the lattice represented the document relations between the terms in a rather vague way, and the actual distributional information on which classification is based, though it is more precise, cannot be expected to generate much more strongly defined classes. The assumption that we should look for weakly connected classes for retrieval purposes can, however, be contested: though distributional relationships in general are irregular and weak, some sets of items may be much more strongly connected than others; and it is at least possible that these may be of more value in retrieval than the more weakly connected groups, so that we should confine our classification to these.

The retrieval character of a thesaurus

We come finally to what I have called the retrieval properties of a classification. What this means may not be clear, but the general idea can be indicated by an example. A given classification has a particular property, namely that of being selective, if it tends to retrieve only a small number of documents, or at any rate a small proportion of the collection, when it is used in searching. The important point is that the effect of the classification as a means of obtaining documents can be distinguished from its effect as a means of obtaining relevant documents. It may be that if a classification is selective, it promotes precision rather than recall, but this does not necessarily follow. Recall and precision have to do with the relation between relevant documents and documents retrieved: they depend on the numbers of documents retrieved, but the two are not the same; and it is convenient to have some way of describing the behaviour of a classification in terms of the way it retrieves documents, whether these are relevant or not. We can then relate the performance of a classification, as it is expressed by recall and precision, to the way the classification partitions the collection. The retrieval properties of a classification, though they are perhaps less obvious than their linguistic or classificatory ones, are as important.

Now we were primarily interested in a keyword classification as a recall device; and we therefore thought that our classes should have the retrieval property of being wide-ranging or comprehensive, so that the substitution of term classes for terms would tend to retrieve a fair number of documents, rather than only a few: this would presumably tend to promote recall. This was again the natural consequence of starting with the lattice. Moving up the lattice in the scale of relevance procedure tended to bring out many more documents, because documents were obtained not only for the new terms, but for all the terms under it. We did not think that we wanted a selective classification because we did not think that this would lead to any improvement in recall, compared with terms, and these were just what we were trying to improve on. But there is no very good reason for concluding that a classification cannot promote recall, and still be selective.

This depends crucially on the nature of the document collection, and it is here that the intimate relation between the choice of classification properties, on the one hand, and the nature of the keyword vocabulary and the character of the document collection the vocabulary represents, on the other, is most obvious. But it will be clear by now that all the properties of a classification depend on the vocabulary and collection: if there are no strongly connected sets of keywords, for example, there is no point in looking for them; and the particular relationship between the different properties of the classification in a given case will be based on the characteristics of the keyword vocabulary in question: strongly connected classes may or may not be selective, according to the distribution of the words in each class throughout the documents. In more general terms, the effect of a given classification will ultimately depend on such features of the vocabulary and collection as the typical length of a document or request word list, the size of the collection, the size of the keyword vocabulary, and the distribution of the terms throughout the vocabulary on which the frequency of occurrence of individual terms, and hence their co-occurrences, depend. We have found that these can have a much more marked effect on the behaviour of classifications in retrieval than we thought when we began, and they must therefore be taken into account in the construction of the classification in a wholly explicit way.

We said earlier that we discovered from our experiments that some of the assumptions we started with, when we thought of constructing a keyword classification because we wanted to overcome the defects of simple keyword retrieval, were mistaken. How wrong were we in fact? First, the object of a classification: we started by emphasising recall rather than precision; and we have concluded by thinking that precision is at least as important as recall. Second, the properties of the classification: we have not changed our attitude to its semantic character, though it must be admitted that we have not gone into this question very thoroughly; we have, however, concluded that object-based classifications, and also tight rather than loose classifications, that is classifications containing strongly as opposed to weakly connected sets, may be desirable, given our revised view of our purpose; and we have also come to the conclusion that we are rather more interested in selective classifications than we thought. All of these conclusions are of course relative to our experimental collection; but we hope to show that much of what we have learned holds for other collections too.

24

In the chapters which follow, I shall examine our approach to automatic classification, within this framework, in more detail. We have not, as just mentioned, gone further into the linguistic aspects of keyword classification, though some conclusions can be drawn from our experiments and those which have been carried out elsewhere. These will be discussed in Chapter 10. Most of our effort has been put into the techniques required to obtain classifications of the kinds we have considered, and Chapter 3 will be concerned with the various approaches to automatic classification we have investigated, and with the work we have done on related problems. We should, however, look first at the detailed questions which can be asked about the use of classifications as indexing devices. The general belief is that keyword retrieval is unsatisfactory, because it is evident that specific keyword searches can fail to select relevant documents because they do not match on the actual request words. But as Cleverdon, for example, has shown, we have to look more carefully at the real performance of keywords, that is at the overall performance of keyword matching systems, before we can attempt to substitute something better[8]; we have to know exactly what we want a classification to do. This detailed discussion of the performance of a keyword classification naturally involves its retrieval properties. I shall therefore consider both the purpose of our classification, and its retrieval properties, in the next chapter, before going on to its classificatory properties. I shall then return to the problems presented by the character of the keyword vocabulary and document specifications. This will complete the set of chapters on our approach to automatic keyword classification which constitutes the first section of the report: and the description of the actual experiments we have carried out will follow.

Historical Note

The general idea of exploiting statistical associations to form a thesaurus automatically, for use in indexing and retrieving documents, was a salient feature of research in mechanised documentation from about 1958 to 1966; and most of the main points involved in this and the complementary area of automatic document classification were raised in the work done by Baker, Borko, Doyle, Giuliano and Jones, Maron and Kuhns, Needham, Speigel and Bennett, Stiles, and Williams, in particular. Unfortunately, the experimental side of research in information retrieval proper was comparatively undeveloped then, and these discussions of the character and value of statistical associations were not generally followed by serious large-scale experiments of the appropriate kind. Most of the tests were concerned with the feasibility of automatic classification, rather than with its evaluation by retrieval. Overall, the most important experiments involving actual retrieval have been Giuliano and Jones' and subsequently Lesk and Salton's.

25

For a general view of the subject, and representative papers by the main workers in the field, towards the end of the first period of enthusiasm, see Stevens, M. E., *Automatic Indexing: A State-of-the-Art Report*, Monograph 91, National Bureau of Standards, Washington D.C. (1965), and Stevens, M. E., Giuliano, V. E. and Heilprin, D. (Eds), *Statistical Association Methods for Mechanised Documentation, Symposium Proceedings* (1964), Miscellaneous Publication 269, National Bureau of Standards, Washington D.C. (1965).

REFERENCES

1. NEEDHAM, R. M. and PARKER-RHODES, A. F., *The Theory of Clumps*, Cambridge Language Research Unit, M.L.126, mimeo (1960): NEEDHAM, R. M., 'A Method for Using Computers in Information Classification', *Information Processing 62: Proceedings of IFIP Congress 1962* (Ed. Popplewell), Amsterdam, 284 (1963): NEEDHAM, R. M. and SPARCK JONES, K., 'Keywords and Clumps', *Journal of Documentation*, **20**, 5 (1964): JACKSON, D. M., *Automatic Classification and Information Retrieval*, Doctoral Dissertation, Cambridge (1969): SPARCK JONES, K., 'The Theory of Clumps', *Encyclopedia of Library and Information Science* (in press)
2. CLEVERDON, C., MILLS, J. and KEEN, M., *Factors Determining the Performance of Indexing Systems*, Vol. 1, Design, Parts 1 and 2; CLEVERDON, C. and KEEN, M., *Factors Determining the Performance of Indexing Systems*, Vol. 2, Test Results, Cranfield (1966): SALTON, G. (Project Director), *Information Storage and Retrieval*, Scientific Reports Nos. *ISR 7–10*, The Computation Laboratory, Harvard University, 1961–5; Nos. *ISR 11–14*, Department of Computer Science, Cornell University, 1966–8. As references to these publications will be frequent, the Cranfield project reports will be cited as *Factors* and the SMART project ones as *ISR*, with appropriate volume and chapter references. Much of the SMART project material is reproduced in SALTON, G., *Automatic Information Organisation and Retrieval*, New York (1968)
3. For the original development of the argument see NEEDHAM, R. M. and SPARCK JONES, K., 'Keywords and Clumps', *Journal of Documentation*, **20**, 5 (1964)
4. *Factors* 1, 1, Chapter 4; *Factors* 2, Chapter 2
5. *ISR–13*, Chapter IX
6. *ISR–13*, Chapter IX; the account of Lesk's experiments which follows refers to this chapter
7. HARPER, K. E., 'Some Combinatorial Properties of Russian Nouns', The Rand Corporation, Santa Monica, Calif., RM-5077-PR (1966)
8. *Factors* 2, Chapters 4 and 5

FURTHER READING

DOYLE, L. B., 'Semantic Road Maps for Literature Searchers', *Journal of the ACM*, **8**, 553 (1961)
DOYLE, L. B., 'Indexing and Abstracting by Association', *American Documentation*, **13**, 378 (1962)
GIULIANO, V. E. and JONES, P. E., 'Linear Associative Information Retrieval' in *Vistas in Information Handling* (Ed. Howerton and Weeks), Vol. 1, Washington D.C. (1963)

Chapter 2

Indexing Languages, Recall and Precision

SUMMARY

This chapter is concerned with the precise purpose for which a keyword classification is required, and with the retrieval properties which it should have to satisfy the requirements imposed by this purpose. How, in other words, should we use a thesaurus to set up an indexing language? A keyword thesaurus is generally regarded as a recall device, because it permits term substitutions; and the assumption is that we should exploit it as such, and work with term classes instead of single terms, because the recall capacity of unclassified keywords is poor. This belief is shown to be mistaken, at least for our test collection: for this, maximum recall is quite high, while precision is less high than might be expected. To obtain an improvement in retrieval performance over keywords by using a classification, therefore, we have to promote precision as well as recall, especially in the middle matching levels. If recall/precision curves are used as retrieval performance indicators, the keyword performance curve has the familiar sagging shape; and improving recall or precision alone will not remedy this: what is required, moreover, is not a systematic improvement in both at all matching levels, but a relatively greater improvement in the middle section of the curve as opposed to the ends. The question which then arises is whether a classificatory indexing language can incorporate useful precision devices, apart from the use of class coordination, which simply follows if we start with coordinated keywords and substitute classes for keywords in our request and document specifications; and we also have to ask what the combined effect of various recall and precision devices will be. A classification in itself can, in fact, act as a precision as well as a recall device, if overlapping classes are permitted, because these discriminate keyword senses. We can also weight classes by their relative frequency for a source list of request or document keywords, and further possibilities are represented by different methods of combining keywords and classes in specifications. We can, that is, set up a number of classification-using indexing languages designed to promote both recall and precision. The fact that they are intended to promote precision as well as recall means, however, that we want our language to be selective rather than comprehensive in retrieval. In thinking about the retrieval properties of our classi-fication in other words, it presumably follows, if we are not interested in recall alone as we thought, that our classification itself should be selective as opposed to comprehensive: we at least want any language incorporating it to be selective, and we may wish to achieve this not merely by various methods of manipulating our classes to form request and document specifica-tions, but by ensuring that the classes themselves are selective because they are, for example, exclusive rather than inclusive.

Retrieval performance

We have already seen that a classification of the kind with which we are concerned can be considered, in principle, either as a recall device, or as a precision device; but when we started work on our project we were more interested in the recall problem. This was because we could see that searches with unclassified keywords miss useful documents, and we thought that the object of our research should be to deal with this defect of keyword re-trieval. It is, however, true to say that we had very vague ideas about the

27

behaviour of systems using keywords, and we therefore had no real idea of the kind of retrieval performance we were trying to improve. We were able, however, to obtain some of the necessary information by carrying out a proper keyword retrieval experiment for our test collection*, and by referring to results obtained by the Cranfield and SMART projects[1]. Our experiment was of the simplest and most obvious kind: we simply matched keywords on all levels of coordination from n down to 1, where n is the total number of keywords in each request, for a test set of requests; and we then totalled the numbers of retrieved and relevant documents on each level for the set and calculated recall and precision ratios of the usual sort. I do not want to go into the propriety of this procedure here, since it depends on a straightforward and well-established method of using keywords to retrieve documents, the important point being that it gives us the kind of information we need about keyword retrieval, in a sufficiently satisfactory and indeed usefully transparent form; the problems of averaging over requests containing different numbers of keywords, and of measuring performance, are discussed in Chapter 5. For the purpose of discussion it is convenient to imagine that we standardise crude results of this sort in some way, so that we are dealing with precision at standard recall values.

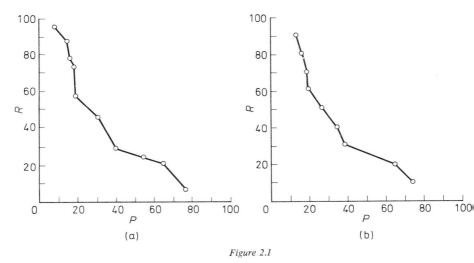

Figure 2.1

We thus replace a recall/precision graph of the familiar kind exemplified by (a) in Figure 2.1, in which the actual levels of the keyword matches are indicated, level n having greatest precision, by the tidier version of (b).

If we now imagine that we are given the retrieval performance of unclassified keywords in this form, we can see, in a quite definite way, what

* A detailed description of the test collection is given in Chapter 7.

28

improving on it might involve; what, that is, can we say we want, if we express our requirement in terms of a different curve?

The form of improvement in retrieval performance

Suppose that we have a given performance curve for keywords. We now say that we want to substitute a keyword classification for these keywords because the retrieval performance of the unclassified keywords is defective in some general respect. It is natural to think that a given indexing language behaves in the same way at all matching levels, so that if we substitute another language which is intended to differ from it in some general respect, we get a performance curve of the same shape, though its position relative to the graph axes is different. Thus if we are considering keywords, the only difference between their performance at the highest level, where a request specification is completely satisfied by a document, and at the lowest, where the specification matches at only one point, is in the relative distance of the documents from the request; we have the most complete specification of the request at the highest level, and so obtain documents which are very close to it, and the most incomplete, and hence most inaccurate, specification at the lowest level, and so obtain documents which are further from it. We should, therefore, have a smooth transition as we

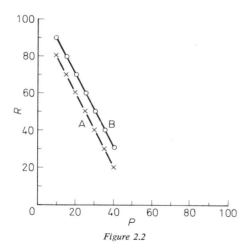

Figure 2.2

descend from the high levels to the low ones, from the relatively high precision and low recall which is in practice associated with close request matches, to the reverse which is usual at low levels. If we now substitute some other language for keywords, which is intended to overcome a characteristic defect of keywords and therefore expressed in terms of the relation-

29

ship between recall and precision, we will expect an improvement in retrieval performance, but a pattern of performance which resembles that of keywords. We expect, that is, to find that the performance of the new indexing language is consistently related to that of the old.

What, then, would an improvement in retrieval performance look like? Suppose that we say we want better recall, while precision remains the same, i.e. that we are comparing two languages A and B, where B is intended to overcome a specific defect of A, namely its inadequacy in recall. We can illustrate the relation between the two languages, using unrealistic, but convenient, straight curves, where we also imagine that the standard recall values coincide with keyword matching levels, as in Figure 2.2.

At a given recall level, the precision value is the same for both A and B, but the recall value is different. The point here, however, is that we have assumed that we have improved recall by retrieving more relevant documents altogether with B than we did with A. But now suppose that A in fact reached 100 per cent recall at the lowest matching level, namely 1: what happens if we substitute B? We get the result shown in Figure 2.3.

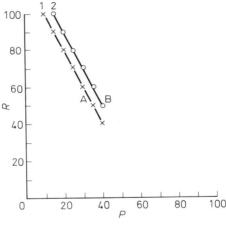

Figure 2.3

In this case, we have reached 100 per cent recall for language B at level 2, and have therefore obtained the maximum recall with a better precision value than that for the maximum recall for A, namely 15 per cent instead of 10 per cent; we can thus say that in improving recall we also improve precision. The same effect could of course be achieved with a cutoff at 70 per cent recall in the first case.

In saying that we want to use a classification to improve recall, therefore, we may have two rather different aims. We may on the one hand want to retrieve more relevant documents in total, or we may be interested in pro-

30

moting relevant documents so that we can use a cutoff in searching which gives us better precision for the same recall: for clearly, if with language A we obtain 70 per cent recall at level 1, and only 60 per cent at level 2, and we want to obtain 70 per cent at level 2 with language B, we have to ensure that relevant documents are pulled out at higher levels for B.

In both of these examples we have behaved as if the two languages differ in only one respect, namely the greater recall capacity of B. The assumption is that we are happy with the precision performance of A, so that we are not trying to improve on this explicitly, though we get the incidental improvement that follows from better recall, for a given recall level. More generally, however, we may want to find a language, say C, which has a superior performance in terms of both precision and recall, than any given language which does not reach 100 per cent recall and 100 per cent pre-

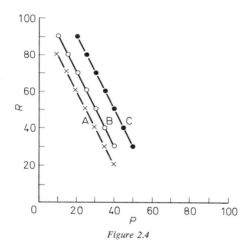

Figure 2.4

cision, like language A in the first example. A successful language C would then have a performance curve which compares with those for languages A and B in the first illustration, as shown in Figure 2.4.

These points are of course quite straightforward; but we need to be very clear about what we want to achieve in terms of retrieval performance. In principle, the optimum performance is 100 per cent recall and 100 per cent precision right from the start, that is right from the highest level. It is quite unrealistic to suppose that this can be achieved, though the serious problem in this field is that we do not know what the optimal performance for a set of requests and a given collection is, and hence what we should aim at. Moreover, experience shows that we can in practice expect some sort of middling performance, which can be schematically represented by a diagonal curve from top left to bottom right of a graph. We have, that is, to work with the results of matches at different levels, because we cannot hope to obtain all and only the relevant documents at first; and this gives us an extended curve representing the relationship between recall and precision at successive matching levels. Generally speaking, we can expect an inverse relationship between the two, with a higher precision than recall at high levels, and the reverse at low. The curve then represents the change in the relationship over the set of levels. The overall balance between precision and recall is even in this case, and improvement is thus clearly a matter of improving both on recall and precision in a consistent way over all the levels. The relative balance between recall and precision may, however, differ: we can have a language which is better on recall than precision, like Q in

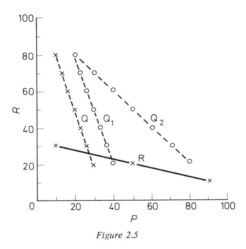

Figure 2.5

Figure 2.5, or one which is the reverse, like R. We would then clearly be interested in improving on these in different respects, namely in precision for Q, and in recall for R. These examples show, however, that improvement is more complicated than we have envisaged it hitherto. While we can in general say that we want to move towards the optimum represented by a dot in the top right-hand corner of the graph, we are obliged in practice to be more specific than this; and while we can say, broadly, that we want to improve Q, say, in precision, this is not quite right. While we can replace Q by Q_1, which represents a consistent improvement in precision, what we really want is the more marked improvement in precision at higher levels than at lower ones of Q_2. We may find ourselves, that is, wanting to improve performance in one respect by different amounts at different levels, or, if we are interested in both recall and precision, in improving performance in different respects at different levels, or in looking for different balances between the two at different levels.

32

Keyword performance

We are now in a position to consider what the actual performance of keywords is, and what trying to improve on it would amount to. The general assumption that we want a keyword classification because it should give us better recall implies that the recall capacity of keywords is poor, while their performance in terms of precision is reasonable. This suggests that the typical keyword performance curve has the general form of curve 1 in

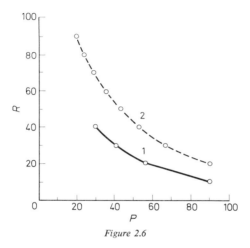

Figure 2.6

Figure 2.6; and our aim in using a classification would be to produce a new curve like 2. The actual keyword performance we obtained for our test collection when standardised, however, as described in Chapter 5, is as shown in Figure 2.7.

It is quite different from the curve one might expect, on the assumption that keywords have a high precision capacity and poor recall capacity: this curve shows high recall, combined with not conspicuously good precision over much of the curve, though a respectable precision maximum is reached; but the fact that similar curves have been obtained in other experiments, for example by Cleverdon for the larger collection of which ours was not a part, show that this result is not a freak[2]. More particularly, this shape of curve is obtained, as we shall see later, because on the one hand many relevant documents do not contain all or most of the request terms, while on the other, many request terms occur in a large number of documents.

But what sort of improvement in performance should we try to obtain in this case? Curve 2 in Figure 2.8 represents a simple improvement in recall over the given curve 1; but the sagging shape of the curve suggests that what we should try for is the result represented by curve 3. A simple im-

33

provement in recall is hardly worth while, because almost maximum recall is obtained anyway by level 1, so the only gain is in being able to make a cutoff; and though recall is not very good at the highest matching level, so that we do gain something from a classification giving us curve 2, the overall improvement in performance represented by curve 2 is not really good

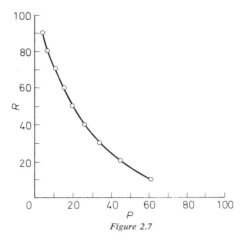

Figure 2.7

enough. We should try to obtain the relatively greater improvement in the middle levels which is typical of curve 3 as well. In doing this, moreover, we are essentially looking for an improvement here in precision as well as recall, because this is what the change in the shape of the curve amounts to. It is in any case clear that we want some improvement in precision

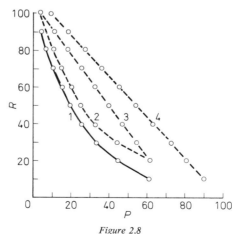

Figure 2.8

34

because it is very low at low levels, and the maximum reached at the highest level is only 80 per cent. So the final conclusion is that we should aim at a performance curve like 4.

The important point about curve 1, indeed, is what it tells us about keywords. It suggests that keywords do not behave in quite the same way at high levels and at low levels; and if this is true, the consequences of substituting classes for terms may not be wholly predictable. This is, of course, a particular instance of the general problem which is presented by the performance differences which occur at different coordination levels because the character of a request specification is changed by being reduced: for partial matches do correspond to a reduced specification. What we have to do now, therefore, is look more closely at the way keywords work in retrieval, and particularly at the effect of reducing keyword specifications, in order to see what is likely to happen if we try to substitute classes for keywords.

There is little doubt that, at high levels, keywords are characterised by fairly high precision, and low recall. If a sufficient number of request keywords match a document specification, the chances are that the document is relevant; but few documents are like this. The general assumption is that keywords are fairly selective, especially in combination, but that their extractive power is low, so that we should not obtain too many documents, and hence not too many false drops, even at low coordination levels, even if this means that we also miss relevant documents. It is usually believed that the characteristic retrieval property of a keyword indexing language is that it is selective rather than comprehensive. But it is a disagreeable fact, at least for our test collection, that individual keywords may retrieve a very large number of documents, and that they are not particularly selective even in combination, on low levels, as we shall see in detail later. Their performance at low levels is therefore characterised by greater recall, but less precision, than might be expected.

In this situation, the simple argument for substituting a keyword classification for keywords, namely that it will improve recall, does not look so compelling. It is true that it would be agreeable if recall could be improved, if only because this might enable us to apply a cutoff to reduce the actual number of documents inspected, given that very large numbers of documents are retrieved at low levels. But it is arguable that we ought to be trying to improve precision at low levels as much as recall: if keyword recall is reasonably good, and precision comparatively poor, we ought to concentrate on precision. A second problem is that to improve recall absolutely, if the maximum level of 100 per cent has not been reached, we have to enlarge the retrieval capacity of our system, and it is conceivable that this may actually degrade precision. If we try to obtain more documents with a classification, that is, or indeed try to improve recall by promoting relevant documents to higher levels, it is possible that we may reduce precision, especially at high levels, and this is not something we want in the circumstances; improving recall at the cost of precision would only be justifiable if a really conspicuous improvement in recall was desirable, and as this does not seem to be the case, we should not do anything which might degrade precision.

From the foregoing, it follows that we should be as interested in precision, in thinking about the use of a keyword classification, as in recall; and the question we have to ask now is what can we expect of a classification? Have we any good reason for thinking that a classification could be used to improve on keywords in the ways we want one to?

Now if it is the case that a classification does function as a recall device, and assuming that it does perform at least as well as, and possibly better than, keywords alone, we might expect to obtain either curve 2 or curve 3,

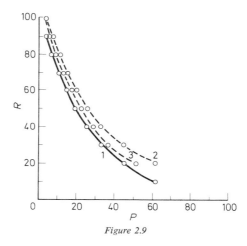

Figure 2.9

curve 1 being the keyword curve, in Figure 2.9. Curve 2 represents a gain in recall without loss of precision, curve 3 some loss of precision in return for the gain in recall. In both cases it is assumed that the substitution of classes for terms will probably lead to an overall increase in the number of documents retrieved, because more alternative term combinations are allowed to match, but that the relationship between the precision and recall ratios will not differ as much in the case of curve 2 as of curve 3, because more relevant documents have been obtained.

But now, is it likely that a classification of the kind we have been considering will act solely as a recall device? We have on the contrary seen that an overlapping classification can in principle promote precision because we can use class matches to control keyword matches, in the sense of ensuring that the right senses of words match, as well as to supplement them. The important question, therefore, is whether we can expect any real gain overall, because the fact that a classification may eliminate some of the irrelevant documents which are obtained with keywords may be counter-balanced by the fact that a classification may retrieve more documents altogether while pulling out the additional relevant documents which are not obtained with keywords. While a classification can in principle function as both a recall device and a precision device, that is, so that we can in principle look for an improvement in both respects over keywords, which is what we want, can we in practice expect a classification to promote both recall and precision? Or will we get an increase in the number of documents retrieved which is not confined to relevant documents, because the precision device represented by the overlapping classes is not powerful enough to eliminate irrelevant ones. The same problem of course arises if we are not interested in raising the maximum recall, because it is fairly high already, but are interested in promoting relevant documents, to obtain better recall at higher matching levels; we may only succeed in doing this by also promoting irrelevant documents, so we may get no improvement in precision.

These questions are very awkward ones. We can, of course, say that the actual results we obtain when we work with classifications give us our answers: and clearly, if we obtain a performance curve for a classification which is better than the keyword curve in all respects, we have achieved what we want; the classification is functioning both as a recall and as a precision device. However, we may still wish to understand what is happening in detail, and we may also want to plan our experiments, rather than simply carry them out at random; and for these reasons, we should try to describe the relation between keywords and keyword classifications. The problem is that the relation between the retrieval performance of a request in keyword form, and in its corresponding class form, may be quite complex in detail; it depends on the distribution of words in classes, and in documents, and it is therefore extremely difficult to predict what the effect of using a classification, as opposed to keywords, will be. Direct comparisons are made more difficult too, if matching is geared to coordination levels: when a keyword can occur in more than one class, the total number of classes for a request may be quite large (up to 45 in our tests, for example, compared with a maximum of 11 keywords), and when the number of classes per keyword varies, it is impossible to say that any level of class matching corresponds with some level of keyword matching, particularly since the same class may be generated by more than one keyword. Of course this does not matter from the point of view of comparisons between performance curves as wholes; but it is a disadvantage from the research point of view, because it makes the analysis of what is happening in detail so difficult. If we have a class match on level 3, for instance, this can correspond to a match on one, two or three keywords. This is not very informative, if we are trying to find out what happens when we replace keywords by classes at different levels, and the only way of doing this properly is by a complete analysis of the class membership and document distribution of the request keywords, and this requires a large amount of work.

Methods of using keywords and classes

In this situation, we decided that the best approach would be to consider various ways of using classes to characterise requests and documents, which would enable us to see how classifications and keywords are related, and also, hopefully, to see how classification can influence recall and precision. We have so far simply assumed that keywords constitute one indexing language, and keyword classes another; but we can in fact set up keyword class descriptions in more than one way, so that we have different indexing languages. If we are considering keywords and keyword classifications, we have a range of possible indexing languages. Two of these are of course quite straightforward: we simply use coordinated keywords, or the corresponding set of classes, to describe a document or a request. As we saw earlier, we can say in Cleverdon's terms that, starting with the base keywords, we have a language with a null recall device in the first case, and the classes as a recall device in the second, and a language with coordination as a precision device in the first case, and with coordination and sense specification as precision devices in the second[3].

The use of simple keyword or class lists can, however, be regarded as rather crude, because no attempt is made to take into account the fact that some items in a specification are more important than others. We have not explored ways of modifying a keyword list by weighting, largely because we were not given the necessary information about our collection; but Salton has found that weighting keywords by their frequency (actually in abstracts) noticeably improves retrieval performance[4]. We have concentrated mainly on the treatment of a classification, but a more sophisticated use of keywords as a base for classification would be possible: it would be easy, for example, to weight classes to match their source keyword weights. A rather more subtle alternative is to set up the class description for a request or document in such a way that a similar effect is achieved, though without the explicit use of term weights: this again is a way of making the class description more discriminating. The simple substitution of classes for terms is clearly rather crude, precisely because it only takes the occurrences of the terms into account; it does not reflect any of their other properties; and though these may not be explicit, it may be possible to make inferences about them. If we weight terms directly, and then their corresponding classes, we are incorporating an additional precision device in our classification; but we may be able, given an overlapping classification, to obtain an analogous effect, without needing the term weights, and in fact in a more sophisticated way, as follows.

Suppose we take the term list for a request or document, and list all the classes for these terms; it is quite probable that some of these classes may be generated by more than one term in the initial specification: the classes themselves were obtained from collocations, and one or more of these collocations may well occur in a given request or document. We may then say that the class specification of the request or document should consist, not simply of a list of classes, but of a list of classes to which weights are attached, reflecting the number of different keywords they are generated by.

Suppose, for example, that we have a request with three terms, a, b and c, which occur in three classes, as in Figure 2.10. In this case we will obtain a class specification in which C1 and C3 have weight 1, and C2 has weight 2. This is clearly like giving terms a and b a greater weight than c; but the important point is that the class overlaps enable us to obtain something more refined than the simple term weighting.

Figure 2.10

For in assigning a greater weight to C2 than C1, we are weighting one sense of a, namely that defined by C2, as opposed to the other, which is defined by C1. If we weight our terms to start with, on the other hand, we are not weighting what is presumably the relevant sense specifically in this way. We can of course weight classes by their frequency in this way, if we do not have an overlapping classification, because we may still find that more than one of the listed terms occur in the same class; it is merely that as we already have an overlapping classification we can exploit it to give a more discriminating weighting.

Selecting classes in this way gives us another class-using index language, which differs slightly from the first one because it incorporates an additional precision device, namely weighting, as well as coordination and class over-lap. We can obtain yet another language, which also incorporates weighting, though in a more drastic way, as follows. Suppose again that we have a term list which generates a class list in which some classes are repeated. We may then say that the class specification of the request or document concerned should consist not of a simple list of all the classes, or of a list in which some items are weighted, but of a list only of the classes which are repeated because they are associated with more than one class term. For the previous example, for instance, we retain C2, and reject C1 and C3. This is clearly a form of weighting, and it is also one which gains in effect, like the previous one, if it is used with an overlapping classification. In this case, however, we are saying that some classes are so unimportant that they should be eliminated altogether. The effect on the example is rather extreme, but with the typical request or document list, which is much longer, a more moderate result would probably be obtained. This selection of some classes could, moreover, be combined with a weighting by frequency of the retained classes, as in the previous case, to produce an even more sophisticated result. The general effect of all these weighting methods is, however, the same: we select (or emphasise) classes for some term senses only, either

39

by selecting classes for some terms only, or by selecting only some of the classes for a term; we are presupposing that some terms, or rather some term uses, are more important as characterisations of the request or document.

Now in all of these cases, we are considering more complex ways of using classes, on the assumption that the keyword specifications from which our class specifications are derived are themselves thrown away: once we have substituted classes for terms, we lose the information that the requests or documents were originally characterised by certain specific terms. A rather different possibility is suggested by the idea that the performance of keywords can hardly fail to be better than that of classes in some cases, that is at high coordination levels rather than low ones, because the combination of the keywords ensures matches on their correct senses only, while the fact that class overlaps permit this too is counterbalanced by the fact that classes allow matches on other words which may not be appropriate. Can we, therefore, combine keywords and classes in some way, to obtain an indexing language which maximises the advantages obtainable from each in some way, and in particular avoids losing the valuable information represented by the base term description. In keyword retrieval we perhaps do not gain as much benefit from this as we should, because keyword retrieval has other disadvantages; and it would be nice if we could somehow use classes to help us to gain more.

The general approach to doing this is as follows. We form a combined request or document specification, consisting both of keywords and their classes; we preserve, that is, the distinction between the source keywords and their class-mates which is lost if we simply substitute classes for keywords; and in the actual process of retrieval we look for matches under both heads, but with a preference for direct matches on the source keywords as opposed to indirect matches on their class-mates. We say, therefore, that matches on some members of our classes are more important than matches on others. This again is clearly a form of weighting: we are regarding the source keywords as more significant, the additional ones as less so, though they are still valuable enough to be used. In this case, therefore, we are expanding our specification to include more terms, with a view to promoting recall, but in such a way that precision is maintained, and, hopefully, more effectively than we may be able to maintain it with classes alone.

It naturally becomes somewhat difficult to be clear about the distinctions between the various recall and precision devices which are being used in these more complex languages. The total amount of information contained in the keyword and class specifications of a request or document is very large, and it can be exploited in many different ways. We can, for instance, add a class weighting of the kind we examined previously to the keyword weighting we have just considered. Suppose, for example, that we have a request or document specification consisting of the keywords a, b, c and d,

40

and that these occur in some classes with other terms, such as e, f, etc., as in Figure 2.11.

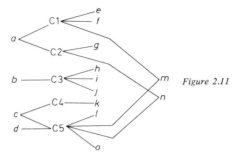

Figure 2.11

Now the drastic class weighting scheme we discussed earlier would select class C5 to represent the specification, so that we would permit matches on any of the keywords c, d, l, m, n and o. We can clearly combine this with the keyword weighting we have just considered, so that we say that we will permit preferred matches on the source keywords a, b, c and d, and additional matches not on any of e, f, etc., but only on l, m, n and o.

This suggestion in turn opens up a further possibility. We have so far spoken either of keyword matches or class matches; but this is of course slightly misleading, because class matches are keyword matches: when we substitute a class for a term, we are simply substituting matches on any of a set of keywords for a match on a single keyword. We have, however, hitherto thought only in terms of allowing matches on the whole set of keywords contained in a class, if we are using classes. But we can in fact use classes as a more selective device for expanding a given keyword list. Suppose, for instance, that we have an initial list of request terms, a, b and

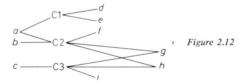

Figure 2.12

c, and that they occur in classes, with other terms, d, e and so on, as in Figure 2.12.

In principle, if we substitute the classes C1, C2 and C3 for the given keywords, we permit matches on any of d, e, f, g, h or i, as well as on a, b or c. But as g and h occur in more than one of these classes, we may conclude that they are especially closely related to the initial set of keywords, and we may then say that these keywords only should be selected to enlarge the initial set consisting of a, b and c, so that we obtain the revised set a, b, c, g and h. This again is a way of exploiting the classification both as a recall and as a precision device, or rather as two precision devices, because we have not merely the selection of the initial word senses which is supplied by overlapping classes, but also a selection of only some additional words to supplement the original specification. We could of course use this procedure together with a weighting of the initial request or document keywords of the kind we considered earlier: it would then give us, for the example illustrated in Figure 2.11, not the secondary keywords l, m, n and o, but the secondary keywords m and n.

It will be evident that there are many ways of using a classification, some of them rather baroque; I have just listed some of the possibilities, but other methods of substituting classes for keywords, or of combining them, could certainly be devised. Any of these methods could also be combined with the use of explicitly weighted keywords, to give more alternatives. We have not been able to try very many of these different indexing languages, but we have experimented with some of the possibilities; and we should be able to learn something about the retrieval potential of keyword classifications from the tests we have carried out with simple keywords, simple classes, classes with frequencies, and combined keywords and classes.

Search strategies

What sort of retrieval performance we get with these languages will of course depend also on the actual search procedure we use. The matching algorithm is basically independent of the indexing language which is used to describe documents or requests, in the sense that we can define our procedure in principle without any reference to a specific language. We can, for example, say that our matching algorithm consists of a search with a full request specification, whatever this is, and a further search with successively smaller partial specifications. The details of the matching algorithm, however, clearly depend on the properties of the languages which are actually used for the specifications, though this is perhaps not so obvious if we look at the straightforward languages. Thus if we have simple coordinated keywords, the natural procedure is to start with full list searches, and to continue with searches with progressively reduced sub-lists; this gives us the familiar result with documents retrieved on successively lower coordination levels. The simple class language suggests a similar procedure, though it is, as we have seen, difficult to attach any significance to individual levels, because the actual numbers of classes involved are of no significance. This is at any rate the search procedure we have adopted, though it has rather disagreeable consequences at low recall levels, where very irregular performance curves are obtained because the successive reduction in the number of classes does not correspond in a straightforward way with the keyword characterisation of the documents. The procedure suited to the weighted class language is equally obvious: here we simply demand a class frequency for a class characterising a document which is greater than, or the same as, its frequency for the request; this requirement is simply superimposed on the search for matches on these classes at the class coordination levels.

The fact that the indexing languages and search strategies are closely related, however, is brought out by the way in which the combined languages we have examined are used in retrieval. In these cases we have searched primarily with the coordinated source keywords, on different levels, in the way in which we would search if we were using these keywords alone; and we have then treated further class matches, or additional keyword matches, as extra keyword matches, so that any documents which match on these additional keywords are moved up from the level to which they were assigned on their source keyword matches.

We have in fact tried two alternative ways of specifying further classes for matching. One, the 'inclusive' mode, considers classes associated with any non-matching request keywords. The other, 'exclusive', mode considers only classes not associated with matching words. The former is less restricted because matches on classes which contain matching as well as non-matching keywords are allowed. Thus if we imagined that we were using a specification which consisted of keywords and classes, *tout court*, or thought simply of working with a full specification first, and then a reduced specification, we would fail to obtain the right effect: we have to preserve the distinction between base keywords and additional keywords, or classes, during matching.

The logical way of looking at the use of a classification in retrieval as a whole, therefore, is to say that we have a variety of indexing languages which differ in the recall and precision devices they incorporate, where these devices are largely provided by a classification; and that we use the same search procedure with all of them. This is, moreover, the correct way of looking at the situation: we do have a variety of different indexing languages, and we do use what is essentially the same matching algorithm with all of them. However, the fact that the way the matching algorithm works in detail depends so much on the character of the language suggests a rather different way of looking at the situation, and we have indeed looked at the relation between index languages and search procedures in this way during our experiments. We have behaved as if we have a single classificatory language, and a whole battery of different search algorithms which exploit the classification in different ways designed to promote recall and precision according to our interests. We have, as it were, incorporated the recall and precision devices in our search strategy, rather than in our given document and request specifications. This is largely a consequence of the way our programs work: the retrieval program is provided simply with document and request keyword specifications, and with keyword class lists, and it then proceeds to manipulate these in different ways, according to our choice of what we describe as modes of retrieval. A particular choice of mode triggers off a specific way of manipulating request and document specifications, given the initial keyword lists and the corresponding simple lists of classes. We have therefore found it easier to describe our actual experiments in terms of a single classificatory indexing language, or rather in terms of two indexing languages consisting respectively of keywords and classes, and a range of retrieval procedures using them. It must nevertheless be emphasised that what we have been concerned with, from the theoretical point of view, is a range of different indexing languages: what the results of our experiments really tell us about are the effects of different languages, and not the effects of different matching algorithms.

REFERENCES

1. *Factors* 2, Chapter 4; *ISR–11*, Chapter V; *ISR–12*, Chapter III
2. *Factors* 2, Chapter 4
3. *Factors* 2, Chapter 2
4. *ISR–11*, Chapter V; *ISR–12*, Chapter III

Chapter 3

Classification Techniques

SUMMARY

This chapter deals with the most important part of our theoretical work, namely that on classification techniques. We started with the assumption that loosely knit and overlapping classes were what was needed for retrieval purposes, and we began our experiments by applying the grouping procedures derived from the theory of clumps which were intended to produce this kind of classification. It is possible to characterise individual classification procedures in terms of quite general properties, and it seems fairly clear that classifications with some of these properties are not appropriate where keyword classification is concerned: we do not, for example, want hierarchical or exclusive term classifications. We can, however, distinguish different kinds of multiple classification, again by referring to general properties such as whether classes are necessarily based on individual elements or not, whether they depend only on similarity connections within a class or on both internal and external connections, and so on; and for any kind of multiple classification which is characterised by some combination of these properties, we can list a variety of specific class definitions. In working with the theory of clumps we were concentrating on a set of definitions of one particular kind; but these did not give very satisfactory results, and this led us to question the assumption that this was the kind of classification we required. We realised that it was necessary to investigate other kinds of multiple classification, and we set up a frame of reference for doing this by establishing four types of classification, namely 'strings', 'stars', 'cliques' and 'clumps', which would allow systematic comparisons between different classifications in the retrieval context. The consequences of using specific class definitions could be properly understood, and the differences between classifications clearly exhibited, by referring to their relations within the common framework. The four types themselves, and the representative class definitions of each type with which we have actually worked, are described. The role of the definition of similarity on which these class specifications depend is also discussed, and the similarity coefficients we have studied are described.

The use of clumps

The general character of our approach to automatic classification for retrieval, and our justification for it, were outlined in Chapter 1. In this chapter we have to look at the specific classification procedures we have developed, and at the classificatory properties of the keyword groupings they produce. We started, of course, with more than a general idea of the kind of classification we wanted and the way it should be obtained; we began with grouping techniques which had been developed under the general heading of the theory of clumps, and which represented particular ways of implementing the basic approach to classification we thought we should adopt for retrieval purposes. These particular definitions were designed, therefore, to generate classifications which permitted comparatively weakly connected, overlapping classes. We wanted overlapping classes because we wished to distinguish the different senses of words in the way that these were distinguished by the various affiliations of words in the original lattice; and we were therefore interested in class definitions which allowed as much overlapping as followed naturally from the co-occurrence information about words on which the classification was based. We wanted weakly connected classes because we recognised that the general distribution of word co-occurrences over a set of documents is liable to be irregular and (from the abstract point of view) haphazard. This is not simply because the information about word relationships contained in a collection of document occurrence lists is incomplete: these irregularities are a consequence of the fact that words are used, purposively, in different connections in different texts, and we want our classification to reflect this irregularity in the way in which the lattice reflected it. The work on the theory of clumps therefore concentrated on definitions generating classes depending on stronger internal connections than external ones, rather than on internal ones only: we thought that looking for maximally connected classes, or cliques, would be a mistake, for example. This interest in, as it were, reproducing the lattice also meant that we excluded class definitions depending on single elements: looking for sets of comparatively well-connected items could be described as an attempt to pick up the denser areas of the lattice network. At the beginning of our project, therefore, we thought that we would be concerned with the application of some current clump definitions on a larger scale, and possibly with the investigation of alternative definitions, should these turn out to be unsatisfactory: for although we believed that one particular kind of classification was suited to retrieval, we recognised that different definitions of this kind could generate classifications which differed in detail; and some of these might be more appropriate than others, if only because, as subsequent experiments have shown, the particular character of the set of objects which is being classified can influence the classification to a surprising extent.

Two other legacies of the work on the theory of clumps must be mentioned. One is that we were interested in general classification techniques, which were suited to quite different applications, rather than in methods which were designed specifically to suit our retrieval requirements. We have, in fact, been obliged to change our ideas about the consequences of the retrieval application for the kind of classification technique we should develop. But the fact that when we began we thought in terms of a particular application of a general theory is very important; the general work on classification has been of great value because it has acted as a frame of reference for the particular work on the retrieval application, even though our views about the status of retrieval classifications have changed. The study of classification in general on which our initial research was based has meant that we have been able to distinguish purely classificatory considerations from retrieval considerations; we have been able, in looking at the performance of a given classification, to separate features of the classification which follow from the grouping technique we have been using from those which follow from the properties of the material we have been using, and from those which follow from the retrieval use of the classification. We have also learned a great deal from applications in other areas, such as archaeology, which have again served to bring out the particular consequences of the retrieval application.

The second important aspect of our work on classification which is derived from the research on the theory of clumps is the emphasis we place on the practical side of classification. We have always confined ourselves, that is, to 'technological' definitions, or definitions which can be successfully applied on a large scale without an altogether unreasonable consumption of computer time. Some approaches, though they have attractive theoretical properties, lead to such computational complexity where large universes of objects are involved that they cannot be regarded as realistic methods of grouping for applications, like the retrieval one, which necessarily involve large sets of objects. We have to think, in our own case, for instance, of techniques which can be applied to thousands of keywords. It is true that improvements in computers mean that we can describe an increasing number of procedures as feasible; but we still have to accept some limitations: any class-finding algorithm which commences: take all the subsets of the universe set, is not an algorithm we can contemplate applying to tens of thousands of objects. We have always felt that these practical considerations are of considerable importance, if automatic classification is to be of any value where it is most needed, namely in those cases where the universe is large enough to preclude effective manual classification; and we have therefore concentrated on class definitions which can be applied without too much difficulty. It is of course the case that a class definition may not naturally lead to a search procedure (other than the exhaustive examination of subsets, which is always theoretically possible), so that the propriety of the particular method of obtaining classes on such a definition has also to be established. This naturally leads to problems concerning the exhaustiveness of the classification. Whether it matters that a classification is not exhaustive is one of the interesting questions about the relation between classification theory and classification practice which arises in the retrieval context to which I shall return later.

Bearing these points in mind, we can now turn to the details of our work on classification. We have so far behaved as if the formation of a classification depends solely on the application of a particular grouping technique to the co-occurrence information we can extract for our keywords from their occurrences in our initial document lists. But it is more correct to say that the classification process has two stages, because the normal procedure is to compute a connection or association or similarity matrix for pairs of terms from this initial information about co-occurrences; and the class-finding procedure is then applied to this matrix. Different choices of similarity coefficient are possible, so that we have to recognise that the

47

matrix-formation procedure and the group-finding procedure are separate components of the classification process as a whole, which both require consideration. It is, however, convenient to start by considering class definitions, on the assumption that we are given a similarity matrix in which the notes of simple co-occurrence between terms have been replaced by more complex coefficients. It is also useful to establish a terminology for talking about the different aspects of classification, given the very varied ways in which such words as 'connection' and 'similarity', for example, are used in this field. I shall therefore use 'association' to refer to any number of co-occurrences for a pair of terms, so that two terms are associated if they co-occur at all; 'co-occurrence' to refer to the actual number of their co-occurrences; 'connection' to refer to a non-zero similarity between a pair of terms; and 'similarity' to refer to the actual value of the connection. In many cases 'co-occurrence' and 'association' can be used interchangeably, as can 'connection' and 'similarity'. In discussing class definitions I shall also abandon the specific reference to keywords or terms; I shall use the more general terms 'object' and 'element' instead.

The research on the theory of clumps which preceded our project appeared to show that satisfactory definitions of clumps could be based on the general notion of 'cohesion': a class or clump is obtained if the cohesion between a set of objects and the remainder of the universe, which is expressed in terms of the ratio between the similarities within the set and between the set and its complement, is minimised. This clearly follows from the general idea that we are looking for relatively well-connected sets of objects: we want a class definition which maintains a balance between the internal and external connections of a set, or between what may be described as the internal coherence of a class and its separation from the remainder of the universe. The first such definition which was considered was as follows. If A is the set of objects constituting the putative clump, and B its complement, SAA is the total of similarities between the members of A, SBB the total between the members of B, and SAB the total of similarities between all the members of A and all the members of B. The cohesion function, G, is then defined as

$$G = \frac{SAB}{SAA + SBB}$$

This function, which can be referred to as the arithmetic cohesion function, is symmetric, so that both of the sets into which the universe of objects is partitioned are strictly clumps; though conventionally only the smaller of the two is taken as a clump. Unfortunately this definition is objectionable because a fairly cumbrous search procedure is needed to find clumps. In general terms, clump-finding involves an iterative scan over the universe of objects to see whether shifting objects from one side to the other of a given partition between a potential clump and its complement will reduce the current value of the cohesion function; but in this particular case one set is liable to disappear completely and an elaborate resetting of the partition to prevent such a collapse is required.

The natural alternative is the geometric cohesion function

$$G = \frac{SAB^2}{SAA \times SBB}$$

with which a wholly simple scanning and shifting search procedure may be combined. This definition, which we will call the SAB^2 definition*, was the first we actually tried with our test collection: earlier experiments with it in other fields appeared to be satisfactory, and it seemed to have the right properties for our retrieval application.

First experiments with clumps

Unfortunately, we found that the retrieval performance of the classification we obtained with this definition was poor, and that the classification itself had odd properties. A very large number of terms were not classified at all, while the other classes were, generally speaking, large. The poor retrieval performance, compared with terms alone, could be attributed to the defective character of the classes which were obtained: the unclassified terms were treated as unit classes, and so behaved like the corresponding terms, which meant that the other classes were necessarily responsible for the less good performance of the classification. At the same time, any benefits which we were supposing could be obtained from classes could not be obtained for all the unclassified terms, so that no improvement over single terms could be looked for in these cases. This unsatisfactory result was, moreover, not due to the particular properties of the keyword vocabulary being classified: we have obtained similar results with the variant vocabularies I shall describe later. The character of the classification obtained with any class definition of this sort will also depend on the coefficient used to compute similarities, but again tests with different similarity definitions did not give conspicuously better results; and it was therefore clear that the classification did not perform well because it was not suited to material with the general properties of that under study. This was basically because a keyword in a fairly dense document collection, characterised by reasonably long word lists, tends to have a fair number of similarity connections, some of which may be strong, but many of which will be weak. Now the general intention of the SAB^2 definition is to identify relatively denser areas of the connection network; it does not depend exclusively on individually strong similarities, but on the aggregate value of the similarities between a set of objects, so that the members of a class may be linked either by a few strong similarities,

---

* This abbreviated way of referring to clump definitions, as opposed to the conventional one using numbers, has been adopted to make the discussion of our experiments in later chapters clearer.

or many weak ones (or both, of course). If any of the objects being classified have a relatively large number of connections, however, it will almost certainly be the case that these objects get pulled out of classes, as it were, as soon as they get put into them, because their aggregate similarities with the usually larger complement of a putative clump will tend to be bigger than their similarities with the clump; and the net result will be that some objects do not get clumped at all.

Essentially, these difficulties arise with the SAB^2 definition because it is symmetric: the connections between the members of the complement B of the putative clump influence the formation of the clump as much as its own internal connections and the connections between the two. This is clearly objectionable. It is true that the class definition may not have been the sole cause of the trouble; it is clear that many of the weaker connections in a large similarity matrix like the one under discussion are not really significant, and if these connections are removed, this will presumably reduce the chances of an object being pulled out of a clump by the aggregate effect of many small similarities. But doing this in practice does not seem to deal with the problem of unclassified elements in a radical way. It can also be argued that terms with many connections, which were often unclassified, should not in fact be classified, just because they have too many affiliations to justify their assignment to individual classes: they should form unit classes. But such objects may have some individually strong connections which might justify their assignment to some classes; and the grouping procedure in any case did not treat such objects in a consistent way: some were classified, though some were not. It was also the case that some terms with few connections were not classified; and while it can again be argued that if such terms are not classified this can correctly indicate an absence of any significant connections, it did not seem to do so in practice. We in fact thought that there might be some justification for giving very frequently occurring terms, which are normally the ones with many connections, special treatment, by removing them from the set of objects to be classified altogether and treating them as independent unit classes, on the grounds that their many connections tend to disturb the grouping propensities of other terms, even if the classification algorithm correctly treats them as unit classes. From the retrieval point of view there are good reasons for treating such terms as unit classes, as we shall see later, and this somewhat crude way of doing it is likely to be more effective than any classification procedure, which can hardly be expected to cope with the various problems presented by what can be described as idiosyncratic objects in a thorough and consistent way.

Quite apart from the fact, however, that objects with many connections can present problems for any classification procedure, there is no doubt that the SAB^2 definition is not wholly satisfactory. This is clearly shown by the result obtained with a reduced vocabulary from which very frequent terms had been eliminated. The general character of the classification was the same as before, that is to say, there were still a large number of unclassified items, combined with some miscellaneous, generally large classes. Now it is true that it is not easy to know what the effect of different facts about objects on their classification should be, and how much weight we should attach to such facts as the number of connections of an object, their relative strength, and so on; but we felt that the classifications produced by the SAB[2] definition were defective because as many as one-third of the objects in the universe were not classified, and this did not seem to be justified by the relationships among the objects. We believed, therefore, that a better retrieval performance could be obtained with a classification in which more of the connections between objects were exploited: not only do unclassified objects lack affiliations which may be useful; classes of the kind we obtained lack objects which may, so to speak, give them a rationale. We felt, therefore, that we could legitimately look for a fuller classification, and since the defects of the classifications which were based on the SAB[2] definition could be attributed to its being symmetrical, we decided to investigate cohesion definitions which were concerned only with the properties of a putative clump, and not with those of its complement as well.

The first such definition we investigated was as follows: if NA is the number of elements in A,

$$G = \frac{SAB}{SAA} \times \frac{NA^2 - NA}{SAA}$$

We did not, however, feel very happy about this definition either, largely because it produced large and very heavily overlapping classes. We unfortunately could not test any classifications based on this definition for purely practical reasons associated with the size and number of classes involved; but we thought that they were most unlikely to give good retrieval results because they would retrieve very large numbers of necessarily mostly non-relevant documents. We also felt that the definition was not explicit enough, for research purposes. If a class definition is intended to hold a balance between the internal coherence of a clump and its external separateness, it is useful to have a definition in which these two components are clearly distinguished, so that we can study the effect of changes in the balance between the two. We therefore revised this NA definition to obtain a fourth cohesion function as follows[1]:

$$G = \frac{SAB}{SAA} \times \left(\frac{NA^2 - NA}{SAA} - \left(\frac{100}{P} \times \frac{SAA}{NA^2 - NA} \right) \right)$$

Here 100/P is a constant which can be given a chosen value in advance to place more or less weight on the internal coherence of the potential clump A. This definition, particularly with one value of P, produces classifications which do not suffer from the specific defects of those obtained with the SAB[2] and NA definitions: the assignment of objects to classes is more complete, and the classes are generally smaller and better differentiated.

The retrieval performance of the classifications obtained with the 100/P definition is also better, and this can presumably be attributed to these differences in the character of the classifications. We cannot be absolutely certain about this: the construction of clump-type classifications is a complicated business, and it is always difficult to correlate the characteristics of its retrieval performance with the properties of a classification. But it does seem to be the case that the distinctive properties of the 100/P classifications which I have just listed are responsible for their better performance; from the retrieval point of view, those of the other classifications are defects. This point cannot be emphasised too strongly: whether we regard a classification as acceptable or not depends on its retrieval performance. In one sense, any classification is acceptable: it is incorrect to say, for example, that a classification is a bad one because some objects do not fall into any classes, or because it contains many large classes. Remarks like this are only legitimate if what we mean is that the classification is defective because some objects are unclassified, and this is the reason why it does not work well in retrieval. Evaluative remarks about the classificatory properties of classifications must always be interpreted in this way: the importance of the purpose for which a classification is required is shown by the fact that we want our classification to have such and such classificatory properties, because this means that it will work well, although this may lead us to a classification which is perhaps not the most obvious or natural one, from the point of view of the information about the objects with which we are working.

A more comprehensive approach to classification

Now though the 100/P definition gave better results than the others in our first experiments, these were still less good than those which were obtained for keywords alone; and the generally inadequate performance of these clump-type classifications, compared with that for terms, suggested that the theories about the kind of classification we require for retrieval purposes, with which we started our project, were themselves mistaken. We had assumed that a loose classification, based on a definition which did not impose strict conditions on class membership, was appropriate, as well as one which was overlapping. But the fact that even the best of these classifications did not do very well led us to suspect this whole theory of retrieval classification. At the same time, we found that Salton's list of the criteria for a successful retrieval thesaurus, which was based on experiments with different manual classifications, included the requirement that classes should be small and strongly connected[2]. It is of course not necessarily the case that a class must be small to be well connected, but this tends to be true in practice: so saying that small classes are wanted can be interpreted to mean that well-connected classes are wanted. We therefore felt that the idea that we wanted loosely connected classes was perhaps mistaken, though we had no reason to abandon the belief that we wanted an overlapping classification: and abandoning our original view of retrieval classifications led us, in turn, to think that we should look again at the whole question of what a retrieval classification should be like.

We felt, therefore, that it was necessary to revise our plan of research, to allow a much more comprehensive study of classification in the retrieval context. Our initial approach was much too narrow. It was clear that we had no real justification, or at least did not have sufficient justification, for our assumption that the particular kind of classification with which we have been concerned was what was required; and that we were mistaken in trying to find the best classification of this particular kind, when we had not demonstrated that this type of classification was indeed the right one. We were forced to conclude that any attempt to compare specific classifications, like those based on different clump definitions, would be pointless if it was not tied to a broader analysis of classification in the retrieval context. A number of algorithms for constructing retrieval thesauri have been proposed, and these are naturally associated with some general belief about the kind of classification which is suited to retrieval. But these general beliefs, as we have seen, are often not examined with the critical attention they deserve, and they may not even be made explicit. This is clearly very unsatisfactory. A more important point is that no serious experiments covering a wide range of classifications have been carried out, so that any tests which have been made of particular classifications are deprived of a frame of reference. It is therefore extremely difficult to evaluate the results of these experiments, other than by direct comparisons with terms alone; and this is not sufficient to show, even if a classification does better than the terms, that the classification is a particularly good one. The general absence of a real context for these experiments means, for example, that it may be difficult to attribute the relative success of a given classification to what may be described as its macro properties, or to its micro ones, that is to its being a classification of a certain kind, or to its being based on a specific definition. This in turn means, for instance, that we may not be able to say that the performance of a particular classification could probably be matched by that of another which could be obtained more economically, and so on.

Our difficulties in trying to draw correct inferences from our first experiments with clumps made us aware, then, of the lack of a general frame of reference for detailed comparisons between retrieval classifications. We realised, in particular, that individual classification algorithms should be clearly related to general kinds of classification, if the effects of using them are to be properly interpreted. The fact that a particular kind of classification is required may be as important as, or more important than, the fact that a specific form of this classification is needed; and we cannot, therefore, conclude that some classification is what we really want, at least in some circumstances, unless we have shown, not merely that it is a good classification of its kind, but that it is a classification of the right kind.

A simple frame of reference

The original object of our project, to investigate the use of the theory of clumps for retrieval purposes, was therefore replaced by a much more substantial one, that of studying a range of classifications of different kinds, including clump-type classifications, but contrasting these with others. For this purpose we set up a frame of reference for classification experiments which we hoped would enable us to collate the results of different experiments in a systematic rather than an *ad hoc* way. This classification framework covers four types of classification, under which a variety of individual definitions may be subsumed. It must be emphasised that these types are not intended to exhaust all the kinds of classification I discussed earlier: though the arguments which led us to consider clump classifications no longer seem to be compelling ones, we can still exclude hierarchical classifications, if we are interested in keyword thesauri. The framework is confined to the multiple classifications without levels which seem to be more suited to our retrieval purpose. It could of course be broadened to include other kinds of classification, if this was thought to be desirable, but it is comprehensive enough as it stands to cover most of the class definitions which have been proposed for handling extracted keywords; it includes, that is, those kinds of classification which were considered earlier in relation to clump-type ones, namely classifications in which classes are based specifically on individual objects, as opposed to those which are not, and classifications which impose absolute conditions on class membership, as well as relative ones. The broad classificatory properties of classifications can, as we saw earlier, be combined in different ways, to give particular kinds of classification; our frame of reference is confined to those kinds which are not hierarchical and not exclusive: it is, however, convenient to categorise these kinds of classification in a rather more detailed way than that which follows simply from their description in terms of the general properties of being individually based, and so on, which we have considered hitherto. We have in fact divided these kinds of classification into four types, which represent a subcategorisation of the kinds given by particular combinations of the general properties; particular class definitions are then assigned to the appropriate type.

Now it must be admitted at once that this framework is extremely crude: it would probably be difficult to defend the categorisation it embodies on the level of classification theory, or at least to maintain that it is immaculate in all its details. It was proposed as a device for controlling classification experiments within a given context, and we have found it invaluable for this purpose. It has in fact made it possible for us to think about and test proposed classifications in a well-organised and fruitful rather than in an undirected and *ad hoc* way. It is true to say that the idea of grouping class definitions according to their high level properties, as a way of simplifying and systematising experiments based on them, has made all the difference to our research. Our experience with the particular framework we set up has suggested various modifications to it, but we feel that it is basically fairly satisfactory. The fact that the use of this framework has made it much easier for us to correlate different experiments is not, however, its only advantage. It has another important consequence, namely that of reducing the enormous number of possible experiments which could be carried out if direct comparisons were made between specific classifications derived from individual class definitions, in which every such classification is regarded as distinct from all the others. This is because particular classifications can be taken as representatives of their types, or at least, if the use of single representatives is thought to be rather rash, given that it would be difficult to show that we had found the best representative, we can at any rate confine ourselves to only a small number of classifications which can be regarded as sufficiently representative of the type, when taken together. We want, therefore, to identify both the best type of classification, and its best examplar; but we can hopefully achieve the first, not by extended comparisons between large numbers of classifications of each type, but by comparatively restricted comparisons between selected examples. We can then concentrate on more detailed investigations of different versions of the same type.

Our classification framework, then, has given us a handle to turn our experimental engine with; and we have found it a very good handle, though it is such a simple one. It has enabled us to identify the interesting features of experiments which have already been carried out, and to plan future comparisons. It seems to us, moreover, that while the division of multiple classifications into these types may look crude to the advanced theorist, it does represent important distinctions between classifications of this general sort: at least, we maintain that it would not be so useful if it was not well founded.

Four types of classification

It is helpful, in considering the four types of classification we have worked with, to say that they are characterised by increasing sophistication, so that type 1 classes are the most simple, and type 4 the most complex. This is a remark both about their logical nature, and that of the search procedure which is typically associated with each. Perhaps the best way of introducing them is by an illustration, giving an example of a class of each type, as in Figure 3.1.

In these figures, the nodes are objects, the links similarity connections

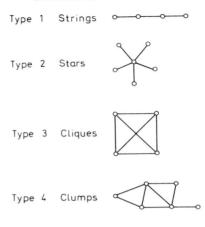

Figure 3.1

between the members of the class which hold it together, that is internal connections on which the existence of the class explicitly depends. Thus strings can reasonably be regarded as the most elementary form of class: we take a specific element, find an element connected with it, and then an element connected with the latter, and so on. With stars, we take an individual element, and select a series of elements connected with it. We obtain a clique by identifying a set of elements which are all connected with each other. Clumps, on the other hand, depend only on a greater density of connections within the set than outside it; the clump diagram is therefore rather misleading because the complementary external connections are omitted.

This is clearly an extremely simplified view of these types of classification; but it is useful to start in this way, before we look at them in more detail. Some of their specific properties can in any case be disregarded here: we can more profitably look, for the moment, at the main features of each type, and at the more striking resemblances and differences between them. Thus we can say, to begin with, that if we consider only those very general classificatory properties of groupings we considered earlier, that we get the following characterisation of our types. Strings and stars are based on individual objects, while cliques and clumps are set based; and strings, stars and cliques impose absolute conditions on class membership, while clumps are relatively defined.

Turning now to their other properties, we can distinguish strings and stars on the one hand, from cliques and clumps on the other, by the way in which they depend on the connections between their members. Strings and stars may depend explicitly on only some of the actual connections between the objects in a set; while cliques and clumps refer explicitly to all of them.

Thus we may have an actual pattern of similarity connections between the members of a string or star as shown in Figure 3.2, for instance: the dotted lines indicate connections which exist but are not exploited, the others the connections on which the string and star depend.

Figure 3.2

As far as cliques or clumps are concerned, on the other hand, there are no connections between the members of a set which do not play a part in the characterisation of the set. This may appear to be a trivial point, but it is in fact an important one, because it is the actual pattern of connections which matters when a class is used in retrieval, as we shall see later. The individual connections between the members of a set are of course thrown away once the set has been found: a classification when it is used in retrieval consists only of lists of terms, but it is obvious that the original connections determine the value of the class. The fact that the specific connections are thrown away incidentally marks the difference between a classification and an association map or network, and indeed between a classification and our original lattice. Some information is thrown away, in return for a simplification which also sharpens up the real groupings and divisions among the objects, and in fact adds information by establishing relationships between objects which may not be directly connected. In talking about the different structures of these types of class, therefore, we are not implying that this is relevant to the actual manipulation of classifications, only that it is responsible for the classifications.

The general remark that the types represent an increasing sophistication in the characterisation of a class is borne out in a number of ways. To start with, as we have seen, strings and stars depend on individual elements, and cliques and clumps do not. This is not a statement about the way they are built up, because clumps may be generated from single elements, but a statement about the logical structure of the classes. From this point of view it is reasonable to say that classes which necessarily depend on single elements are simpler than those which depend on the relationship between a number of elements. We have a rather similar transition from definitions based only on the connection between one element and another, to definitions based on the connection between an element and a set of elements: a given element appears in a string or star solely in virtue of its connection with one other object, namely the base element; an element is added to a clique or clump, on the other hand, because of the way it is connected with the remainder of the objects in the set. This requirement may be formulated in different ways: in cliques a given element must be explicitly connected with all the other elements; in clump-type classes, the requirement may be put in terms of the ratio between the average or sum of internal connections and external ones, and so on, without any reference to specific connections with specific elements.

These distinctions lead, in turn, to what is perhaps the most important difference between the more elementary types and the more sophisticated ones. This is in the relation between an individual class and the universe of objects, as this is reflected by the relationship between the pattern of connections inside the class and the whole network of connections for the universe. The object of a clump-type definition is to identify the sets of objects which are associated with denser areas of the network: a class is obtained if a set of objects are relatively well connected and are seen to be separated from their environment. This is certainly not true of strings and stars, and it only applies to cliques in a sense: in practice, in the ordinary very incomplete network, a clique may in fact represent a well marked-off cluster of items; also may not, since a clique depends on many connections, and so may be surrounded by elements which just miss being members. The important point about strings and stars and cliques, as opposed to clumps, is that classes of these are set up without any reference to the distribution of connections as a whole in the relevant area of the network: the search for the members of a class is limited to the connections between the given element and its immediate neighbours. It then obviously follows that we can perfectly well obtain a star or string and even clique which represents a relatively empty part of the network, so to speak, which would never

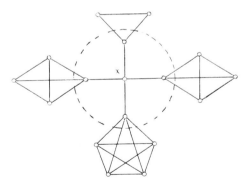

Figure 3.3

be allowed to form a class if we were interested in clumps, for instance. This is easily illustrated by the (rather improbable) example of Figure 3.3, in which we have a complete network of connections, as indicated, and the star based on the element x which is marked by the dotted circle.

In this case, the star based on x in fact represents the weakest part of the network as a whole: it contains unconnected elements, and is surrounded by much more dense sets of connections which in fact define four cliques. We get a similar 'anomaly' if we have the complete network shown in Figure 3.4 and have the string given by proceeding from the element x to y.

Figure 3.4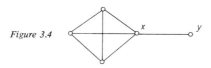

The rather less extreme way in which this situation may arise in connection with cliques can be illustrated by two examples, as shown in Figure 3.5. In the first case we have a set of items which are relatively well separated from the remainder of the universe, because the set as a whole has only the two connections indicated by arrows outside itself; the set as a whole might well form a clump, but only a, b, c and d would form a clique. In the second

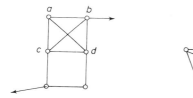

Figure 3.5

case, a, b and c form a clique, although they are themselves linked to many elements which are linked to one another quite strongly.

It is in fact the case that classes like stars can perform quite well in retrieval, which perhaps looks paradoxical from the classification point of view; the implications of this situation will, however, be considered later, in the analysis of the results of our experiments in Chapter 10.

The increasing sophistication also matches the increase in the number of specific class definitions which are possible under the different heads. The alternatives in the first two cases are fairly trivial. For strings, we could set up various criteria for choosing the next element in the string, though the only really sensible one is to take the element which is most strongly connected with the last given element, or at least an element which is sufficiently strongly connected with it. In principle, the formation of a string should terminate naturally, either by looping, or because we have exhausted the connections of the element we are currently looking at. But in classification practice, principles may be modified (for very proper reasons connected with applications), and an obvious additional constraint on strings is to impose some upper limit on the length of a string which does not terminate naturally; the specification of the maximum length of a string is clearly a variable to which a given value can be assigned to suit the purpose at hand.

In a sense, permitting a string to continue until it terminates naturally would not, if the result were at all long, be in the spirit of classification: we are really interested in those elements which are relatively near to one another, and while we may be interested in the fact that this is because they are linked in a string, there will naturally come a point where we have the class structure we are interested in, but our set of objects no longer satisfies the other requirement, that the members of a class should be relatively near one another. There is therefore every reason for adding a subsidiary specification of the length of a string to the definition. In the same way, if we choose to base strings on a sufficient rather than the strongest connection, we have to say what constitutes a sufficient connection, and here too we have a choice of specification. In general terms, that is, it is convenient to distinguish the alternative definitions of a type of class, in this case of a string as a series of maximally connected items or as a series of sufficiently connected ones, from any subsidiary alternative specifications which are associated with the definitions, in this case, of length for either string definition, and of connection threshold for the second.

The choices for stars and cliques are very like those for strings. Thus the only obvious way of selecting the members of a star is to take either the elements which are most strongly connected with a given object, or those which are sufficiently connected with it. In the first case we clearly need to specify a cutoff, so that we choose only the most strongly connected of all the elements, but the cutoff can be chosen to suit the requirements of a given application and the character of the data with which we are working. In the second case, the level of connection can be adjusted as required. We again, however, have an initial choice of definition and subsidiary choices for the specification associated with each. With cliques we do not have a choice of definition, but we do have one of specification, in that it is often only sensible to look at sets of elements which are reasonably strongly connected with one another, and we may therefore apply a threshold which will ensure that cliques do not depend on any weak connections. The level of the threshold can then be adjusted, as before, to suit the universe being classified and the purpose for which the classification is required.

The range of choices for clump-type classifications is much wider, as is shown by the existence of a comparatively large number of definitions of a clump or cluster, and of a range of associated specifications. Broadly speaking, the definitions cover the strength of connections within a class, and between it and its complement, both individually and in total, and the form of the connections between an object and a class, and hence within a class; we may say that an object must have more internal connections than external ones, or a greater strength of connection, and so on. We have in fact only worked with the three definitions based on the notion of cohesion which were given earlier, namely the SAB^2, NA and 100/P definitions. We can again, however, adjust the values of a variety of subsidiary specification parameters to suit particular operational requirements, though in this case we have a wider range of specifications than for previous types of class, to match the generally greater complexity of the clump definitions. We have, of course, a choice of value for the constant P if we use the 100/P definition; but another specification is associated with all three clump definitions. This concerns what was called the gradient test. This was designed to smooth clumping by inhibiting transfers of elements to or from a potential clump, either if the cohesion function would not be significantly reduced, or if the change would be too catastrophic. We thus have a choice, in clump-finding, of applying the test or not, and if we do apply it, subsidiary choices of the maximum and minimum changes in the value of the cohesion function that we are prepared to allow. In fact, as we shall see, this turned out to be a pointless complication, despite its initial attractions.

Both for cliques and clumps, we in principle have a further specification, namely that of the starting position for a search. The choice of a suitable starting procedure naturally cannot arise for element-based classes like strings and stars, and the question is only of technological interest for cliques and clumps if we want an exhaustive clique or clump classification, because the fact that particular starting positions lead to certain classes does not matter if we find all the classes. The question is of interest, however, if we have no means of ensuring that our classification is exhaustive, other than the impracticable one of testing every subset of the universe, and so have to accept the fact that our classification may only be a partial one: in this case, the type of class we get with a particular starting procedure is of interest. The clique and clump definitions we have discussed do not lead naturally to any effective procedures for finding exhaustive classifications, and we are therefore obliged to try any procedures we can find. In this connection, however, purely practical considerations are important: we want starting positions, and also class-formation procedures, which enable us to find classes quite quickly; and for this reason we have worked only with single starting elements in forming clique or clump classifications. The actual class formation procedure has also been kept simple in both cases: for clumps it consists, as we have seen, of an iterative scan of the universe, while for cliques, a single ordered scan only is made. Order-dependent classification procedures like these are clearly inadequate on general grounds, in the sense that they cannot be guaranteed to produce exhaustive classifications, but the individual classes are of course acceptable, and the set of them which is found may constitute an adequate classification for the purpose in question, as we shall see in Chapter 10. In any case, the fact that we have not examined any alternatives in the way of starting positions and search procedures, like the use of random partitions or several connected starting elements, has meant that we have not included either as specifications associated with the types of class in question, though we could clearly include slots for them in principle; we have concentrated primarily on the characteristics of the types of classification themselves.

From the foregoing it will be evident that each type of classification is intended to get round some difficulty of classification, that is, to represent some particular idea of what a classification should be like; cliques, for example, are intended to satisfy the information requirement that a class is a tightly knit set of objects, while strings or stars take into account our intuitive recognition of the fact that objects may fall into a class, although they are not directly connected, because they are linked by connections with common items. But we naturally have a trade-off: we satisfy one intuitive requirement at the cost of another; the beliefs on which strings and cliques respectively are based, for example, are incompatible. So that if we can say that a particular type gets round some particular difficulty of classification, we can also say, from another point of view, that it suffers from some defect. No one type, then, can be regarded in the abstract as the best type of classification: this can only be determined by the results we get when we apply our procedures in a given case. We cannot, moreover, predict what the effect of using a specific type of classification will be: this can vary with the character of the data being classified to a surprising extent; cliques, for example, can be large in relation to the universe, or small, or heavily overlapping, or almost exclusive, depending on the property characterisations of the objects being classified, and their resemblances to one another. Alternatively, we may find that quite different types lead to very similar classifications again because the material being classified has certain features. A final possibility is that different classifications may give comparable results when they are actually applied. These points can, however, be more usefully discussed in connection with the results of actual experiments, and I shall therefore go into them more fully later, in the analysis of the results of our tests in Chapter 10.

Now I have so far emphasised the importance of comparisons between the types of classification; but the existence of many alternatives where clump-type classes are concerned is a useful reminder of the need for experiments with more than one representative of each type, though we can reasonably assume that we need not investigate very many different alternatives in each case; in practice, comparisons between several alternatives of a given type, and between types, in relation to our data and our application, should enable us to identify appropriate definitions and specifications. It will, however, be clear that different definitions and specifications of a given type may lead to classifications which are quite unlike one another, even if they are of the same kind: a simple change of the threshold on connections for cliques, for example, may have a quite radical effect; and we should therefore try several alternatives, so that we can distinguish the consequences of using a particular definition or specification of a given type, from that of using the type itself. But it will hopefully be the case that a selective investigation of some sample classifications of each type, rather than an exhaustive one, will be sufficient to show whether any classification of the type in question, whatever its detailed properties, will perform well. We have in fact tried only one form of string, representing one choice of definition and of specification; three of star, representing one definition and three alternatives for one specification; three of clique, again representing one choice of definition or three alternative specifications; and about a dozen forms of clump, covering the three definitions with two alternative values of P in the 100/P definition, combined in various ways with the two gradient options and different values for the gradient test (though not all of these during classification have been fully tested in retrieval, for practical reasons); but this has been sufficient, in our view, for us to be able to draw some quite definite conclusions about retrieval classification, at least for our test collection.

Similarity coefficients

Before listing these classification options in detail, however, we should look at the other component of the classification process, namely the measurement of similarity. We have so far simply assumed that we have defined the similarity of a pair of objects, and have the matrix giving the similarities for all the pairs of objects, that we can set up alternative similarity definitions which will give different results, both for a specific pair of elements and for a universe of objects, and that these can then lead to different classifications although we use the same classification procedure in each case. A very large number of coefficients have in fact been proposed for various purposes, and if we regard them all as similarity coefficients in a broad sense, though they may be called similarity, resemblance, association, co-occurrence or dissimilarity coefficients, we in principle have a wide range to choose from. It will be remembered that we have found it convenient to distinguish the co-occurrence array, in which the simple co-occurrences of terms in documents are noted, from the similarity matrix in which the information about the co-occurrences of a pair of terms is replaced by the value of a resemblance coefficient. This is a natural distinction to make, because we can separate the initial facts about the property relations of two objects from any inference we draw from these about their likeness, and it is also convenient from the computing point of view. It may be the case that the initial co-occurrence information is not processed in this way so that the co-occurrence array is treated as if it were a similarity matrix; and it may also be the case, in a particular program, that the similarity of a pair of objects is directly calculated from their property lists, without the use of an intermediate co-occurrence array: but doing this depends on the existence of co-occurrences, and this means that we have a procedure which is logically like the general one, though the actual program is different. We can therefore say that in general we start with simple information about the properties which are possessed by individual objects, that we use this to obtain a co-occurrence array noting shared properties, and that we then exploit this array to establish the similarities between pairs of objects. What we are interested in, therefore, are the alternative definitions which can be set up to do this, which I shall call similarity definitions, whatever they may be called elsewhere.

Some of the definitions which have been proposed are quite complex; and some of them are in fact not suited to the retrieval application, because they are designed for quantitative rather than qualitative data. We nevertheless still have a choice, given the range of coefficients listed, for example, by Ball[3], but we have in fact worked only with a few, comparatively simple, definitions. This is because we have always felt that the choice of a class definition is more important than that of a similarity coefficient: though different definitions may lead to differences of detail in the way the relations between objects are represented, it can be argued that these should not influence the overall pattern of classification very much, given a robust classification algorithm. This is indeed the central problem of classification. It is also possible to maintain that these simple definitions are very satisfactory from the logical point of view, as representations of our intuitive feelings about resemblances between objects, though we have also concentrated on simple definitions because they are computationally preferable. A rather different point is that the technological restrictions on classification procedures, like our inability to make exhaustive searches for classes on some definition because it will take too long, mean that our classifications may be rather crude, and we are therefore unlikely to gain anything from being very sophisticated about our similarities. The final question is whether it matters if we get different classifications if we use different similarity coefficients, any more than it matters if we get different results from different class definitions, if they work equally well; but this is a question to which I shall return when considering the results of our experiments. In the present context the point which must be emphasised is that in the process of classification as a whole we have a slot which has to be filled by some definition of resemblance, and that in investigating the use of classifications in retrieval, we should look at different definitions, to see how they interact with the specification of a class to give us particular classifications, and hence particular results when we apply these classifications.

Thus our approach to the treatment of similarity has been to work with relatively simple definitions, rather than complicated ones, partly because these appear to be satisfactory in principle, given the general character of our material, partly because they match our generally rather straightforward approach to the treatment of a class, and partly because they make for easier computing. Our general experience, as we shall see, has been that the choice of one of these definitions rather than another does not appear to affect. the performance of classifications, using the same class definition based on them, very much; but if we should find that we are mistaken, it is easy to try out new coefficients, at least of the kind which do not require more information about our objects than we have available.

The foregoing explains why we have worked mainly with the very simple coefficient which is attributed to Tanimoto[4], which defines the similarity between two objects a and b as

$$S_{a,\,b} = \frac{\text{total number of shared properties}}{\text{total number of different properties}}$$

or, in terms of the co-occurrences and occurrences of a and b as

$$\frac{\text{total co-occurrences } a \text{ and } b}{(\text{total occurrences } a + \text{total occurrences } b) - \text{total co-occurrences } a \text{ and } b}$$

To compute this, we clearly need only the simple co-occurrence array which we can derive from our initial data by noting the number of occurrences of each object, that is the number of properties it has, and the names of the objects with which it co-occurs, or shares a property, with the number of co-occurrences, or of shared properties, in each case. It is evidently only necessary to store the non-zero entries in the matrix, and even if these are duplicated, because the matrix is symmetrical, the fact that in the retrieval case, unlike some others, we may find that the matrix density, or proportion of non-zero entries, is as low as 10 per cent is an important practical point.

The value of this coefficient does not, however, reflect wide variations in the number of objects which are described by different properties: agreement in a property is regarded as equally significant whether the property is assigned to 3 objects or 300, out of a total of 400, say; but it can be argued that agreement in a rare property should be regarded as more significant than agreement in a common one. We should, therefore, weight agreement in a property by its frequency, so that instead of adding 1 to the numerator or denominator of the coefficient for a property, we add $1/n$, where n is the total number of objects possessing the property in question. This information is strictly incorporated in the co-occurrence array which is used to generate the similarity matrix: we simply apply the Tanimoto formula to the content of the cells in a co-occurrence array worked out in one way or the other. But it is convenient to say that what we have is two similarity definitions, which we refer to as the unweighted Tanimoto and the weighted Tanimoto definitions respectively.

For a number of reasons, we have worked mainly with the unweighted Tanimoto definition; but though we have excluded really complex coefficients, there are other simple ones. Two of these have been fairly extensively investigated and used by the SMART project[5]. One is the 'logical overlap coefficient', LO, and the other is the 'cosine correlation coefficient', CC, defined respectively as

$$LO = \frac{\sum\limits_{i=1}^{t} \min(v_i, w_i)}{\min\left(\sum\limits_{i=1}^{t} v_i, \sum\limits_{i=1}^{t} w_i\right)}$$

and
$$CC = \frac{\sum_{i=1}^{t} v_i w_i}{\left[\sum_{i=1}^{t} (v_i)^2 \cdot \sum_{i=1}^{t} (w_i)^2 \right]^{\frac{1}{2}}}$$

where v and w are t-dimensional vectors.

The first of these is *prima facie* inferior to the unweighted Tanimoto definition, and we thought that there was no real point in considering it, given that Lesk has concluded that the cosine correlation coefficient works better for associative purposes[6]. We have, however, tried the latter, for comparison with the two previous definitions, though the fact that Lesk works with quantitative property lists, because he notes the frequency of occurrence of a term in a document, which we do not, means that the comparison is only a partial one. It is in fact not clear that this coefficient is really suited to qualitative property lists, or logical lists, as Lesk describes them; at any rate, it does not appear to give better results, for our material.

The weighted Tanimoto coefficient also appears to make very little difference, presumably because there is little variance in the distribution of the properties. It can, however, be argued that we should also take into account any differences there may be in the relative frequency of occurrence of our objects in a more explicit way than this is already done by the Tanimoto coefficients: if two objects occur very frequently, and hence possess many properties, the fact that they share a property or properties is presumably much less significant than the fact that two objects which possess only a few properties have some property in common. We have indeed investigated this question, but not directly, by trying to set up a suitable similarity definition; we have instead modified the actual vocabulary which is being classified, as we shall see in Chapter 4.

The character of the similarity matrix which is actually presented to the grouping procedure may, however, be determined not only by the choice of the similarity definition, but by the application of some test to separate significant similarities from non-significant ones. It is quite reasonable, in many cases, to regard very low values of the similarity coefficient as non-significant, and so to disregard them. The most obvious way of doing this is by using a global threshold and rejecting any similarities below it; but this is rather a blunt weapon, because some low similarities may be significant. A more satisfactory alternative, though we have not tested this seriously, is to apply a significance test, essentially to the co-occurrence array, to decide whether the extent to which two objects are associated is more than would be expected, given their respective occurrences: if they are not sufficiently associated, no attempt is made to work out their similarity. In each case, however, we have an adjustable parameter which can be used to influence our similarity calculations, in the way in which we can control the operation of the various class definitions we discussed earlier by the specification of a similarity threshold or star size, for example.

Summary of test classification procedures

In our experiments, then, classification is a two-stage process involving the construction of a similarity matrix for object pairs, and the subsequent identification of groups of similar objects; and it will be clear that if each of our similarity definitions may be combined with each of our class ones, we have a wide range of possible classifications to investigate, especially if we try several values of each adjustable parameter in each case. We have in fact not tried every such combination, partly because some are not very sensible–combining a low matrix threshold with strings is futile, for example –and partly because some tests are impracticable or seemed to be unnecessary. But the number of tests which could be carried out was still large enough, especially when the alternative treatments of the term vocabulary and classificatory document descriptions which will be considered in the next chapter were taken into account, to force us to make a selection, even though the number of alternatives in most cases was not large: we only considered two global matrix thresholds, for example. The principles on which this selection of combinations was based will be outlined later: what we can do now is give the complete list of the various alternatives under the headings of similarity and class respectively that we have examined in at least one experiment; this is a useful way of summarising the whole description of our main research on classification and of indicating the range of our investigations.

Thus Table 3.1 overleaf shows that we have examined three similarity coefficients, to which we have applied a global threshold, at one of two levels. The table also shows that we have examined at least one classification of each type; under strings we have considered only links by the strongest similarity, and one maximum length; under stars we have again taken the most strongly connected elements, up to three alternative maximum sizes of set; under cliques we have considered three alternative minimum thresholds; and under clumps we have investigated three clump definitions, with two alternative specifications of the constant P for the 100/P definition, and the option of a gradient test with two alternative values for the maximum and minimum. The reasons for the particular choice of alternatives in many cases, like those of global threshold, are to be found in our data, and will be considered later; the important point here is that we have experimented with some genuine alternatives, at least in some of the many places where a choice can be made: the classification process as a whole depends on many decisions, and we have to see what these can lead to.

Table 3.1 brings out the fact very well that we have a much wider range of choices with type 4 classes. It also shows how complex the classification process is as a whole. It is difficult to deny that the choice of a class definition is more important than that of a similarity coefficient, but it is easy to see how the choice of a particular coefficient can influence the classification

Table 3.1

SIMILARITY

Definition	Control	Level
unweighted Tanimoto ⎫ weighted Tanimoto ⎬ cosine correlation ⎭	threshold	⎰ 7 ⎱ 19

CLASSIFICATION

Type	Definition	Specification			
strings	strongest link	length 7			
stars	strongest links	size ⎰ 8 ⎨ 6 ⎱ 4			
cliques	links above threshold	threshold ⎰ 13 ⎨ 16 ⎱ 21			
clumps	⎰ SAB^2 ⎨ NA ⎱ 100/P ⎰ P = 1 ⎱ P = ½	⎰ no gradient test ⎱ gradient test	⎰ max ⎱ min	⎰ 100 (i.e. none) ⎰ 95 ⎱ 5 ⎰ 0 (i.e. none)	

Bracketed items are alternatives

we obtain. In one sense type 4 classes are particularly susceptible to differences in the computation of similarities, both because more connections are inspected, and also because relatively weak connections play a part in the formation of classes of this kind in a way that they do not in the others. It is likely that any really strong connections, which are the ones that matter for strings, stars and cliques, will, as it were, come out in the wash, whatever definition is adopted. It is also true, however, that the other types of class, and strings in particular, are such that differences in the calculation of similarities can radically influence the formation of a class, in a way which is unlikely with clumps: if the highest similarities for a given object differ, according to how they are computed, this will change the direction of the string generated from this object, for example. In a similar way, the use of a precise cutoff in the construction of stars, or of a threshold in the formation of cliques, may lead to the exclusion of elements where one similarity matrix is concerned, which are included in the star or clique if another matrix based on a different coefficient is used. In principle, we want our classification procedure to be impervious to small changes in our universe of objects: we want to identify its more salient features; but it will be evident that different choices at different points in the process can lead to very different descriptions of our objects, and this is what we must indeed expect if we deliberately opt for different approaches to classification.

Whether these different choices lead to the different results we might expect when we apply the classifications is, however, another question. This is partly because there is more to a classification than its individual classes, and partly because the way classifications behave in retrieval may be less straightforward than we expect. On the first point, it is sufficient to notice here that it is easy to see that differences in similarity matrices can lead to differences in the classes generated from a given single element, for instance; but it may be the case, if we are considering overlapping classifications, that a connection which is picked up in the class in one case, and not in the other, still brings two elements together in another class, in the second classification. Thus if we proceed from a to b in a string in one case, and from a to c in the second, we may still find that a and b are linked in the second classification, say in the class derived from b; this is what is meant by the statement that any really important features of a set of objects should be identified by any classification procedure; we are interested in the common class membership of objects, and we have assigned a and b to the same class in each case, though this is not obvious at first.

What happens when we use term classifications in practice, for retrieval, presents rather different problems. This may depend on the characteristics of the individual term vocabulary and document collection. But this point leads us to the central problem of the whole field, namely that of the relation between theory and practice, given that we are seeking to apply specific classification techniques in an ill-understood situation: it may be that differences between classifications do not matter as much as we might expect them to, because of the way in which classifications actually work in retrieval. This can, however, be more appropriately considered in the light of actual experience, and I shall therefore return to it when I attempt to evaluate our whole project, and try to reach some conclusions about the general properties of automatically obtained keyword classifications and their value in retrieval. But before going on to the account of our experiments in Section II, we have to consider the effect of the characterisation of our keyword vocabulary on the effectiveness of a retrieval classification. This will be the subject of the next chapter.

REFERENCES

1. This definition is due to D. M. JACKSON; for a fuller discussion of these clump definitions see his Doctoral Thesis, *Automatic Classification and Information Retrieval*, Cambridge (1969)
2. *ISR–11*, Chapter IV
3. BALL, G. H., 'Data Analysis in the Social Sciences', *Proceedings of the Fall Joint Computer*

Conference, 1965: AFIPS Conference Proceedings, **27**, Pt. 1,533 (1965); and also SOKAL, R. R. and SNEATH, P. H. A., *Principles of Numerical Taxonomy*, London (1963)

4. TANIMOTO, T. T., *An Elementary Mathematical Theory of Classification and Prediction*, I.B.M. Corporation, New York (1958)

5. *ISR–13*, Chapters IV and IX

6. *ISR–13*, Chapter IX

Chapter 4

Vocabulary Characteristics

SUMMARY

In this chapter the effects of various features of the vocabulary being classified are considered. Though we initially believed that all the terms being classified should be treated in the same way, it turns out that this has undesirable consequences when the classification is used. The relative frequency with which keywords occur in the documents in a collection is, in fact, very important: if frequent terms occur in classes, for example, they are likely to lead to the retrieval of large numbers of usually irrelevant documents. It seems, therefore, that the distributional properties of a vocabulary should be taken into account in the classification process, so that, for instance, grouping is restricted where very frequent terms are concerned, and so on. We have in fact investigated four ways of treating our initial term vocabulary, representing the complete classification of all the terms, restricted classification of frequent terms with unrestricted grouping on non-frequent ones, and the suppression of frequent and non-frequent terms respectively altogether, with a view to showing how the distributional properties of the vocabulary influence retrieval. This has been done by using different vocabularies as inputs to the classification procedure for convenience, but it must be emphasised that different ways of treating keywords can in fact be built into the classification process itself, or at least into the computation of similarities.

Keyword lists

When we began our research, we thought that the character of the actual list of keywords being classified would not present any problems. There are many difficulties about the selection of keywords as representatives of objects, but we regarded these as outside our terms of reference. Keyword classification procedures should be designed to apply to any list of words which is regarded as a document description, however it has been obtained. In the original experiments with the lattice, we used lists of keywords which were selected by hand, but there is of course no reason why we should not use automatically obtained lists, provided that we are convinced that these are satisfactory as descriptions of our documents. A related question is the source of these lists. They can in principle be derived from the entire text of the document, or from its abstract or title, or even from its citations or bibliography. The problems of fully automatic indexing have been extensively studied, and a variety of experiments comparing manual and automatic indexing, using titles, abstracts, and full document texts, have been carried out, in the context of our own area of research, by the SMART project[1]. It has not been shown that automatic methods are better than manual ones; but it also appears that they do not necessarily work less well, and which alternative is adopted depends to a considerable extent on economic considerations.

We have, however, worked with a test collection which was indexed by hand, for rather different reasons. The value of a keyword classification as a means of characterising documents will naturally depend to a considerable extent on the reliability of the keyword listings from which it is derived, and for which it is substituted, though one object of a classification is to compensate for inconsistencies or inadequacies in the use or selection of keywords. Our test collection was very fully and carefully indexed under Cleverdon's aegis*, and we felt that our lists could therefore be regarded as good as can be got without unnatural effort. This meant that they would be a satisfactory base for experiments in classification: we would be able to attribute the poor performance of any classification in general to the classification itself, or to our method of using it to index documents, rather than to defects in the document lists we are working with, though individual lists may of course be unsatisfactory. The comparative fullness of the lists was also important. The relative exhaustivity of keyword descriptions appears to affect their value very much, longer lists being more useful than shorter ones, though there is an upper limit beyond which gains from the assignment of some keywords are outweighed by losses due to the assignment of others: there comes a point where a keyword may correctly describe a document, but the description may be unhelpful and even confusing in retrieval from the collection as a whole. Cleverdon's experiments suggest, however, that lists as long as those we used are of the right sort of length for maximum usefulness, at least for this collection[2].

In general terms, therefore, we thought that we were working with suitable lists, and that our problem was simply one of processing these lists, or rather the complete vocabulary contained in them to obtain classification. We assumed that the terms would all be treated in the same way, because there were no real differences between them as descriptive items characterising the documents. When we came to apply our classification procedures to the vocabulary, however, we found that the results we obtained suggested that this view of our terms was rather naive. In Chapter 3 we saw that terms which had many connections had a marked effect on the formation of SAB[2] clumps: the large number of connections they possessed meant that they were generally not classified themselves, and their presence disturbed the grouping of other terms. The other clump and class definitions were not upset in this way: these terms appeared to fall into classes in a quite natural way, as indeed they can be expected to in the case of strings and stars, where the formation of classes is quite independent of the number of connections possessed by the objects being classified. But we found that the retrieval performance of all the classifications in which the full vocabulary was processed was not very good; it was indeed less good than that of the terms alone, and this was clearly unsatisfactory.

This poor performance could not be ascribed to the classification procedures which were used, or to any of the methods of exploiting the

* See Chapter 7.

72

classifications in searching, because it was true of a variety of different classifications and indexing techniques; and we were reluctant to attribute it to the use of classification. Further investigations suggested, moreover, that the reason for the poor performance of these classifications was to be found in the presence of very frequent terms, that is terms occurring in many documents, in the vocabulary being classified. Terms which occur very frequently tend to be those which have a great many connections; and the combined effect of their frequency and their multiple connection, even if they are grouped in a classification in an apparently satisfactory way, is to degrade retrieval performance. The SAB[2] clump definition responded to multiply connected terms in a way which led, not merely to a classification which did not work well, but to one which looked odd; in the other cases classifications which did not work well were obtained, though they looked more satisfactory. This shows, however, how misleading the appearance of classifications can be, and how important it is to judge them only by their performance. In this context none of the classifications was really satisfactory, and we realised that this was probably due to the inclusion of very frequent terms in the classification.

Keyword frequency

The consequences are clear enough. It is evident that any frequently occurring term will of itself tend to pull out a large number of documents, though if we are considering term retrieval, the use of others as well will usually reduce the number. If frequently occurring terms appear in classes, moreover, this means that in class matches, any document containing a frequent member of a class will be obtained for any request which was initially formulated using its other members, even if these occur very rarely. It is further the case that as frequently occurring terms tend to have many connections, the chances are that they will occur either in classes with many other terms, or in many classes, though with fewer terms in each case; and this means that this feature of class matching, where frequent terms are involved, will be more pronounced. We can, therefore, expect to find that the occurrence of such terms in classes leads to the retrieval of many documents which are unwanted, though it may also enable us to obtain some relevant documents. The unwanted documents are obtained because frequent and multiply connected terms accompany rarer and less well-connected ones in classes, so that when a request contains one or more of the latter, we obtain documents characterised by the latter. It must be admitted that in some actual cases, documents relevant to requests containing rare terms are only obtained through the class relations between these and the more common terms which instead occur in the document; and it is also true that this kind of indirect match is what a classification is intended to achieve. But it seems to be the case that if very frequent terms appear in classes, more false drops than relevant documents are obtained, so that the overall performance of the classification is less good than that obtainable from the terms alone. A further problem arises when frequent terms themselves are used in requests. In this case we may obtain irrelevant documents even in term matching; but if these terms occur in classes, perhaps with other frequent terms (which is quite likely because their frequency may lead to their co-occurrence), we may do even less well than we do with the terms alone. If frequent terms in fact have few connections, we can perhaps permit them to appear in our classification, on the grounds that they can help to retrieve wanted documents, and that their few connections will probably mean that they behave more like unclassified terms. But as we can in general expect them to have many connections, it is possible that we should treat them in some special way in setting up our classification, so that the unfortunate consequences of their uncontrolled appearance in classes are mitigated or avoided altogether. This conclusion has also been reached by Salton and Lesk[3], who argue that very frequently occurring keywords should not be permitted to appear in thesaurus groups, for the reasons we have been discussing; they should be treated as unit classes instead.

We have here, in other words, very good examples of the influence of the purpose for which a keyword classification is required on the way in which it is set up. Saying that we should treat frequently occurring terms in a special way is clearly only one statement among the many that can be made about the need to treat some items in a keyword vocabulary in a special way because they have some distinctive distributional property. It is the distributional property of frequent terms which accounts for their behaviour in retrieval, and it is clear that if such terms do behave in an idiosyncratic way, we have to take this into account when we construct a classification of these terms which is also to be used for retrieval. In the case of frequent terms we want, if we wish our classification to work better than terms alone, to damp down the clearly undesirable feature of frequent terms, namely their tendency to retrieve a large number of irrelevant documents. But it will be evident that terms can have other distributional characteristics which influence their retrieval behaviour, and that we should in principle consider all of these in trying to choose the right classification algorithm; we may in particular wish to exploit some property of our term vocabulary because it has a good effect on retrieval, as well as counteract the bad effects of another. The questions we have to ask about a term vocabulary we are classifying, therefore, are: what distributional properties does it have? and how do these affect retrieval using the terms?

These questions are far from easy to answer. Very frequent terms are the most obvious example of items which may require special treatment: thus if a term occurs often in a collection, which nevertheless does not consist of documents on precisely the same subject, it seems fairly clear that many documents containing it will not be relevant to a request which is presumably intended to select only a small part of the collection. But suppose that we have a term which occurs only rarely: documents containing it are likely to be relevant to a request in which it occurs, but there will probably be other documents not containing it which are also relevant to the request. It is not, however, only the distributional properties of individual terms which count: the distribution of terms with different distributional properties in the term vocabulary as a whole also matter; thus if the proportion of very frequent terms is high it becomes more difficult to avoid irrelevant documents, while if the proportion of rare terms is high, we may have difficulty in obtaining relevant ones. But the important point is that the effects of the distributional properties of a vocabulary or retrieval are quite different according to whether we are working with terms only, or with a term classification. If we are working with terms, we are not interested in the distributional properties of the vocabulary in themselves: what matters is how this vocabulary is used in requests. Retrieval performance, in this case, is determined by the way in which the vocabulary which characterises a collection is used to formulate requests. If, for example, frequent terms never occurred in requests, their frequency could not lead to the retrieval of irrelevant documents and hence poor precision. It is the relation between the use of the same vocabulary for documents and requests which matters. It is the fact that a request contains a term which occurs frequently that makes its frequency significant. With a classification, on the other hand, the presence of a frequent term in a class may influence the retrieval performance of a request not containing the term, if one of the request terms occurs in the same class as the frequent one. At the same time, the effect of frequent terms is clearly liable to be much more marked if they actually occur in a request.

Now it can be argued that the occurrence of, say, a frequent term in a request should not be regarded as a defect of the request; in principle a request is formulated in a way which represents its author's interests, and if it contains a word which retrieves many documents, its author should not object: in a sense, any documents retrieved by a request cannot be irrelevant to it. We should not, then, attempt to differentiate our terms, and to treat those with certain distributional properties in a special way. But this attitude is far too naive (at least, as long as we assume blind requests, so that the author of a request cannot know that the use of a certain term may retrieve half a collection): the author of a request can say that some of the documents it retrieves are irrelevant; a request can be formulated in different ways, some of which will be more effective than others in retrieving relevant documents given the way the documents are described: and the object of a retrieval system, which is presented with only one formulation, should be to exploit the information which it has about the documents and to modify the request to make it as effective as possible. The same holds for frequent terms as descriptions of documents: in principle they correctly describe documents but in practice they may not be so helpful.

We should, therefore, consider the distributional properties of our vocabulary when we construct our classification. It is of course true that what documents are retrieved for a request does not necessarily depend on the distributional properties of a single word. The fact that a particular term occurs very frequently, or rarely, is not the only factor influencing retrieval with this request. A request is usually initially formulated with more than one keyword, so the chances are that a frequent term will be accompanied by one, or more, less frequent ones, and that a rare term will be accompanied by other less rare ones. In principle, therefore, we have other terms which will reduce the range of request document matches in the first case, because we are looking for documents containing other terms as well as the frequent one; or we have other terms which may enlarge the range of matches in the second: we may accept documents which contain other terms, though they do not contain the rare term in question. In practice, however, we find that full, or even almost complete, request specifications are not matched by many documents, even if these are usually relevant ones; and if we use partial specifications, with a view to obtaining more documents, the retrieval results will be increasingly determined by the distributional properties of individual words. So we have to consider how we should react to these. This is where the classification comes in: the object of a classification is in fact to act as a substitute for a full request: it supplies additional terms which may match instead of the given ones: and it can clearly achieve the best results in doing this if it does this in a systematic way based on the characteristics of the vocabulary. The use of several terms in a request may make retrieval with the request relatively impervious to idiosyncrasies of the vocabulary, but only in a rather haphazard way; we may be able to design our classification to correlate requests and document descriptions in a more sophisticated way, in which the idiosyncrasies of the document descriptions are not disregarded, but are taken into account.

Keyword distribution and classification procedures

The question now, therefore, is how we can take the distributional properties of our term vocabulary into account in forming our classification. It would be possible in principle to set up a similarity definition which was designed to take the relative frequency of terms into account: this would complement the weighted similarity definition we have discussed, which is designed to assess the frequency of properties. We could, in particular, try to set up either a similarity definition, or a class one, which treated very frequent terms, or terms with many connections, in some special way, so that their grouping tendencies were restricted. But it would be very difficult to do this in a way which, for instance, reliably generated unit classes for these terms; we might also find that even if we could do this in theory, it might make the whole classification process too expensive. So we decided, for experimental purposes, to adopt an extremely crude approach, which consisted simply of deleting all connections for the most frequently occurring terms, so that they never contributed to the similarity matrix on which grouping was based; they would then be added to our list of classes automatically, as unit classes. Though this is a crude procedure, its objective is a respectable one: saying that frequent terms should appear in a classification, but in the restricted way represented by their occurrence as unit classes, is one way of dealing with the consequences of their frequency; we retain them because matches on the words themselves may be useful, but we do not permit them to have any class-mates, so that they are involved in indirect matches.

We were somewhat surprised to find, when we did this, that it had a quite radical effect on retrieval: a very much better performance than that associated with the uncontrolled grouping of the whole vocabulary was obtained; and a noticeable improvement over the performance given by terms alone was also obtained, which meant that the use of a controlled classification could contribute to retrieval. The full details of these experiments will of course be given later, in the description of our actual tests, though it is worth noticing here that these results are some of our most important ones. The point of immediate interest about them is that they suggested that we should make a rather more careful examination of the characteristics of our term vocabulary as a whole, with a view to seeing how these characteristics may influence retrieval. We were of course obliged to carry out several experiments using different frequency levels, to test the effect of different cutoff points for selecting terms for deletion from the vocabulary to be grouped. But quite apart from this, we became interested in the whole question of the characteristics of the initial vocabulary, and how we should take these into account in constructing a keyword classification for retrieval purposes. We realised, too, that we had two questions to consider, namely how our vocabulary described the documents, and how it was used in the requests, because we recognised that we could not try to adjust the treatment of the term descriptions of the documents to optimise retrieval performance unless we knew what the characteristics of our requests were.

In general terms, therefore, we need to consider, as part of the process of choosing a classification procedure, the relative distribution of terms in the vocabulary, whether it contains very frequent terms or very infrequent ones, and whether there are many or few of each. When we take this information together with the facts about the length of document term lists, the number of terms and documents we get, and together with similar information about our requests, we will have some idea of the way the vocabulary characterises the documents; and we can then seek to use this to choose the most appropriate approach to classification. In real life, we cannot, of course, know what our requests are like; but we can probably rely on samples, or past experience, and we can in any case consider different ways of treating the vocabulary, according to what they may be like, by using what we can learn from a situation in which we have test requests to work with.

Now it is true that we can collect all this information and hope to use it; but it is not easy to see how these different factors interact to determine retrieval performance, and we thus cannot say that in a given situation we should construct our classification in a certain way, if we are to optimise performance. For this reason, we decided to look at the way our term vocabulary described our documents in more detail, to try to understand how the different descriptions and characteristics of the terms affected retrieval with our test requests; we might then be in a position to choose classification procedures which should have the right effects, given our knowledge of the features of our terms and their consequences. Thus we started with the full vocabulary, which we regarded as a base; this was the obvious way of using our given index description, though this did not imply that these actually gave the best performance. We then compared the retrieval performance of various sub-vocabularies with the base performance, in an endeavour to see how terms with the properties in question contributed to the overall performance of the full vocabulary. We examined, in particular, one sub-vocabulary consisting only of frequent terms, and another consisting only of the remaining, non-frequent terms. Detailed descriptions of these vocabularies, and of their retrieval performance, are to be found in Section II. The results in general were, however, as we expected, namely that recall was good, but precision was poor with the frequent terms, while the reverse was true of the infrequent ones, though, as we shall see, the recall capacity of the requests when formulated in infrequent terms was better than might have been expected.

The question we then asked ourselves was: how does classification affect the performance of these vocabularies? What happens, for instance, if we apply the same grouping algorithm to them? We wanted to find out what the effect of the different vocabularies was, which could be a way of identifying both the vocabulary and algorithm which would give the best results when used in retrieval.

This way of looking at the situation was, however, rather misleading. We can say, in the context of the present chapter, that we were interested, not in classifying different vocabularies, but in classifying the same vocabulary, which had been processed in some way. In principle, we were interested in applying various classification procedures to different similarity matrices: because different similarity matrices is what the different vocabularies are equivalent to. That this is really the case is suggested by a reference back to the earlier contrast between the complete classification of the full vocabulary, and its partial classification. We obtained unit classes by fiddling with the input to the classification process, but we could in theory have achieved the same result by an appropriate choice of similarity coefficients, which would have led to the selection of certain items as unit classes by the classification procedure, or at least by some classification procedure. We could similarly imagine ourselves suppressing these unit classes altogether, as part of the classification process as a whole: we might, for instance, construct our matrix in such a way that objects disappeared, so to speak. This idea looks odd at first; and its propriety might also be questioned because we are interested, for test purposes, in comparisons between unclassified terms and classified terms, and it might be thought that comparisons are only legitimate if keyword descriptions of documents and requests are the same in both cases: there is apparently something odd about comparing retrieval with a request containing seven terms, say, in one case, and only three, which lead to classes, in the other. But we can, in fact, say that we start out with the same thing, which is what matters, but that as part of the classification process we suppress some terms altogether, either because they are frequent or because they are infrequent; they do not appear in the classification, even in the form of unit classes, and so are not allowed to characterise requests or documents at all. They have been suppressed by the classification, because this may make the classification work better. This is a legitimate thing to do from the point of view of describing documents and requests and using them for retrieval. What we have in principle, in other words, is a variety of ways of processing a given vocabulary, which we can imagine is done in the classification process itself, at the stage when we construct the similarity matrix: in one case we take the vocabulary, and process it in such a way that our classification procedure groups all the terms; in the second, we take the vocabulary and form a matrix which generates unit classes for some terms, though it groups others; in the third we process the vocabulary in such a way that the classification algorithm fails to form any classes of any kind for some terms, namely the frequent ones, so that they disappear altogether; and in the fourth, we do the same for infrequent terms.

The foregoing clearly shows, for example, that we could in theory process the vocabulary so that infrequent terms formed unit classes, though we have not done this because we could not see that it would be useful from the retrieval point of view; and we can in general try to arrange our procedure so that terms with any particular distributional characteristics are treated in a certain way: it is merely that distinguishing either frequent terms only, or infrequent ones, seems to be the obvious thing to do. We could, moreover, try any combination of these approaches. Thus we might have some terms grouped, some terms treated as unit classes, and some suppressed altogether, if we thought their characteristics justified this treatment. It is indeed worth noticing that the deletion of terms occurring only once in the collection, which we carried out at the beginning of our project to give us the term vocabulary I have referred to hitherto, could itself be regarded as an operation of the classification procedure like those we have been considering, though it was in fact *ad hoc*; we could have arranged things so that these terms had no similarities and so were eliminated in grouping. In this chapter I have referred to the deletion of infrequent terms, but I have assumed that these can include terms occurring more than once; but deleting terms which occur only once simply represents a choice of a similarity definition which makes the cutoff at a lower point.

What we have, therefore, are distinctions we would like our classification procedure as a whole to make, though we have in practice made them before classification because this is easier; and the fact that we have done this means that we have described our experiments in terms of the classification of four different vocabularies, rather than of one. We have distinguished the full vocabulary, in which all terms are grouped, from the 'restricted' one in which some terms are excluded from the classification procedure, and from the ones containing only frequent, or non-frequent terms, respectively, because this conforms with our experiments; the fifth vocabulary, including 'once' terms, has not been used at all. This is a confusing way of describing the situation, because we should in principle refer to one vocabulary and different ways of treating it in calculating similarities, but this has been forced on us by practical considerations.

However, these detailed points should not obscure the important general problem which underlies them. This is that there must be a limit to the extent to which we can improve retrieval performance by substituting keyword classes for keywords, when the class descriptions of requests and documents must be derived from their keyword descriptions; the substitution represents a modification of the initial descriptions, and clearly, though this modification is intended to preserve the essential content of the description while changing its form, there must be a point where modification changes content as well as form. We have to behave, in other words, as if the given keyword form of a request is right from the library user's point of view, and that what we want is to manipulate it, using our knowledge of the descriptions of the documents, in such a way that we hope to satisfy the user. The fact that we might be more successful in giving the user the documents he really wants if we were given a different request to start with is irrelevant, or rather, it leads us to the notion of interactive retrieval, which I am not taking into consideration here.

REFERENCES

1. *ISR–11*, Chapter V; *ISR–12*, Chapter III
2. *Factors* 1,1, Chapter 4; *Factors* 2, Chapter 5
3. *ISR–11*, Chapter IV

SECTION II

Experiments

Chapter 5

Test Environment and Experimental Design

SUMMARY

This chapter is the first of the sections devoted to our actual experiments, as opposed to their objectives: in it the particular problems we have been concerned with in investigating the use of a keyword classification are related to an information retrieval system as a whole. A retrieval system as a whole has a number of components, or is characterised by a number of factors, which influence retrieval performance; and a proper appreciation of experiments designed to examine a particular component is only possible if the relation between this component and others is clearly seen. The aspects of a system with which we have been concerned in studying thesaurus classifications are therefore described in terms of Cleverdon's analysis of system factors: from this point of view, we have been concerned almost exclusively with 'software' factors, as opposed to the environmental, operational and hardware aspects of a system, the only exception being the actual retrieval performance of a system, or its output of relevant and non-relevant documents in response to searches, which is an operational factor. Evaluating keyword classifications clearly requires a measure of retrieval performance, and for this information about the system output is needed. The general problem of establishing a measure is, however, that of identifying any other components which have to be taken into account, and of relating these to one another in a suitable formula. We have not been able to proceed here much beyond the standard recall/precision ratios; but while we admit these are inadequate, they are useful to start with. Further problems arise, however, in comparing these measures for different tests: some kind of normalising is required for legitimate comparisons where system differences prohibit straightforward ones. This again presents problems, and for purely practical reasons we have done no more than provide an interim solution based on a very crude standardisation of the initial recall/precision plots. In designing our experiments, however, we have been obliged to do more than provide performance measures: even though we have confined ourselves to some components of a retrieval system only, the number of parameters or variables they involve is very large. Truly systematic tests would require a study of the effects of assigning different values to each of these, in all their combinations, so that the effect of each choice, in all circumstances, could be demonstrated. But this is clearly impracticable, and we have therefore used a test design in which every value of each variable in turn is studied in a 'base environment' defined by constant values of the other parameters, with cross checks in which some changes in the values of other variables are made, against those in the value of the given variable.

Problems of experimentation

This section of the book will be devoted to a description of our actual experiments, which are presented in part for their own sake, and in part as illustrations of the kind of investigation which is required in the study of automatic keyword classification. They are, however, of interest for a further reason since they can also be used to show what the problems of experimentation in information retrieval in general are, and how they may be approached.

In Section I we presented our basic problem, namely can we obtain a better retrieval performance with a keyword classification than we can obtain with keywords alone, and if we can, can we construct such a thesaurus automatically? We considered the main questions which follow— that is, what sort of classification procedure should we implement to generate our thesaurus, what sort of indexing language should we use to set up, and what sort of vocabulary characteristics should we take into account in constructing it—and we outlined the approaches we have adopted in investigating these questions. It will be evident, however, that there are many aspects of an information retrieval system as a whole that we have not touched on so far: the physical form of document storage, and of the search output given to users, are two random examples. In principle, if we wanted to implement our classification-using system in practice, we would have to consider points like this; but they have no immediate bearing on our main problem, and we can therefore disregard these particular questions for the moment. It is a mistake, however, to think that we can study our main problem in complete isolation: we have, on the contrary, to see how the particular component of an information system which is represented by the use of a keyword classification fits into such a system as a whole. This is because a retrieval system is a very complex structure; it contains many components which interact to determine its overall perform- ance, and which may be related to one another in complicated and un- obvious ways. The size of the document collection and its subject homo- geneity play a part, for instance: they influence performance not only in the narrow sense of obtaining relevant documents on which we have concen- trated so far, but in the wider sense which covers the scale of searches, volume of output, and so on. But the size and subject matter of the collec- tion are clearly only two of the factors influencing the performance of information systems as wholes: there are a variety of others; and it is obvious that some of them must influence the results we obtain when using a thesaurus.

If we are interested in a given component of a retrieval system, like a keyword classification, therefore, we must identify the other components of the system and see how they are related. This is essential if experiments designed to test a particular component are to be of any value. When we come to carry out experiments we must be quite clear about the specific role of the component we are examining in the system as a whole; we have to identify the other components of the system which constitute its environ- ment, and we have to note the particular characteristics of these compo- nents in the specific system we are working with. Without this analysis we cannot design satisfactory experiments or evaluate the results we obtain from them properly: we have to be sure that we are correct in attributing different results to changes we make in the particular component we are examining, such as changes in the classification, and that they are not due to other factors.

The fact that the whole process of document description and retrieval is ill understood means that it is not easy to make this analysis of a system, and to list the various factors which are involved in its operation. The Cranfield and SMART projects have, however, provided prototype frames of reference which can be taken as starting points. Cleverdon's analysis of the factors determining the performance of information systems as wholes is particularly valuable[1], and I shall therefore use it to describe the specific system which constitutes our test environment. An additional reason for doing this is that we have been working with a document collection and set of requests obtained from Cleverdon, and the use of a similar frame of reference makes it easier to compare our results with his. Cleverdon did not, however, investigate the use of automatically obtained keyword thesauri[2], and though these have been tested by the SMART project[3], our own experiments in this area have been much more exhaustive. We have in particular made much more detailed analyses of factors which are involved in the construction and use of these classifications, that is of the various sub-components of the classification component of the retrieval system itself. In considering our test system as a whole, therefore, I shall provide a much more detailed description of this part of it, within the framework supplied by Cleverdon's analysis of information systems in general.

Components of a retrieval system

We can start, then, by considering the components of a retrieval system as a whole. The list of these components includes any feature of the system we have to take into account in describing its operation and judging its performance; but we can disregard some of these because they are not relevant to our research problem. In considering a system in all its aspects we have, for example, to notice the kind of people running it, because their training and experience affect its performance; and any measure of the performance of an information system as a whole, assuming that such a measure could be set up, has, for instance, to cover the economic aspects of its operation, like the cost of storing a document, or of making a search. It is easy to see that the complete description of a system, and the overall evaluation of its performance, present very serious problems: but these are problems which we can to a considerable extent avoid here; we are interested only in one feature of the performance of a system, namely its ability to retrieve all and only the documents appropriate to a request, or its 'effectiveness' as Swets describes it[4], in so far as this is affected by the way we describe documents and requests, and manipulate these descriptions. It is clear that some of the other properties of a system, like collection size, are relevant here, though it must be admitted that they are not taken into account directly when we measure performance in the restricted sense just mentioned. Given that we are working in an experimental situation, in other words, we can distinguish those features of our system which are relevant to our interests, because they influence the behaviour of the component we are studying from the other features which characterise the system as a whole: the relevant features constitute what can be called the test environment; they represent aspects of the system which should in principle be covered by a performance measure which was designed to give a complete account of the effect of using a classification for the retrieval of wanted documents, though we have in fact been working with a much more limited measure. This division of system features into relevant and non-relevant is indeed justified not only by the fact that we are interested in one part of the system, but because our system is set up in a way which is suited to experiments, and not at all in a way which would be appropriate if it were a regular working one. This means, for example, that its economics are quite eccentric, though it must be emphasised that it is possible to envisage what a working form of the system would look like.

In the discussion which follows, then, the factors which are involved in a retrieval system as a whole, and which should therefore be covered by any measure of what can be called system performance, are briefly described, so that the necessary background to the more detailed analysis of the factors, which matter from our research point of view is provided. The factors which are relevant to the use of a classification are those which should in principle be taken into account in any measure of what may be called retrieval performance, that is performance in the narrow sense referred to earlier, rather than system performance. The particular features of our experimental system which fall under these headings thus constitute the test environment surrounding our actual classifications; and the listing of the factors influencing the use of a classification is therefore followed by the detailed description of our actual experimental material. In this whole discussion, I shall make use, as mentioned earlier, of Cleverdon's treatment of the subject, but the analysis of those parts of the system in which a keyword classification is directly involved will be more exhaustive.

Cleverdon initially distinguishes four main classes of factor, covering all the aspects of an information retrieval system, namely

> Environmental factors
> Software factors
> Operational factors
> Hardware factors

The first heading 'environmental factors', covers at least four features of a system, namely the

> subject field
> collection size

questions asked
relevance needs

We have not investigated the effects of differences in these factors explicitly, as Cleverdon, and Salton and Keen, have done[5], because our tests have been confined to one particular document collection containing papers on one subject, and to one set of questions and one set of relevance lists. The distinctive features of these components of our test environment must be noted, but we cannot make any very reliable inferences about their effect on our results, though the comparisons between these test documents and request sets and others which have been made by Cleverdon and, more particularly, Salton are very helpful: they suggest that there is nothing really unusual about them.

Software factors

The software factors listed by Cleverdon include the

level of exhaustivity (of the indexing)
form of the index language
search strategy

In the most obvious sense, we have not examined the first of these: we have not, that is, investigated the effect of using keyword lists of different lengths on retrieval; we have simply worked with the fullest word lists provided by Cleverdon's indexers for our documents. But it is possible to regard the use of a classification as representing an increase of exhaustivity, because an initial keyword list is expanded for matching purposes to include the class-mates of the words in it; and the use of the different vocabularies I discussed in Chapter 4 also represent changes in exhaustivity which are in principle induced by classification. We can, therefore, say that we have studied the effect of changes in exhaustivity, though these changes are not the result of different attitudes to the initial extraction of keywords from documents, but of different ways of processing the extracted vocabulary. The type of index language represented by a classification is of course our main interest. We have, however, confined ourselves to comparisons be-tween languages incorporating a keyword classification in different ways; we have not made explicit comparisons between these and other languages of different kinds. But we can take advantage of the comparisons between languages of different kinds, including thesaurus languages, which have been made by Cleverdon and Salton, to infer what the performance relation between languages we have tested and those we have not would be.

In discussing index languages, Cleverdon distinguishes different 'base units', as we may call them, namely single extracted words, extracted phrases [his 'simple concepts'], and assigned descriptors, from the various recall and precision devices which may be applied to document descriptions initially consisting of a set of base units of a certain kind. A particular combination of a specific kind of base unit, recall device and precision device then constitutes one index language[6]. For Cleverdon any grouping or classification of keywords is a recall device, while weighting is a precision device. Naturally, these distinctions are not always easy to maintain: if the base units are phrases, for example, these necessarily incorporate a particular precision device, because any syntactic linking of words acts as a precision device; and as we have already seen, regarding a classification only as a recall device may be much too simple a way of looking at it. Within limits, however, Cleverdon's analysis is very useful, and we can therefore say that what we are doing, in studying different classifications and ways of using them, is examining different index languages which all share the same base unit, namely single words, and one precision device, namely coordination, while we are experimenting with the different recall devices represented by different classifications, and also with various additional precision devices; the use of class frequencies is, as we saw in Chapter 2, one such precision device, and it will be clear that the special treatment given to various sections of our vocabulary we considered in Chapter 4 also acts as a precision device.

In his own experiments, Cleverdon examined four forms of classification, namely those containing groups of variant word forms, of synonyms in the strict sense, of quasi-synonyms, and of hierarchically related items, and he investigated languages containing the recall devices represented by these forms of classification, both singly and in combination[7]. We have not chosen to regard the grouping of word forms as a form of classification, though it clearly technically is one: we have grouped variant keywords to form terms which we regard as our base units for further classification; this is convenient, and it also matches Salton's practice. Both Cleverdon, and Salton and Keen have established that the substitution of terms for keywords has a good effect[8], and we can therefore reasonably start from here and look at the effects of further classification.

It will, however, be clear from the earlier discussion of our approach to classification that we cannot correlate Cleverdon's list of three forms of classification in any detailed way with the different classifications in which we are interested; we can, it is true, say that we are not working with hierarchically structured classifications, though it must be remembered that the relations between specific words that may be given by a hierarchy can also be given by a non-hierarchical classification; but it is evident that the linguistic distinction which Cleverdon makes between synonym and quasi-synonym classifications should not be looked for in the kind of automatic classification with which we are working. The distinction between these types of group is a natural one from the point of view of manual classification, as we have seen, but it is not one that we can rely on automatic techniques to make; and we indeed argued earlier that the attempt to make it was mistaken from the retrieval point of view. Neither can we expect to obtain automatic classifications which can be treated as if they represented straightforward combinations of the types of class which Cleverdon distinguishes. Thus Cleverdon investigated a classification containing word groups consisting of both synonyms and quasi-synonyms; but there is no reason to suppose that our classifications could in general be described in this way.

There is no point, in other words, in our trying to fit our classifications into Cleverdon's slots. The reason why any attempt to do so would not be helpful is clear: Cleverdon did not go into the problems of classification in much detail, and his categorisation of the different recall devices they may represent covers only some of the broad linguistic distinctions that can be made between classifications: classifications as recall devices are differentiated by their semantic rationale. From this point of view, we are interested in classifications in which word groups are based on a semantic rationale which Cleverdon does not mention, namely that of textual co-occurrence. But it will be obvious from the statement that we are studying the use of a co-occurrence based classification as a recall device, that is a grossly inadequate description of what we are doing. We have noticed that a keyword classification has many properties of different kinds, and it would be more accurate to say that we are regarding each of these as a recall device: thus dense, tight classes like cliques give us one form of classification or recall device, while clump-type classes constitute another recall device. The whole situation is much more complex than that allowed for by Cleverdon's analysis, and we should therefore think in terms of a much wider range of classificatory features, both linguistic and others each of which can be regarded, in principle, as a recall device, so that a given classification may incorporate a number of these devices in combination. We thus arrive at the position that in studying term classifications, we are investigating a set of index languages which are each characterised by a variety of recall devices associated with a particular approach to classification, and by a variety of precision devices: the latter include not only coordination, which is logically independent of the use of a classification, but other devices which are associated with classification.

The third software factor considered by Cleverdon is the actual search procedure which is used to obtain documents. In general terms we can choose how far we go in searching with successively reduced requests, in attempting to obtain further documents, and how much we control the reduction by saying, for instance, that some partial requests are permissible and others are not. (This assumes a non-interactive situation: if we have interactive searching, we have a more complicated situation, though the basic questions of how far, and in what way, we permit modifications of the initial request remain.) In our experiments we have in fact permitted exhaustive and uncontrolled searching, mainly because we have wanted to see what sort of retrieval performance we get when we use classifications in retrieval without any interference, so to speak, but also because any attempt to control the formation of partial requests, by, say, giving the classes associated with some terms special treatment, is very awkward to implement. At the same time, the combined term and class matches discussed in Chapter 2 do represent controlled searches.*

From the foregoing it will be evident that in considering classifications we are not attempting the wide range of comparisons, involving many different system factors, that have been carried out by Cleverdon and Salton. In the experiments carried out by the Cranfield and SMART projects, the relations between different factors have been more extensively investigated than they have been in our own[9]. It might indeed look as if the area we are interested in is so small that our results are of limited interest. But this is not so, for three reasons. The first is that as we can tie our experiments in with those carried out by these projects, we can use the results obtained by Cleverdon and Salton to make comparisons between the systems they have studied, and those we have investigated, and so widen our area of research by indirect methods: this is the important advantage to be gained from working with a common collection, and within the similar frameworks supplied by similar analyses of retrieval systems. The benefit is of course mutual, in the sense that results of experiments carried out under any one of the projects can be used to supplement those obtained by one of the others. The second reason why our research area is a less limited one than it might appear to be lies in the fact that Cleverdon, and Salton and Keen, have concluded that index languages incorporating keyword classifications seem to work better than many others[10]; and this means that we are working in what may be described as the area of maximum interest in the study of indexing languages as a whole. The third and most important reason is that the range of alternative classifications studied by both of these projects has not been large, though the number of variables which is involved in the constructing classifications is so great that the list of alternative classifications which could be studied is enormous. There is, therefore, every justification for a much more comprehensive set of experiments, based on a more exhaustive analysis of the classification process, than has been carried out hitherto. That these investigations are required is indeed shown by the substantial variations in retrieval performance we have obtained with different classifications; recall/precision curves as unlike one another as those given as curves 1 and 2 in Figure 5.1 can be generated by classifications of the same vocabulary (which gives term retrieval curve 3), and even by classifications based on apparently very similar principles. We cannot, therefore, treat any results based on only a few classifications as reliable indications of the con-

---

* The fact that we have confined ourselves to exhaustive one-off searches with requests taken as they come does not mean that we are not interested in interactive retrieval. It is evident that substantial improvements in performance can be achieved by interactive techniques; but we wanted to establish what may be described as base-line retrieval performance before considering the possibilities of interaction. For some results with interactive techniques in this context see *ISR–12*, Chapter V, and *ISR–14*.

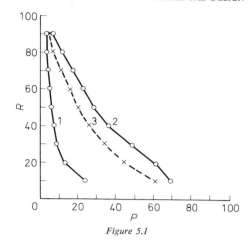

Figure 5.1

tribution which a keyword classification can make to retrieval: we have to investigate a sufficient number of alternatives to ensure that our conclusions are well founded. Thus we have to test alternative classifications in the first instance on the same collection and request set, that is in a constant test environment; and we have then to see what the effects of changes in the other relevant factors are, by trying different collections, request sets, relevance judgements, search procedures, and so on. We have only made a beginning in this direction, but this is, if nothing else, of value in indicating the lines on which further experiments should be planned.

Operational factors

The third group of factors listed by Cleverdon are the operational ones. These include the time taken for indexing and retrieval, the cost of personnel, the clerical effort which is involved in running the system, and so on. In a very broad sense, these factors can also be regarded as economic ones, because time and effort and people mean money, but it is clearly necessary to distinguish the fact that it takes longer to do a search in one system than in another from the fact that this will generally mean that a search is more expensive in the first case than the second. With one important exception, Cleverdon himself did not investigate these operational factors, and realistic remarks about them can hardly be made in the context of a primarily research project, in which the way a system is set up is designed for test rather than ordinary working purposes. The fact that all procedures are carried out automatically is a concession to research convenience for example, and does not represent an attempt to set up a practical system. We have not attempted to simulate a working system in its entirety, since we have been concentrating only on one part of a retrieval system; our methods in running our test system as a whole have been quite different from those which would be natural in real life, and we cannot, therefore, infer anything very directly from them. This does not of course mean that the components of the system concerned with classification are not genuine: we have, for instance, to use a real document collection and real requests if we are to learn anything about the value of classifications; but we can implement our search procedures, say, in any way which is convenient from a research point of view without this affecting our judgements about the value of classifications: thus the fact that it takes so and so long to make a search in our experimental system has no significance. We must indeed separate those features of the classification and class-using process itself which must necessarily be those of a working system from those which need not. We have to use real documents; but the details of, say, the classification program can be determined by experimental considerations, rather than those which apply in real life, though it must be emphasised that we must be careful about the extent to which we allow ourselves to behave in an unrealistic way. This is clearly demonstrated by the fact that we would reject any classification algorithm, however good its product, if it took a week to group ten terms. We should be able to draw some conclusions from our experiments about the characteristics of working systems based on the same principles; and we can do this, as we shall see when the results of our experiments and the inferences to be drawn from them are considered.

Although we have not examined operational factors in general, we have naturally made one exception: Cleverdon regards retrieval performance, in the restricted sense in which we have defined it, as an operational feature of a system, and we have of course been concerned with this. We cannot say anything about classifications without referring to it, though measuring it is the major problem of information retrieval research which accompanies that of identifying the components of a retrieval system. Before we go into this question, however, we can briefly consider the fourth class of factors which characterise a system, namely the hardware factors. These include the type of store used for the documents, its updating ability, and so on. It is not always easy to separate these factors from the operational ones, but the remarks just made about operational factors other than retrieval performance apply to these too. Cleverdon did not explicitly examine any hardware factors at all, and we have not done so either, though they are clearly of some importance in any system which depends on a computer at some point, as a system using an automatic classification must do. We shall therefore return to them later, in the discussion of what may be called the applications side of using an automatic classification, as opposed to its theoretical side.

Summary of test components

Before going on to discuss the measurement of retrieval performance, we can usefully summarise this discussion of the factors involved in retrieval systems in general, and the specification of those with which we have been concerned in our experiments, by an illustration. In Table 5.1 the complete list of factors noted by Cleverdon[11] are given, and the details characterising our experimental material are filled in for those factors which are relevant to our research. The description of the test collection is amplified in Chapter 7; that of the features of our test index languages is rather brief, and should be supplemented by references to Chapters 2, 3 and 4, and to Chapter 8; each classification of course acts as the base to a separate language, so the total number of languages tested is large. The organisation of

Table 5.1

Environmental factors	
Subject field	aerodynamics; specialised
Collection size	200 documents; homogeneous
Questions asked	42; distinct, single themed, in total covering much of the collection; varying numbers of starting and retrieving terms, and of relevant documents
Relevance needs	not graded
Software factors	
Concept indexing	manual indexing using whole document texts, most exhaustive of those provided
Indexing language	single terms:
	recall devices: classes of terms; precision devices: overlapping classes of terms; class frequencies; term/class combinations (cf. searching); vocabulary restriction
Search strategy	coordination at all levels; controlled searches with term/class combinations
Operational factors	
Subject coverage	small
Time ⎫ Effort ⎬ Personnel ⎭	(time, effort and skill went into the initial indexing, but these factors were not otherwise taken into account, given the special test circumstances)
Clerical routines	(special for testing)
Retrieval performance	recall; precision
Hardware factors	
Type of store ⎫ Input ⎪ Expansion capacity ⎬ Updating ability ⎪ Output ⎭	(special for testing)

the table should not be taken too seriously: it is quite clear that the identi-fication of the factors involved in an information retrieval system, and of their relationships, presents many difficulties; we feel that Clever-don's analysis should be treated as a useful framework for describing our experiments, but that this should not be taken to imply that it is wholly correct.

Retrieval performance measures

We now come to the very difficult problem of measuring the performance of a retrieval system, even in the limited sense of performance to which we have confined ourselves. How should we present the results of retrieval tests?

To start with, we must be careful to distinguish retrieval performance as an operational factor, or set of factors, characterising a system, from what we have hitherto called retrieval performance, which is represented by a measure. We can, that is, list various features of a system which are associated with the consequences of searches, which are on a par with other features like the character of the search strategy, or the time taken to make a search: the features in question have to do with the properties of the docu-ments related to requests. When we come to measure retrieval performance, that is the effectiveness of the system as a means of retrieving required documents, we should clearly take these operational retrieval factors into account, but it seems fairly obvious that we should in principle also incor-porate in our measure other relevant factors, like the size of the collection and the character of the requests. The difficulty is that it is not at all obvious how such a factor as the subject field covered by a collection, which clearly has to do with retrieval performance, should be given a precise value and incorporated in a retrieval measure.

The general problem of measuring retrieval performance has been very widely discussed, both on its own, and in the wider context of evaluating system performance as a whole[12]; but there appears to be no simple solu-tion to it, and it is possible to object to any of the specific measures which have been put forward. We clearly have three points to consider:

(1) the factors to be taken into account as constituents of the measure;
(2) the way in which these are related to one another and incorporated in a formula; and
(3) the way in which a series of measurements describing different sys-tems are to be evaluated and compared.

In the experimental context we have an additional constraint, namely that we want a performance measure which can be computed in a reasonably economic manner using information that is readily available.

The specific retrieval factors which should be taken into account in measuring performance evidently include

(*a*) the relevant documents retrieved,
(*b*) the non-relevant documents retrieved,
(*c*) the relevant documents not retrieved,
(*d*) the non-relevant documents not retrieved.

Whether there are any other specifically retrieval factors is not clear; but the first three of these at least normally appear in performance measures. The extreme difficulty of incorporating other relevant factors, like the size of the request set, in such measures in a meaningful way has, however, the effect that they are generally left out; the fact that they are listed or otherwise described in accounts of retrieval experiments shows that their importance is recognised, though the correct method of responding to it is not obvious. We thus have the situation that in practice retrieval performance measures cover only some of the factors which should properly be considered, and they should therefore be regarded only as partial rather than complete measures. It would in principle be better if these partial measures were given some other name, like search performance measures, to avoid confusion; but retrieval performance measures is the common name for them, and I shall therefore use it: in what follows, then, the expression retrieval performance measures will be used to refer to the kind of measure which is in practice used to characterise retrieval performance, though these measures take only some of the factors which should be incorporated in a really adequate performance measure into account.

Recall and precision

The customary approach to setting up a limited performance measure is to start with the well-known recall and precision ratios which are derived from the retrieval factors (*a*) and (*c*), and (*a*) and (*b*), respectively; thus as percentages, recall, *R*, is defined as

$$\frac{\text{the number of relevant documents retrieved}}{\text{the total number of relevant documents}} \times 100$$

and precision, *P* is defined as

$$\frac{\text{the number of relevant documents retrieved}}{\text{the total number of documents retrieved}} \times 100$$

We have, that is,

$$R = \frac{a}{a+c} \times 100, \quad \text{and} \quad P = \frac{a}{a+b} \times 100$$

Much has been written about these ratios: of particular interest in the present context are Cleverdon's discussion, and the analyses by Salton,

Keen and Swets[13]. As descriptions of performance they clearly have defects: thus the numbers of documents involved, which are of interest from the operational point of view, are not apparent in the final figures; the two are not independent, and so on. It must also be admitted that these are only two ways of extracting information about a system from the list of factors given earlier; these ratios do not, for example, take account of (d), that is the success of the system in not retrieving irrelevant documents. This factor can be incorporated in another ratio, which is usually called the fallout ratio, and is defined as

$$F = \frac{\text{the number of non-relevant documents retrieved}}{\text{the total number of non-relevant documents}} \times 100$$

We could presumably in principle set up other relationships between the various factors, though we have of course to consider whether doing so tells us anything interesting. A more important question is whether the ratios like these are taken together to represent retrieval performance as they stand, or whether they are given further processing or are related to other factors to obtain another characterisation of performance.

We have not gone into any of these questions in detail; and we have indeed adopted what might be described as a rather simplistic approach to the problem. The reasons for this are, however, quite respectable: we have preferred to concentrate the efforts of our rather small project elsewhere, and we have felt that as these are problems on which other people are working, there is more point in our taking over any satisfactory measures which they may devise, than in trying to set up our own without going into the problem properly. It is also the case that though recall and precision ratios are widely deplored, they are also widely used, and there is everything to be said for presenting our results in a form which, though it is inadequate, means that they compared with those obtained by other projects. In what follows, therefore, I shall simply describe the approach we have adopted to measuring performance, and comment on the main points connected with it, without going into these in any detail.

To start with, then, we accepted the idea of working with recall and precision. The question which follows is how, if we initially establish these relationships between factors, we proceed to set up further relationships which represent another step in the direction of a unified performance measure. The normal way of doing this is by pairing two ratios and exhibiting their relationship in a graph plot. Thus if we imagine ourselves having two specific values for recall and precision for a given request, say 60 per cent and 30 per cent respectively, we can represent this very trivially, using a graph, as in Figure 5.2. This is a well-established idea, and the only difficulty about it is that we have to select two particular ratios from the range of possible ones; though it can be argued that the fact that the ratios are all related to one another means that the choice is to some extent arbitrary. Recall/fallout plots have been advocated, for example, by Swets[14], and they

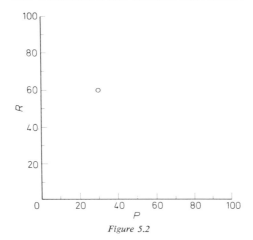

Figure 5.2

have the advantage that all of (*a*), (*b*), (*c*) and (*d*) are used; but we have chosen to use recall and precision for two quite simple reasons: it is undeniable that they represent important aspects of retrieval; and they are very widely used, and there is everything to be said for compatibility. They are also extremely easy to use. Moreover, though it is easy to criticise the recall/precision measure, no-one had proposed any obviously better alternatives.

Two problems now follow: one is how this basic idea should be developed in detail; and the other is that we should seek to extend our recall/precision measure to include any other system information. Again, these questions are very fully discussed in Cleverdon's report and elsewhere: our object here is simply to describe the methods we have used.

The first point is that it is not useful, and is indeed even misleading, to work with a single recall and a single precision value for a request. In the exhaustive searches which are usual, at least in the experimental context, we retrieve documents which match a request less and less closely. Thus if we have a request represented by a set of terms, and match on successively smaller subsets down to single terms, each size of subset gives us a co-ordination level with which we can associate a set of retrieved documents, namely those which are obtained at this level or any higher one. In general, therefore, we can expect to obtain successively larger sets of documents as we proceed from higher to lower levels, because each step will bring out new documents to add to the set obtained by the previous ones. In this case we can obtain, not a single recall/precision point to plot, but a series, one for each level, so that the complete picture of retrieval given by our graph is a curve which in practice has the general form of Figure 5.3*, with high

---

* Individual requests can, however, give very irregular graphs: see Keen's example in *ISR–13*, Chapter II, Figure 12.

precision and low recall at the highest coordination level, and the reverse at the lowest. If we had a request with six terms, for instance, we might get a graph as in Figure 5.3.

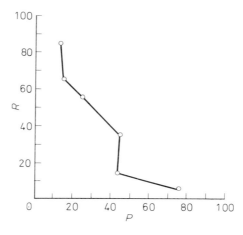

Figure 5.3

This is of course only one way of matching a request against a collection; it is very crude, and it is most convincing when detailed differences in level are significant: as we saw in Chapter 2, this may not be true of classes, and in this case we have to look at the curve as a whole, without attaching any significance to individual points. It is possible to use more complex matching coefficients, like those adopted by workers on the SMART project, which have the advantage that they give a ranked series of documents, rather than successive sets[15]; but it is difficult to maintain that the detailed differences in rank position which follow should be regarded as significant. We have in any case not tried this method of matching, chiefly because of the effort it involves.

We decided to use the simple coordination level method, because it is easier in practice, but it must be admitted that it presents problems at the next stage, when we want to obtain the overall performance for a set of requests, rather than the individual performance for a single request. If we have a set of requests, they will generally be represented by different numbers of terms, or other items, like classes, and so will lead to matches on different numbers of coordination levels. This means that when we try to form a single recall/precision curve for a set of requests, we should in principle take into account the fact that not all the requests could retrieve documents at the highest level associated with the request which contains the most terms. We cannot straightforwardly combine and average the recall/precision figures for two requests, one of which contains three terms and the other six, because the result for levels four, five and six can only represent the performance of one request, and not both. A further problem is that the highest level on which a match can in principle be achieved for a given request may not be the highest level on which an actual match is obtained: we have to distinguish the size of the set of starting terms from that of the set of retrieving terms. The description of the test request set which is given in Chapter 7 shows that this is a serious problem; not only do the requests range from 3 to 11 starting terms: they range from 3 to 9 retrieving terms. Obtaining the overall performance for the set should clearly in principle look at the levels involved in the actual retrieval; and as these may vary very much, any simple-minded attempt to combine the information associated with different requests, on each level, can lead to a rather warped picture of the performance of the set as a whole.

This difficulty is considered at length by Cleverdon, who also examined methods of working out average performance: should we, for instance, combine the information about the documents retrieved for all our requests, and work out the average recall and precision values from these, or should we work out recall and precision values for each request, and then average these? It must be admitted that we have adopted the simplest solution to all these problems, mainly because satisfactory ones make for so much more work. Thus we concluded that we could disregard the problems presented by request variation, and use the first, simpler method of averaging, without disastrous consequences. We felt that the picture of performance that we obtained in this way would not be too distorted, at least to act as a useful guide when we came to sort out our results.

The advantage of ranking is of course that it does not present these problems: a ranking of an entire collection indicating the order in which documents were retrieved in response to a request is independent of the number of matching items. The performance for each request is normalised and averaging is quite straightforward; a recall/precision curve which is the analogue of a curve derived from coordination levels can be obtained by choosing standard recall values, and calculating precision for them. This procedure is adopted by Salton, for example[16]. A further advantage of a ranked output is that it can be used to give an overall single performance figure for a request, or average for a set of requests, indicating the success of the request, or request set, in obtaining relevant documents before irrelevant ones. It can be argued that single figures of this kind are of very limited value, and that more can be learnt from a set; and perhaps the best use of them is as members of a series of performance figures worked out on different principles, which is the way Salton uses them. In this connection, Cleverdon's attempt to simulate ranking, using the output of coordination level matches, should be noticed[17]: this achieved the normalisation needed for the calculation of the single 'normalised recall' figure which was used to characterise the performance of each of the indexing languages he tested, so that it could be assigned a position in a merit ordering of the languages. The particular method used by Cleverdon is open to criticism, in that it does not rank the entire collection, but only the documents retrieved in the process of obtaining relevant documents: this point has been discussed elsewhere, however[18], and I shall not pursue it further. More satisfactory methods of processing the results of coordination level matches to simulate ranking can be devised; but the amount of effort involved is so great that we have not done any work on these lines.

Our basic method of evaluating retrieval performance is therefore an extremely elementary one: and it can be conveniently summarised by an example, as follows. Suppose that we have three requests, A, B and C, containing 3, 4 and 5 terms respectively, and that matching on any 3, 2 or 1 terms in the first case, and 4, 3, etc., in the second, and any 5, 4, etc., in the third, gives us the following sets of retrieved documents.

		A	rel	not rel	B	rel	not rel	C	rel	not rel
levels	1		−	10		2	13		−	15
	2		2	5		2	13		−	10
	3		1	1		1	1		−	7
	4					−	−		1	3
	5								1	−

We now compute the total number of relevant and non-relevant documents which are retrieved on each level and above, for each request, so that we obtain

	A		B		C	
1	3	16	5	27	2	35
2	3	6	3	14	2	20
3	1	1	1	1	2	10
4			−	−	2	3
5					1	−

If we now sum relevant and non-relevant documents respectively, at each level, we obtain

1	10	78
2	8	40
3	4	12
4	2	3
5	1	−

On the assumption that the total number of relevant documents to be achieved is in fact 12, so that two relevant documents were missed, we can apply the formulae given earlier to compute recall and precision values for each level, so that we obtain

	R	P
1	83	11
2	66	17
3	33	25
4	17	40
5	8	100

We can then plot these results as indicated, to obtain a graph as in Figure 5.4.

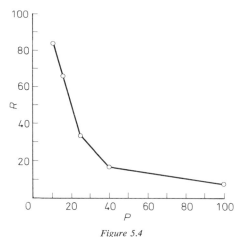

Figure 5.4

Standardisation

Such a graph gives a not wholly inaccurate picture of the performance of a specific set of requests. We found, however, that graphs obtained in this way were very difficult to work with when we came to compare the performance of several sets of requests, or rather of the same set of requests when different indexing languages were used. With matches on class co-ordination levels in particular, the number of points involved tends to be very large, while the variation in relative performance from level to level may be considerable, so that the curves tend to resemble the tracks of crawling insects; this is particularly liable to happen at high coordination levels, where the numbers of requests determining the recall and precision values are so small that wild zig-zags appear: we may have 4 documents, of which 3 are relevant at level x, 3 of which 3 are relevant at level $x+1$, and 2 of which 1 is relevant at level $x+2$. The numbers of documents involved, in other words, are so small that no consistent performance trend is to be looked for. Any attempt to compare curves of this kind directly, therefore, with a view to making some estimate of the relative merits of the retrieval performances represented, is liable to be very uninformative. In consequence, we have been obliged to take a further step and subject our initial curves to a standardising procedure which is intended to exhibit their essential character more clearly, and so make comparisons between different curves easier.

In attempting to compare the performance of different sets of searches representing retrieval with the same set of requests in different forms, we are of course up against a quite general problem: we get into the same difficulty if we are working with quite distinct request and document sets, and want to compare the consequences of using a given indexing language in retrieval across the collections. In this case, however, new problems appear, connected with variations in the sizes of the collections, request sets, and also of the relevant document sets. These variations must in principle be taken into account, but the appropriate ways of doing this are not wholly obvious. The question has been considered by both Cleverdon and Salton, since they have carried out comparative experiments of this type: essentially, further normalisation is required such as is provided, for example, by Salton's 'normed recall' formula in which collection size is indicated[19]. We have, however, been able to disregard this problem, because we have worked throughout with the same test collection; and what our method of standardising recall/precision curves amounts to is a very elementary way of achieving normalisation over a series of requests, of the kind which is more satisfactorily achieved by using a ranked search output.

Our standardised curve is obtained simply by reading off the precision values on the initial curve, at a set of standard recall values. We have in fact used 9 standard recall values, ranging from 10 to 90: this is partly because the middle of the curve is the area of interest, and partly because, on the one hand, few tests reach 100 per cent recall, so no useful comparisons can be made at this point, and on the other, performance at low recall and high precision is very unreliable, for the reason mentioned earlier. The initial curves in this area are very variable, so a simple-minded interpolation would be rather dangerous. The choice of standard recall, rather than standard precision, is based on the fact that the initial curves tend in practice to be more irregular from the point of view of the precision axis, than the recall one, so that readings against the latter are less likely to be misleading. This standardising procedure is of course open to some objections in principle, but the character of the curves to which it is applied in practice is such that the new curves are not wildly different; the desired smoothing is achieved without serious misrepresentation. The process can be illustrated for the example given earlier. Reading precision values off the graph (Figure 5.4) gives us the following values, for the nine standard recall values.

10	20	30	40	50	60	70	80	90
85	37	27	23	20	17	14	12	—

A new graph can then be produced, which is smoother than the old one, as in Figure 5.5.

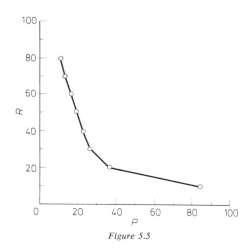

Figure 5.5

Significance tests

Using these standardised curves, representations of retrieval performance, in the very limited sense in which we are considering, can be obtained which are, at least superficially, fairly informative; differences between the performance obtained in different tests with the request set are clearly exhibited. The question which now arises is that of estimating the significance of these differences. This is a far from simple problem. Many tests give more or less the same result in the high recall area especially, and we know that in small-scale experiments variations in high precision are not to be trusted. But it will be evident that it may be extremely difficult to say whether the differences between two curves, like those illustrated in Figure 5.6, are of any importance.

Can the differences between these curves be treated as indications of significant differences in performance? We clearly need to know this, because we can then infer that the indexing language used in one case is better than that used in the other. The most serious attempt to apply significance tests to recall/precision information has been made by Salton[20], and though his methods may be criticised, his attempts to grapple with this problem represent an important advance in setting up the sophisticated apparatus which is needed for serious experimental work in retrieval. Unfortunately, the application of these tests involves a large amount of work, and we have been quite unable to incorporate anything like this in our own program package. We have, however, made use of a simple method of

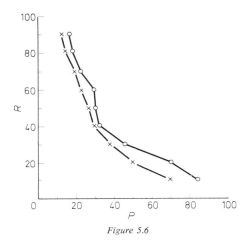

Figure 5.6

characterising differences which prevents us from regarding *any* difference between performance curves as significant, as follows.

Essentially, what we are interested in is not whether there is an important difference between two curves, but whether one curve represents an important and useful improvement over the other. As we saw earlier, we are interested in whether one curve is to the right of another in a recall/precision plot, and in particular in whether classification performance curves are noticeably to the right of our basic term performance curve. A natural way of comparing two curves is to consider some sort of area relationship between them, but the appropriate way of doing this depends on the distinction I have just made. Consider, for example, a graph as in Figure 5.7. Clearly, the two curves P and Q are different; and an obvious way of measuring their difference, and hence of determining whether this is significant, is to measure the area between the curves, i.e. the total area enclosed within the figure of eight, and to compare this with the area enclosed by the graph axes as a whole: if the area enclosed between the curves represents a reasonably large percentage of the whole, we can say that the two curves are genuinely different. Thus in the example applying a percentage threshold of 5 per cent or 10 per cent would mean that P and Q are significantly different.

But now suppose that we are interested, as in fact we are, in whether one curve is better than another, that is in whether the former represents a

104

genuine improvement over the latter. We have already defined performance merit in relation to the axes of recall/precision plots, so that we want to decide whether one curve is sufficiently to the right of another; and we want to do this in a way which depends on the overall character of the curves involved and not on specific features of them. For example, if we have two curves P and Q such that the precision value for P is greater by a factor than that for Q at all recall levels except the highest, where the value for P

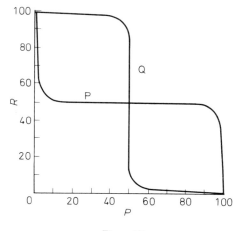

Figure 5.7

is marginally less than that for Q, we do not want this single trivial cross-over to affect the comparison too much. The solution is to compare the two areas enclosed by the two curves as wholes directly, so that when one curve is completely or predominantly to the right of another this is reflected by the fact that it encloses a larger area than the other. In each case, that is, we measure the entire area to the left of the curve, with 100 per cent recall and 10 per cent recall as upper and lower bounds, and we then look at the difference between the two. This means that for the example given above, if we imagine that this represents a pair of recall/precision curves, the result is that the areas enclosed by P and Q respectively are the same, so that neither can represent an overall improvement over the other. Naturally, if there is a difference, we want to know whether this is sufficiently large, so that we have a significant as opposed to a trivial improvement in performance; and the obvious way of doing this is to see whether the difference is greater than some defined proportion of the smaller of the two areas involved. Thus we will say that if we find that the area enclosed by one curve P is larger than that enclosed by Q, we will only accept the difference as important if it is greater than, say, 5 per cent or 10 per cent of the area of Q.

Thus if we consider the more extended example represented by the graph in Figure 5.8, working out the areas enclosed by the curves very roughly gives

$$
\begin{aligned}
A &= 1\ 900 \\
B &= \text{ ,, } \quad +320 = 2\ 220 \\
C &= \text{ ,, } \quad +160 = 2\ 060 \\
D &= \text{ ,, } \quad +280 = 2\ 180 \\
E &= \text{ ,, } \quad +600 = 2\ 500 \\
F &= \text{ ,, } \quad +900 = 2\ 800 \\
G &= \text{ ,, } \quad +\ \ 80 = 1\ 980
\end{aligned}
$$

so that the differences between A and B, C, D, E, F and G represented as percentages of A, again worked out very roughly, are

$$
\begin{aligned}
&\textit{per cent} \\
B &= 17 \\
C &= \ \ 8 \\
D &= 15 \\
E &= 32 \\
F &= 47 \\
G &= \ \ 4
\end{aligned}
$$

Thus if we require a percentage difference of at least 10 per cent of the smallest area involved before we will accept other curves as enclosing significantly larger ones and hence representing important performance differences, we will in this case accept B, D, E and F as improvements on A, but reject C and G. This seems reasonable.

The significance test just described is clearly very rudimentary: and it is mentioned mainly to show that we are not unaware of the need for a significance test of some kind. Its application represents the final stage in the measurement of performance, and we can therefore summarise our whole evaluation procedure by listing the steps involved, as follows:

(1) calculate standard recall and precision ratios, using the total numbers of relevant and non-relevant documents retrieved for the set of requests, on each coordination level;

(2) plot the resulting graph in the standard manner;

(3) read off precision values for 9 standard recall values;

(4) plot a new standard graph from these;

(5) apply the significance test to this graph.

It will be evident that our approach to performance measurement is fairly elementary; but this does not mean that our results are not of value, though our next step should be to adopt more sophisticated techniques.

The foregoing completes the description of our research problem, our approach to it, and the method we have adopted for evaluating the results of our experiments. We can now introduce the detailed survey of our actual

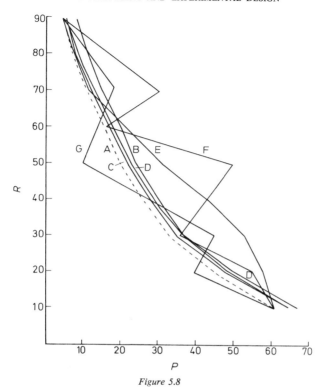

Figure 5.8

experiments themselves with a note on the way we set up the experiments, that is on our test design.

Test design

The need for a test design to control the experiments will be evident when we consider the size of the range of possible experiments. The number of components of the classification and class-using process that we are examining is large enough in itself, and we have several alternatives to consider as fillers for each slot in the process. In Chapter 3 we listed a variety of class definitions, and in Chapter 4 a number of different vocabularies, or at least, a number of what we have chosen in practice to regard as different vocabularies, though they can be regarded in principle as alternative classifications; and in Chapter 2 we considered different ways of using a classification as an indexing language, though in this case we have chosen to represent the range of alternatives as one of search procedures. In practice, it is convenient to distinguish the similarity matrix formation stage of the classification procedure from the class-finding stage, and we can therefore have four main heads under each of which we have at least one set of alternatives to examine, and perhaps several.

If each such set represents one component or variable in the process we are investigating, our experiments should in theory study the effect of changes in each one on retrieval performance; and as these variables interact, this means that to understand the consequences of assigning a particular value to one specific variable, we should first carry out a set of experiments in which the value of this variable itself is changed, while those of all the others are held constant, and we should then cross-check by further experiments in which the values of the other variables are also changed. What this amounts to, if we consider all the variables, is, of course, carrying out tests covering all the possible combinations of all the values of all the variables; and it will be quite clear that the number of variables we are examining is large enough to mean that the number of possible combinations of them is far too big for us to test all of them directly. It is worth commenting on the fact that this is true though we are only working with one collection and request set: the extension of our investigations to cover several collections, request sets, or sets of relevance judgements would make for a substantial increase in the number of possible tests, which serves to show how daunting serious experimentation in this field is.

We are forced, therefore, to be selective in our experiments: we cannot hope to carry out all the possible ones. We must, however, ensure the selection of the experiments we actually carry out is a sensible one; we must choose experiments which are systematically related to one another, if we are to make legitimate comparisons and draw valid conclusions. The combinations of values we consider must be connected with one another. For this reason, we decided that the correct approach would be to choose one particular combination of variable values, or configuration, as a base, and to relate all our other experiments to it. We would, that is, test every alternative for each variable in turn within this configuration, in a systematic way, which would mean that though we did not directly examine some particular combination of variable values, because neither was the base one, we could nevertheless make some inferences about what the effect of using this combination would be, because each value had been individually tested, in the context of the base configuration. This use of a base configuration would, in other words, tie all our experiments together.

The effect of this technique in reducing the number of possible experiments can be seen from an example. If we suppose that we have three variables, with four values each, this gives us 48 possible combinations; if we now select one specific combination as the base configuration, and as well, of course, as testing it, try the effect of substituting the other values of each variable in turn in this configuration, we get a total of 10 experiments, from which we should be able to make some inferences about the combinations we have not tested. The idea can be illustrated diagrammatically, as follows: if we have three variables A, B, C, with four values for each, say

$$A: m \ n \ o \ p$$
$$B: q \ r \ s \ t$$
$$C: u \ v \ w \ x$$

and the base combination uses the first values of each variable, we have
an initial test on $\quad\quad\quad\quad$ $m \ q \ u$
while substituting for A gives $\quad$ $n \ q \ u$
$\quad\quad\quad\quad\quad\quad\quad\quad\quad\quad$ $o \ q \ u$
$\quad\quad\quad\quad\quad\quad\quad\quad\quad\quad$ $p \ q \ u$
substituting for B gives $\quad\quad$ $m \ r \ u$
$\quad\quad\quad\quad\quad\quad\quad\quad\quad\quad$ $m \ s \ u$
$\quad\quad\quad\quad\quad\quad\quad\quad\quad\quad$ $m \ t \ u$
and substituting for C gives $\quad$ $m \ q \ v$
$\quad\quad\quad\quad\quad\quad\quad\quad\quad\quad$ $m \ q \ w$
$\quad\quad\quad\quad\quad\quad\quad\quad\quad\quad$ $m \ q \ x$

from which we can hopefully infer, using $m \ q \ u$, $o \ q \ u$ and $m \ s \ u$, what the result of testing the combination $o \ s \ u$, for example, would be.

It must, however, be admitted that we should be cautious about our inferences; and it is safer to regard such a series of sets of experiments—a set being the experiments covering changes in one variable only—as the absolute minimum number of experiments we have to carry out if we are to say we have investigated the effects of changes in the values of our variables. We will be on more solid ground in drawing conclusions if we have also made some cross checks, that is have also investigated some combinations of values of which all, or at least more than one, are non-standard, since in the base-oriented experiments only one value is non-standard at a time. The more of these cross checks we can make the better, but virtually any should be of value. This is incidentally useful as a way of showing that we have not chosen a really eccentric base configuration, though the character of this configuration should not in principle affect our results: it can be chosen on purely practical grounds, say because it is the easiest to work with. It may indeed be the case that it is impossible to put this scheme into effect in a really tidy way, because some experiments may be too expensive; and we also find that some experiments which would in principle be desirable would be very obviously futile, given the results we have obtained so far. But we have tried to adhere to this scheme as far as possible, so that we can relate the conclusions which can be drawn from one set of experiments, dealing with a particular variable, to those we can draw from another. One point must, however, be noticed: we have chosen a base configuration of variable values as a means of carrying out our classification experiments; this does not mean that the performance given by this configuration is itself regarded as a base: what we have taken is the base retrieval performance, on which we want to improve, in using a classification, the performance given by terms alone; this is our standard of comparison from the retrieval point of view. We must therefore be careful to distinguish the base configuration from the base performance, though we can relate the use of terms in retrieval to the use of classes: in each case, the components of the system as a whole are the same, and we can say that in using terms, we are assigning null values to all the classification variables.

The foregoing describes the principles on which we have based our experiments; but the way in which they have been carried out in detail depends to a considerable extent on the actual programs we have designed for this purpose. The features of our test document and request sets are also relevant, and the account of the experiments will therefore be preceded, first by a description of our program system, which will be given in the next chapter, and then of our data base, which is discussed in Chapter 7; the summary of our experiments and their results appears in Chapter 8.

REFERENCES

1. *Factors* 2, Chapter 2; the references below to Cleverdon's analysis of retrieval system factors relate to this chapter
2. *Factors* 1,1, Chapter 5; see also *ISR–13*, Chapter VII
3. *ISR–11*, Chapter IV; *ISR–13*, Chapters VIII and IX
4. SWETS, J. A. 'Effectiveness of Information Retrieval Methods', *American Documentation* 20, 72 (1969)
5. *Factors* 2, Chapter 4; *ISR–11*, Chapter 5; *ISR–12*, Chapter III; *ISR–13*, Chapters I and X
6. *Factors* 1,1, Chapter 4
7. *Factors* 1,1, Chapter 5
8. *Factors* 2, Chapters 4 and 5; *ISR–11*, Chapter V; *ISR–12*, Chapter III; *ISR–13*, Chapter VI
9. *Factors* 2, Chapters 4 and 5; *ISR–11*, Chapter V; *ISR–12*, Chapter III
10. *Factors* 2, Chapters 4 and 5; *ISR–11*, Chapter V; *ISR–12*, Chapter III; *ISR–13*, Chapter VII
11. *Factors* 2, Chapter 2, Figure 2.1
12. *Factors* 2, Chapter 3; *ISR–12*, Chapter III; *ISR–13*, Chapter II; SWETS, J. A. 'Effectiveness of Information Retrieval Methods', *American Documentation*, 20, 72 (1969); LANCASTER, F. W. *Information Retrieval Systems: Characteristics, Testing and Evaluation*, New York (1968)
13. *Factors* 2, Chapter 3; *ISR–12*, Chapter III; *ISR–13*, Chapter II; SWETS. J. A. 'Effectiveness of Information Retrieval Methods', *American Documentation*, 20, 72 (1969)
14. SWETS. J. A. 'Effectiveness of Information Retrieval Methods', *American Documentation*, 20, 72 (1969)
15. *ISR–11*, Chapter V; *ISR–12*, Chapter III; *ISR–13*, Chapters III and IV
16. *ISR–12*, Chapter III
17. *Factors* 2, Chapter 5

18. SPARCK JONES, K. and NEEDHAM, R. M. 'Automatic Term Classification and Retrieval', *Information Storage and Retrieval*, **4**, 91 (1968)
19. *Factors* 2, Chapter 3; *ISR-12*, Chapter III
20. *ISR-13*, Chapter III

Chapter 6

The Program System

SUMMARY

The series of experiments and the classification and retrieval tests we have carried out required a substantial program package, which is described in this chapter. The package consists of four main sets of routines for forming a similarity matrix, constructing a classification from it, manipulating this classification to provide index descriptions for documents and requests, and carrying out actual searches, with supporting routines for preparing the initial term/document lists and for performing a variety of clerical functions. The activity of these programs can be described in quite general terms, in that a number of units are involved, namely terms, documents, requests and term classes, which can be paired in different ways to give data structures of the standard form represented by a list of items a, each characterised by a list of items b. The procedures followed in the programs can then be described, very generally, as sequences of data-processing operations, mostly of a quite simple kind, which transform a given structure to obtain a new one. This view of the processes involved in our programs in fact leads to the suggestion that they can be described by a general-purpose notation. The routines comprising the programs themselves are designed to be very flexible; the various system components being tested are clearly distinguished, so that different values can be assigned to the parameters which are involved, and different alternatives can be easily examined. Thus the similarity routines permit choices of a similarity coefficient, and of the controls represented by the use of a significance test or matrix threshold; the classification procedures cover a range of definitions of all four types; the processing routines set up the variety of data structures or dictionaries needed for retrieval according to different specifications, by, for example, providing the class lists for requests and documents which replace their original term lists; and the retrieval routines carry out the actual searches, and calculate recall and precision ratios characterising the performance of a given language for a set of requests. In addition a large number of routines for analysing classifications are available, along with the extensive printing facilities which are essential for research purposes.

Program philosophy

This chapter describes the program package we developed under our project for carrying out systematic classification and retrieval tests. The package has a large range of facilities, and though these were initially provided for experiments in the construction and use of keyword classifications, the system as a whole is comprehensive and powerful enough to be used for a large variety of information retrieval research purposes, primarily, but not necessarily, in the area of automatic classification. The programs are therefore worth describing, not only because this description will provide the background for the detailed presentation of the experiments we have carried out which follows, but for their own sake, to illustrate the kind and range of facilities needed for computational information retrieval ex-

112

periments, and to show how much software is needed for satisfactory experimental work in this field. This description will be quite straightforward: the justification for the particular facilities is given in the other chapters on classification and retrieval. As far as comparisons with the program packages developed elsewhere go, the most obvious is with that developed at Harvard and Cornell for the SMART project[1]. This is much more comprehensive as a whole, but in the particular area of classification we probably have a wider range of facilities. Both packages are in any case among the most effective which have been developed so far for retrieval test purposes.

It is convenient to subsume the activities of the programs under four heads, representing successive stages in the construction and use of a classification for retrieval, namely the formation of a similarity matrix for the terms in the given vocabulary, the identification of classes of terms, the assignment of class descriptions to documents and requests, and the use of these descriptions in retrieval. But each of these four stages, as we shall see, covers a whole range of procedures, and it must also be emphasised that the distinctions between them are to some extent arbitrary ones based on programming convenience, rather than on the logic of the retrieval situation. Thus as we saw earlier, we have chosen to regard what are really different ways of characterising requests and documents as different methods of searching. A much more important point, however, is that the divisions between the four sections of the program are far from watertight. Many of the routines are highly generalised, so that they can be applied in quite different circumstances. They may normally be used in a particular way, and so may be described under a particular head, but they can in principle, and may also in practice, be used in other ways. It must be emphasised that this is not a remark about general-purpose subroutines, in the ordinary sense, but about the typical activities of classification and retrieval procedures, which largely depend on listing, sorting and matching. This means that quite general, and hence flexible, programs can be set up, and our package as a whole consists mainly of a set of routines of this kind. These characteristics of classification and retrieval are more fully discussed by D. M. Jackson, who has developed a notation for describing the data structures and operations of a classification-using retrieval system[2]; but I shall discuss the point which is involved very briefly here, because it makes it easier to describe the programs.

The essential point is that it is possible in principle to treat data structures consisting of a list of any items a, described by lists of any other items b, in the same way, and to subject them to a given procedure, in a standard way, to obtain quite different results according to the character of the a's and b's in question. There is of course nothing startling about this: what matters is that it is possible to look at very much more of the apparently heterogeneous activity of a classification-using retrieval system in this way than one might think. This can be illustrated by a reference to our association routine, which simply notes, for any given items a, characterised by other items b, the set of other a's with which each a shares at least one characterising item b. If the a's are terms, and the b's are the documents they occur in, the routine lists all the terms which occur in at least one document with a given term. If the a's are documents and the b's terms, we obtain the set of documents which are related to a given document through a shared term or terms. If the a's are terms and the b's classes, we obtain the set of terms which share at least one common class with a given term. If the a's are classes and the b's terms, we obtain the set of classes which overlap in membership with a given class. In each case, moreover, we obtain new lists which constitute new data structures to which further routines can be applied.

If we have a set of items x, that is, a pair of which can be used to generate data of the a/b form, so that a given pair can be used either way, with the b's describing the a's or vice versa, and this set is not at all large, we have a wide range of possible applications for any general processing routine like the one which lists associations*. Of course it may be the case that a particular pairing or particular application has no obvious utility; but we have found that not only this general approach makes for much more powerful programs, but that it has stimulated a much more enterprising approach to the whole problem of classification and retrieval; the fact that the information and processes involved can be looked at in many different ways has meant that we have been able to consider unconventional ways of using the system as well as conventional ones. For example, we have used the association routine which was initially designed to find the set of terms with which each term co-occurs in the documents, to display the set of terms with which a given term occurs in any class, and so in a sense to form a new classification. The reason for this will appear later; the point here is that this is a non-obvious but useful application of a routine primarily intended for another purpose, which can easily be made because our programs are normally designed so that they can be applied to any data having a standard structure, and most of our data have such a structure. Thus though particular applications of our routines may be regarded as the usual ones, their flexibility in data-handling has been of immense value from the experimental point of view. This is in fact the main advantage of using computers in research in this area: the simple inversion of an a/b description, for example, is a substantial clerical operation when done by hand, but it is computationally trivial; and it is the ability to do something like this so easily which has enabled us to analyse classification and retrieval in a comprehensive way and has contributed a great deal to our understanding of the problems with which we have been concerned. Our program package, then, consists primarily of a number of general, parametrically controlled routines which can be applied to any data in a standard format. They are usually

---

* It will be evident from the previous example that this can include the case where the same items are paired, or where classes are listed for classes.

processing routines for listing, sorting, comparing and substituting items, and for manipulating lists of items, though there are naturally more sophisticated procedures for computing and analysing similarities, identifying classes, and so on. It is surprising how much processing is required for a single complete run from the initial calculation of similarities to that of recall and precision ratios, through the construction of a specific classification and its use in a series of searches, though the programs are very fast. The demands on store space present problems too, though these can be resolved, at least for a collection of the size of our test one, by dynamic allocation. We may, nevertheless, use all the available 40 000 words of a rapid access store in a single test with this collection, and it is obvious that the research with larger collections, which is desirable, will present problems because the store will have to be traded for time, and a complete test even now may take as much as half an hour. Computer costs are of course quite different in research and production, and inferences from research experience may be quite misleading; but the problem as a whole is an important one, and I shall return to it in the concluding chapter.

In describing our program package in detail I shall, as mentioned earlier, make use of four headings representing the four main stages of processing required for a complete classification and retrieval test. Individual facilities will be discussed under the headings representing their regular context of use, though the fact that many of these routines may be used for other purposes must be remembered; some of these alternatives will be indicated, but not all. The system as a whole treats terms, term classes, documents and requests as units, so that sixteen pairings of the a/b form are possible. Only two of these are supplied initially; these are the document/term lists, and the request/term lists. Class/term lists are generated by the classification program, and other pairings are set up as they are required for retrieval. Some lists are not needed for retrieval, but they may be supplied for information, or for other purposes, as we shall see. In the program description I shall generally mention a specific data structure in the context in which it is normally considered for retrieval purposes; but again, the fact that it may be used elsewhere must be borne in mind. In the program description, therefore, I shall describe a particular operation, like that used in the formation of the co-occurrence array, where it is used to process document/term lists to obtain term/term lists, as if this was the only way in which it could be used; and I shall refer to the particular data structure represented by the term/term lists only in connection with this routine. This kind of simplification makes it much easier to describe the action of the programs, because this can then be considered from the natural and most important point of view, namely that of a complete classification and retrieval test. However, the other possibilities, both for operations and data structures, are always there. This is particularly important where the classification routines are concerned; these will be considered in connection with terms and documents, because we are primarily interested in grouping terms by their occurrence in documents, but this is simply a specific application of a quite general procedure which groups objects according to their properties, the terms being the objects and the documents the properties in this particular case.

Formation of similarity matrices

In the first stage, the information about the resemblance between terms on which the actual classification of terms is based is extracted from the initial document descriptions. These are presented in a standard format, with each document followed by its string of term numbers. These 'pre-classification' routines, and the classification routines themselves, are intended to be applicable to any qualitative data, that is to any data where objects are characterised by a simple list of the properties they possess, without any indication of the extent to which they possess them: it will be remembered that we have confined our interest in classification to material of this kind. Our grouping procedures have in fact been applied to a variety of data samples, and we have gained valuable experience from these miscellaneous experiments; we have been able to use them to throw light on the special requirements of classification in the retrieval case, as we shall see when the results of our actual tests are considered in Chapter 10. It will also be clear from my earlier remarks that the input data, though it usually consists of document/term lists can of course be a listing of the incidence of any items b for any items a, and that we may be interested, in the retrieval context, in other combinations of our given set of items. One obvious possibility is to invert the document/term lists to obtain term/document lists, and to substitute grouping documents by their terms for grouping terms by their documents. In this connection, an important distinction must be noted if confusion is to be avoided. In principle, any data structure of listing of the a/b form constitutes an object/property description in the broad sense; but it is convenient to refer specifically to those items which are grouped by the classification procedure as objects, and to the items characterising them on which the grouping is based, as their properties. This distinction must be borne in mind in connection with the description of our grouping procedures: the data are presented in the a/b form, but the a's, though logically objects, are in fact properties from the classification point of view, and the b's, though logically properties, are in fact objects: this arrangement simply makes the programming easier.

The input data are first processed to obtain the co-occurrence array giving the number of occurrences of each term, and the list of terms with which it co-occurs in at least one document, along with the value of the co-occurrence coefficient in each case. The procedure is quite straightforward. We process a single document/term list at a time; the occurrence of each term in the document is noted, and the other terms occurring with it in the list are identified: this requires a term vector in which the occurrences of each term are accumulated, and a dependent list store in which the string of terms associated with each term is formed, the terms being accompanied by the value of the co-occurrence coefficient specifying their relation with the initial term. This coefficient is normally simply the number of co-occurrences of the pair of terms, but an alternative is available in which the addition of 1 for a co-occurrence in a document is replaced by $1/n$, where n is the number of terms characterising the document; this gives us the simple weighting of the properties which leads to the weighted similarity definition discussed in Chapter 3. The basic product of this routine is thus a co-occurrence array in one of two forms. But this can be optionally modified to delete co-occurrences below a specified (usually quite low) value, or by the removal of the actual coefficients altogether, so that a simple association array, listing only the actual terms co-occurring with each given term, or co-occurring more than a specified number of times, is obtained: this can be regarded, from the logical point of view, as representing the use of another co-occurrence coefficient. The formation of the array can also be controlled by the use of a threshold so that only co-occurrences with a value above the threshold are retained. This of course produces the same result as deletion, but the two are quite different from the practical point of view, because the setting of the threshold for deletion can be based on the information contained in the complete array, in the way that the prior threshold cannot.

The co-occurrence array is now used to generate the similarity matrix for all pairs of associated terms which is the normal input to the classification routines. This is of course only true for the genuine co-occurrence arrays: the simple association array in itself constitutes a binary similarity matrix, and is thus input directly to the grouping program. Any plausible similarity definition of the general kind discussed in Chapter 3 can be plugged in here in principle, as long as it does not require more information than is provided by the current input and co-occurrence routines, that is information about the numbers of objects and properties, the size of the universe, and so on, as well as the actual co-occurrence notes. We have actually programmed only the two definitions given earlier, namely the Tanimoto coefficient and the cosine correlation coefficient, though it will be remembered that we have chosen to say that we have three definitions, according to whether the Tanimoto coefficient is calculated using the unweighted or weighted co-occurrences. We can therefore currently obtain a simple unweighted matrix, or a weighted matrix, using the Tanimoto definition, or a matrix based on the cosine coefficient. The straightforward calculation of the matrices using these definitions may, in addition, be modified by the application of the local significance test mentioned earlier, in which the value of the similarity coefficient is only worked out for a pair of terms whose co-occurrence coefficient is higher than would be expected, given their respective occurrences; for this purpose a previously calculated matrix giving the co-occurrences which can be expected on a random basis for items with occurrences ranging from 1 to n, where n is the maximum frequency of occurrence of any item, is supplied. This test may itself be varied by changing the significance level. The similarity matrix when formed may also be thresholded, either for purely practical reasons, to obtain a smaller matrix, given that a set of objects as large as the one we have been working with, which contains 712 items, can easily generate a matrix containing 50 000 non-zero entries, or to eliminate weaker similarities in a crude way based on the assumption that small similarities are trivial ones: a significance test would do this in a more sophisticated way by distinguishing important, though weak similarities from uninteresting ones. The choice of a suitable threshold is made easy by an analysis of the distribution of entries made when the matrix is formed: this gives both the number of entries with each value, and the amount of store which is required to hold a matrix limited to this and higher values of the coefficient.

We have not attempted any elaborate matrix manipulation or permutation routines because our classification procedures in general rely only on the information contained in individual matrix cells or rows; but we can obtain what can be regarded as a squared similarity matrix in an indirect way, by cycling round the co-occurrence routine: the initial co-occurrence array, in its simple associative form, is treated as input data, so that the terms which co-occur with a given term are treated as objects, possessing the property represented by the given term; and a new co-occurrence array is then formed for these which is input to the similarity routine. This is indeed one example of the flexibility provided by our general approach.

The actual matrix construction procedure resembles that used to form the co-occurrence array, with the important difference that the intermediate list store is not required. The co-occurrence routine, as noted, processes one document at a time using a term vector and list store, which is fully unpicked when the co-occurrences for the complete set of document descriptions have been obtained. The similarity routine uses the same term vector, in which the term occurrences are noted, and processes one row of the unpicked array at a time, replacing the value of the co-occurrence coefficient by the value of the similarity coefficient. The matrix is thus stored serially, and an address vector is set up to access individual rows. The construction of the array and matrix is clearly a substantial affair; the associations in their initial list form, in particular, consume a large amount of store space, though only half of this is needed for the similarity matrix. Working with arrays and matrices which can in principle be quite large is of course a general problem of classification practice; the fact that many matrices are not very dense (though 'squared' matrices are an exception) means that we reduce the problem as long as we confine ourselves to non-zero entries; but it will be clear, even so, that the core store may overflow during the construction of the matrix, given the demands of the list processing stage, though the final product itself may still fit in. The matrix itself may, moreover, be too big for the store, and though it is convenient for experimental purposes to have a matrix which can be held in store, because we may want to use it in repeated classification tests, we may only be able to obtain such a matrix by thresholding. Some classification algorithms do not, it is true, depend on random accesses to the matrix, though clump-finding procedures do, and we may therefore be prepared to accept large matrices which will not fit in. But more generally we must be prepared to consider matrices which are too large for the store, even if we subsequently process them to fit them in.

For these reasons, we have designed our programs so that blocks of co-occurrences can be unpicked, and dumped by merging with previously dumped blocks, during the construction of the association array, if the store limit is reached. The co-occurrences obtained from a single row of the input data may indeed cause an overflow, so that a two-level merging, for single-array rows, and sets of rows, may be required. The construction of the actual similarity matrix itself depends on single cells of the array, apart from the object vector, and therefore presents no problems. The routines for these first-stage programs as a whole also illustrate our standard method of manipulating information very well: this involves base vectors and open stores reached from them, where the base vector contains a list of items a, and the open store the concatenated strings of b items. The details in different cases may vary, but the principle is the same: the co-occurrence routines involve a term vector and strings of related terms (though these are stored in a more complex way during the list processing), and the similarity routines also involve this vector and dependent strings, though the initial term vector is replaced by the matrix row address vector when the matrix has been formed.

Class-finding

In the second stage of the processing, the similarity matrix is used to obtain the actual classes of terms. Here there is an initial choice of class type, and a subsequent choice of alternatives under each type, particularly where clumps are concerned. The output in all cases simply consists of the list of classes as found, normally one for each starting element, with the starting element as the name of the class. In the case of clumps information about the clump is also supplied, indicating the size of the clump, the number of iterations required to find it, the values of the set similarities, i.e. SAA, SBB and SAB, and the final value of the cohesion function. The algorithms for finding strings, stars and cliques allow alternative specifications of the length of a string, the size of a star, and the minimum similarity between the members of a clique: these represent subsidiary choices associated with the one particular definition of a string as a series in which each item is followed by the one most strongly connected with it, of a star as the set of items which are most strongly connected with the given item, and of a

119

clique as a maximally connected set of items, respectively. The clump-finding routines are, as already noted, more complex because more choices both at the definitional level and below it are involved. An initial choice of definition can be made, to select SAB^2, NA, or 100/P clumps, with a subsidiary choice of setting for P in the third case. In addition, further options are available, whatever definition is chosen; we may, for instance, decide to retain starting elements in clumps, whether their pattern of connections justifies it or not, or we may simply treat any unclassified element as a unit class; and we may decide whether we want to apply the gradient test to see whether shifting a clump from a potential clump to its complement, or vice versa, is really worth while, or to permit any shifts which reduce the value of the cohesion function, even if this reduction is really trivial. Different specifications of the amount of change in the function we require to justify a shift can also be provided, if we opt for the gradient test.

The actual procedures for finding classes according to any of our specifications are all quite simple. The technique used to find strings is indeed quite elementary: we have only to identify the element which is most strongly connected with the last, either up to a point where a loop is closed, or up to the point where the specified maximum length is reached. All the classes are output with their terms in ascending numerical order: this sorting can be suppressed for strings, so that the actual structure of the chain as found is displayed. Forming stars is just as easy: we simply select the items which are successively less strongly connected to the starting element, until the maximum size is reached (or exceeded, since any items with the same similarity are all included). The clique-finding procedure is slightly more complicated: it requires a term vector indicating set membership, which is scanned to identify terms not yet in the clique; the matrix rows for these are inspected to see whether they are connected with all the elements which are already in the class, and so can be added to it. The clump-finding program is more complex still, though it is similar to the one used for cliques. It again depends on a term vector, but it also requires a 'total similarity vector', giving the total value of the similarity connections between each element and the potential clump and its complement respectively, and a 'set similarity vector' in which the combined similarities between all the members of the clump, or its complement, or between the two, are noted. The term vector is then used to pick up the set membership of each term, and the information contained in its matrix row and cell in the total similarity vector, with that given in the set similarity vector, is used to determine whether a change in its current assignment to the potential clump or its complement will reduce the current value of the cohesion function; if it will, the corresponding alterations to the vector information are made. This scan is repeated until there is either no further change in the allocation of the objects, or a maximum number of cycles has been reached.

The classification routines in general do not make the demands on space as do the earlier ones, apart from the similarity matrix store requirement.

It is worth noticing, however, that this restriction does not apply to stars, because these can be obtained from a single matrix row only, and do not involve the random access to the matrix which is typical of the procedures for finding classes of the other types*. We have not, however, exploited this fact in our experiments, because we have made it a general requirement that the matrix should be held in store, and this naturally simplifies its use even when we are finding stars. Additional space is required for the various vectors, on the other hand, if we are searching for cliques or clumps, but these are not very long, given the numbers of terms we typically work with, and they therefore present no real problem. It is obvious that difficulties will arise as soon as we consider experiments on a much larger scale; but I shall consider these later.

Classification and data processing

We now come to the third set of routines, which process the information contained in the classification, and set up the environment for actual retrieval. If we consider these programs solely from the point of view of the activities which are involved in carrying out a complete grouping and retrieval test, that is, their purpose is to extract and arrange the facts about terms, documents and requests which are needed for searches; but these facts are of interest in their own right, from the research point of view, and this component of our package has therefore been developed so that it can be used to provide us with information about our experimental material whether this is strictly required for retrieval or not. These routines receive the list of classes, as they were found, and are supplied with the original document/term lists on which the classification was based, and the request/term lists; all the various kinds of item involved in the whole retrieval process appear here, and the essential object of these routines is to exploit the relationships between some of them, which are given, to set up new ones. It is in these routines, in other words, that the use of data structures of the a/b form is most evident, because they are largely concerned with the derivation of one structure from others. If we first consider the activity of these routines from the point of view of a retrieval test, it can be divided into two stages, namely the setting up of the document environment, in which the various data structures, or 'dictionaries' as we have called them, associated with the documents are generated; and the setting up of the request environment, which does the same for the requests. In the former, the program is provided with the initial document/term descriptions, and the classification, or class/term descriptions; it then inverts the latter, to obtain term/class lists, and uses the two simple dictionaries consisting of the document/term lists, and the new term/class lists, to obtain document/class listings. The last includes notes of the frequency of occurrence of each class

* Though with some additional processing finding strings could be made equally economical.

for a document, because a given class may of course be generated by more than one term in a document: this information is required for searches in which a document is only retrieved, on a class match, if the frequency of occurrence of a class for a document is at least as great as its frequency in the request specification. The document environment is set up for the entire collection at once; the request environment, which complements it, is however only set up for one request at a time. The routines for doing this are initially given the request/term lists; these are then used, together with the term/class dictionary obtained in setting up the document environment, to generate the request/class dictionary, with frequencies, which complements the document/class dictionary. This is the central activity of the routines from the retrieval point of view, though one essential preliminary is needed: this is purging the initial input class/term lists of duplicates, since the classification program itself may generate the same class more than once: it is the purged lists which form the input to the processing routines themselves. A possibility is also available at this first stage which can be used to illustrate the function of these programs both as part of the retrieval package, and as a source of information about the classifications we are using. We can opt initially for the identification of 'component sets', that is those sets of objects which are classified in the same way by the main classification. These component sets can then be used themselves as a classification, so that they are subjected to the processing described earlier to prepare them for use in retrieval; or they can be output to provide information about the way in which the initial classification, whatever it was, handled the terms.

The production of component sets is thus one way in which these routines can be used as a research tool; facilities for printing out any of the input listings, or dictionaries made from them, are also available: thus a standard 'Examine' run produces the purged list of classes with their terms, the term/class listings, the original document/term listing, and the created document/class dictionary, along with a complementary class/document dictionary which gives the document distribution of the classes with their frequency of co-occurrence for each document. Other data structures, like a term/document listing, can be obtained if required. Information of a more analytical character can also be provided, such as histograms illustrating the class/term and term/class distributions respectively: these are standard, but histograms for other pairs of elements can be generated without difficulty.

These procedures are very typical of the data-handling activities of our program package in general. They also illustrate a general problem of program design in this area, namely that there is a conflict between forethought and repetition: we can set up everything that we may need, but this is liable to consume too much store; or we can set things up as we need them, which may involve repitition. Essentially, we have to arrange a trade-off which is best suited to the amount of experimental material we have, and the character of our computing environment. It will, however, be evident that a fair amount of store is needed, and that as the dictionaries tend to be of very different sizes, dynamic store allocation is required if space is not to be wasted: the program is therefore designed to minimise its use of space as far as possible, by allocating it in this way.

Retrieval routines

The fourth section of the main program is devoted to the actual retrieval routines. These are supplied with the data structures set up by the previous processing routines, and also with a list of the relevant documents for each request. The output consists of the retrieval performance for the individual requests, the overall performance for the set of requests, and an analysis of various features of the data and searches. The output for each request shows the documents retrieved, and the coordination level (however this is defined, for terms, or classes, or matches on a combination of the two) at which each is retrieved. Relevant documents are marked, and the total inclusion of the request specification in the document one is noted where appropriate; any relevant documents not retrieved are indicated, and the total numbers of relevant and non-relevant documents retrieved, for each level separately, are presented. The performance for the set of requests as a whole is displayed both in the form of totals of relevant, non-relevant and all documents retrieved at each specific level, and in the form of totals for each level and those above, which are required for the calculation of recall and precision ratios. The ratios themselves are also provided, and a graph-plotting option for displaying the results is available, though this is not always used. The request/term and request/class lists are normally produced as well, for information, along with an analysis illustrating the behaviour of terms and their classes with respect to the searches: this shows the number of terms per request, of classes, and their maximum and minimum frequency.

This routine represents the general activity of the retrieval program, which is the same whatever mode of searching is adopted. In fact term matching is always carried out, because we use this as a standard of comparison: the choice is in the method of using classes in retrieval. We could in principle plug any reasonably straightforward way of using classes into the program: it is currently designed so that we can opt either for the simple mode of searching, in which class request and document specifications are substituted for their term lists, or for the mixed mode, in which classes and terms are used together. We have two further alternatives in each case, though these are currently both tested at once: thus the program matches in the first mode both on common classes, and on classes subject to the condition that the frequency of a class in a document shall be the same as, or greater than, its request frequency. If the second mode is selected, matches on both exclusive and inclusive class specifications are carried out, that is matches on terms supplemented by matches on any classes not containing these terms, or matches on terms supplemented by matches on any classes in which non-matching request terms occur. Normally, any such additional class matches promote the document to a coordination level one higher than the matching term level, however many matches there are, but the option is available where every class match adds one more level.

The four groups of routines just described constitute our main system: altogether they contain some 10 000 assembly code instructions. They are all needed for a complete test, but they are not all required at once: we customarily form a matrix and then use it to construct different classifications, which are separately processed in retrieval. Carrying through a complete test without interruption is indeed somewhat awkward for operating reasons. For a retrieval test with a previously constructed classification, however, the stage-three and stage-four routines are all required, and as they together consume a large amount of space, they have been designed so that large pieces of the program can be dispensed with while a particular subroutine is being executed. In general, the programs have been set up to permit choices at many stages which can be parametrically specified, and they are built up of successive subroutines so that changes can easily be made, or plugs inserted, if a wider range of choices at a particular point is required.

In this context, the printing facilities we have available are worth a special comment; for though many of them simply reproduce the normal output of a routine, the need for adequate printing in connection with experiments is considerable: producing printouts is very easy, but the value of comprehensible and readable ones where large-scale tests are involved is very great. So I shall not apologise for mentioning this aspect of our system here. We can, for instance, print the association array and similarity matrix, either in its complete form, or as selected rows only: this is very useful for diagnostic purposes if the matrix is at all large. We can naturally print our classifications, but we can also obtain more information about the creation of a clump classification by printing the state of the term vector after each iteration in the search for a clump. For clumps we can also print the information about each clump which is given by the various components of the cohesion function, and so on. From the stage-three processing programs we can obtain prints of all the dictionaries, but also, for example, a 'distribution print' which displays the term membership of a set of clumps in a way which makes comparison easy; the histograms mentioned earlier, and prints of the component sets for a classification, provide additional information. The histograms in particular are a good example, along with the clump vector print, of what may be described as the incidental but useful 'goodies' which can easily be provided with a large and comprehensive system; the information about the size of similarity matrices is another of these. The output of the retrieval program is of course normally presented in printed form.

These four sets of routines together constitute our main program package. But they are supported by a number of miscellaneous routines, mostly for processing either the data which is input to the main programs, or the material which is output from them. Some of these routines are trivial in themselves, but they make our package as a whole more comprehensive and more useful for research purposes. The input preparation routines are, on the other hand, important components of our system as a whole. They include programs for listing all the keywords appearing in a given set of document descriptions, for generating different term dictionaries from this keyword dictionary, and for replacing the keywords in the original document/keyword lists by the appropriate terms, as well as for processing these document/term descriptions; thus we can form frequency counts for our terms, and eliminate terms with more than a specified frequency from the document descriptions. The last is indeed a good example of the kind of supporting routine which is needed if a powerful central system is to be properly exploited. The content of all these dictionaries and lists can of course be printed, and another group of routines is available for replacing the numbers by which the terms are normally represented, both in the document/term descriptions which are input to the main program, and in all the data structures involving terms which are produced by this program, by words. We can, for example, print classes or component sets as lists of words, as well as document/term lists which we would expect to be able to obtain in this form.

Overview of the program package

Finally, some remarks about the operating characteristics of the system as a whole. These are, of course, not directly relevant to any working computational information retrieval system, but we can, as we shall see, draw some conclusions about the operational features of a classification-using retrieval system from our research experience. The operational characteristics of our system are, however, very important from the research point of view. Generally speaking, the requirements which an experimental system has to satisfy are rather different from those imposed by a fully-implemented system, though it must be admitted the difference in scale is not so great as it may appear to be: we have been surprised to find that tests even with 712 terms, 200 documents and 42 requests make much heavier demands, even on a large computer, than we thought at first. A further point is that the demands have not been made at the points we expected. When we began, we thought that our problem was one of constructing classifications on a large scale; but the difficulties here, as we shall see when we look at our experimental results, may be less great than we thought. We have found, on the other hand, that the problems of manipulating all the data required for retrieval, and in carrying it out, impose more strain on the machine than we predicted. It must, however, be emphasised that this is a consequence of our research requirements, and that though both production and experimental information retrieval may present problems of scale, these problems are really different. In the production context, we genuinely have a large bulk of material to be handled, both in constructing a classification and using it in retrieval; but with such a system we could probably rely on greater control over the use of the relevant computer, and we would almost certainly not require the speed in our programs which is essential for test purposes. The scale problem in the experimental context really comes from the need to carry through as much of the work as possible without going outside the rapid-access store: thus in our retrieval procedures, we explicitly rely on having all the necessary information for a complete test with the entire document collection and request set in core store at once, while this would not be necessary in a production environment; the essential need in the research environment is for very fast programs, so that the large number of runs which have to be made to examine the effects of small changes in the system can be carried out at not too great a cost. Our general experience, in other words, and this has doubtless been Salton's too, is that computer testing of even a quite small experimental retrieval system is much more of a business, from the computing point of view, than one might expect, not only because of the need for speed, but also because of the need for a variety of facilities, of a mainly diagnostic character, which have to be provided if research needs are to be satisfied.

Our total program system, then, has been designed for use on the C.U. Mathematical Laboratory computer Titan (an ICL Atlas 2), on which all the work under our project has been carried out. This is a fairly powerful machine with up to 40 000 48-bit words of core store available for object programs, and disc backup as well as magnetic tape. Most of the programs have been written in Atlas assembly code; this has the unfortunate consequence that they cannot be distributed, but the advantage of this approach is that the programs are highly efficient, because they have been set up to exploit the particular facilities of this machine fairly thoroughly. The system as a whole contains some 12 000 instructions, but it is of course divided into component routines partly so that the amount of core space available for the data is maximised, and partly because the operating system used on the Titan does not lend itself to the blanket use of a large program system as a whole, from which a specific routine may be selected, say, simply to produce another printout: it is inconvenient, for instance, to work with more than two magnetic tapes, and though the tapes are addressable, a heavy use of them is time consuming; similarly user file space is limited. For these reasons we have, as mentioned earlier, incorporated dynamic store allocation procedures which automatically concatenate the data structures involved, in the stage-three and stage-four processing and retrieval routines, where the demands on space are heavy. The manipulation of space takes time, but very much less than the time which would be required for a systematic large-scale use of the disc or magnetic tapes.

The amount of time required for a complete test varies very much, according to the combination of options selected; in general the programs are designed to work fast because they are used repeatedly, but special effort has been put into the really repetitive loops, like those involved in the formation of associations, or the iterative search for a clump. Some of the options necessarily impose additional work, however—examples are the mixed as opposed to simple modes of retrieval—and individual programs, like the clique-finding one, are still far from optimal. But some idea of the capacity of the system can be obtained from two examples, one illustrating a combination of options giving a fast test, and the other a less economic one. Thus if we use the vocabulary in which infrequent terms only are grouped, frequent ones being treated as unit classes, constructing an un-weighted Tanimoto similarity matrix takes 5 minutes, forming stars of size 4 takes half a minute, and retrieval by simple class matches takes 6 minutes. If we use the full vocabulary in which all terms may be grouped on the other hand, and if we constructed a weighted matrix, this takes 10 minutes, while forming cliques with a threshold of 16 takes 30 minutes, and retrieval using both terms and classes takes 20 minutes. A reasonable average, over all the options, is perhaps 25 minutes, but the complete series of operations need not, of course, be gone through every time, since the same matrix can be used for many classifications, and the same classification for different retrieval experiments.

From these examples, we can get some idea of the cost of the whole series of tests, which will be described in Chapter 8, and which were required to investigate the various classification and retrieval alternatives we have been concerned with. We have, of course, carried out other tests which are not reported on, and program design has consumed a fair amount of time; the tests described in the next chapter took, however, something like 30 hours of Titan time, which is, we would claim, very fair in research time terms.

Perhaps the best way of concluding this description, and of illustrating the capacities of the system, is by giving two examples of output, the first showing the results of a search for a particular request, and the other a histogram showing the frequency distribution of one set of items a for another set b, in this case classes for objects, which can be obtained with the processing routines. Thus Figure 6.1 shows the documents retrieved on three match modes, terms, classes, and class frequencies, the numbers of matching items being shown and the relevant documents marked; the total numbers of relevant and non-relevant documents retrieved specifically on each coordination level for the three languages are then displayed, the first number in each pair being the total number of documents retrieved, and the second number of relevant ones. In Figure 6.2 the range of frequencies of the classes, and the numbers of objects having each frequency, are indicated.

REQUEST 1

	M1				M2				M3		
R 1302	3			1317	2	2	2	R 1351	1	1	1
1367	1	1	2	1399	1	1	1	1436	1	1	1
R 1437	2	2	1	1443	1	1	1	1451	1	1	1
1467	1	1	1	1572	1	1	1	1574	1	1	1
1575	1	1	1	1576	1	1	1	1578	1	1	1
1597	1	1	1	1605	1	1	1	1656	1	1	1
1667	1	1	1	1672	2	2	2	1676	1	1	1
1677	1	1	1	1681	1	1	1	1682	1	1	1
1683	1	1	1	1687	1	1	1	1691	1	1	1
1695	1	1	1	1703	1	1	1	1706	1	1	1
1729	1	1	1	1787	1	1	1	1788	1	1	1
1795	1	1	1	1919	1	1	1	1920	1	1	1
1921	1	1	1	1964	1	1	1	1966	1	1	1
1967	2	2	2	1974	1	1	1	1981	1	1	1
1983	1	1	1	1984	1	1	1	1985	1	1	1
1987	1	1	1	1989	1	1	1	1990	1	1	1
1997	1	1	1	2061	1	1	1	2075	1	1	1
2077	1	1	1	2081	2	2	2	2099	1	1	1
2104	1	1	1	2111	2	2	2	2153	1	1	1
2154	1	1	1	2274	1	1	1	2313	1	1	1
2317	2	2	2	2319	2	2	2	2321	2	2	2
2339	1	1	1	2341	1	1	1	2342	1	1	1
2367	1	1	1	2391	3	4	4				

LEVEL/DEVICE	M1	M2	M3
LEVEL 0			
LEVEL 1	58	57	57
LEVEL 2	1	1	1
LEVEL 3	8	9	9
LEVEL 4	1	1	1
	2	2	2
	1	1	1

Figure 6.1

128

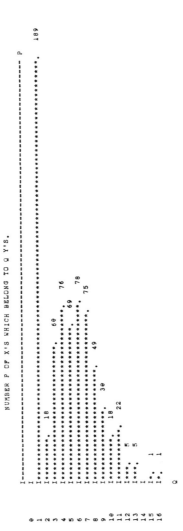

Figure 6.2

129

REFERENCES

1. *ISR–11*, Chapter II; *ISR–14*, Chapter I
2. JACKSON, D. M. 'A Note on a Set of Functions for Information Retrieval', *Information Storage and Retrieval*, **5**, 27 (1969)

Chapter 7

The Test Collection

SUMMARY

This chapter deals with the details of our test material, namely a collection of 200 aeronautical documents, with associated test requests and relevance judgements, which we obtained from the Aslib-Cranfield project, and with the nature of the keyword vocabulary we have classified. The characteristics of the collection are important for an understanding of our results, and an account is given of the initial keyword descriptions and keyword vocabulary, of the term vocabulary and descriptions derived from these by the suppression of morphological variants and rare terms, with which we have actually worked, and of the distributional characteristics both of the term vocabulary and the descriptions. We have found, for example, that about one-seventh of the vocabulary consists of very frequent terms, and that about 16 terms out of 32 in the average document description are frequent ones. Similar features of the requests are examined, and the general features of the request-document term matches, on which we hope to improve by using a classification, are analysed. This analysis shows, for example, that relevant documents may only be obtained by matches on one or two request terms, and, moreover, by matches on frequent terms, so that a large number of non-relevant documents tend to be obtained with them. Clearly, there may be a limit to the extent to which we can do better with a classification than we can with terms alone, given the performance characteristics of terms and the fact that the class specifications of requests and documents are necessarily derived from their term specifications.

The Cranfield Test Collection

The details of the test collection we used for our project are not of great interest in themselves, though the fact that the collection has been used for a variety of experiments justifies some interest in it. But it is rather worth considering as an example, to illustrate the kind of collection feature which has to be considered, both in experimental retrieval and in general retrieval practice.

We naturally wanted, when we began work on our project, to use a satisfactory test collection, that is one for which reliable keyword descriptions of the documents were provided, and for which test requests and relevant document lists were available. We also wished our collection to be a genuine one, that is one containing documents of the kind which are to be found in ordinary scientific libraries, for which sophisticated information retrieval systems are required; we wished our requests to be realistic, in the sense that they are the sort of requests which would be addressed to such a library; and we wished our relevance judgements to be sound ones made by experts. We were not in a position to provide such a test collection (where 'collection' here covers documents, requests and relevance judgements), and our attempting to do so would in any case be open to the criticism that our own collection might not constitute a genuine test of our system. We were also very anxious to use a collection which was being used for other retrieval experiments, so that we could compare the results we obtained for our specific system with those obtained elsewhere.

For these reasons, we decided to work, as mentioned earlier, with a test collection from Cleverdon's Aslib Cranfield project*. We first thought of working with his entire collection of 1400 aeronautical documents, but our experiments have in fact been confined to the sub-collection of 200 documents on aerodynamics which was used in many of Cleverdon's own tests, and has also been used, along with other collections by Salton's SMART project †.

Some comparisons between our own results and those which have been obtained from these two projects will be made in Chapter 10; the point worthy of comment here is that though Salton's experimental procedures have differed in detail from Cleverdon's, the general methods of all three projects have been close enough for us to be able to pool the various results we have obtained from using different indexing languages and retrieval techniques with this collection; this is particularly true for our own and the Cranfield results, but the work of the three projects is complementary, and very useful conclusions can be drawn from them when their results are taken together. Salton has also worked with other collections, so we can (with caution) extrapolate from his conclusions about the behaviour of these collections in different situations, to conclusions about the effect on other collections, of the methods we have investigated for just one of them.

It is true that where there was any divergence in the behaviour of the different collections Salton examined, this was between the Cranfield collection and the others; but the divergence was not great, and it is difficult to maintain that this is not a respectable collection, and that we are not dealing with documents, requests or relevance judgements which would not be encountered in some real retrieval environments.

The bare features of the test collection were mentioned in Chapter 4: the object of this chapter is to describe it in more detail, given that any results we obtain for the classificatory indexing languages will necessarily depend very heavily on the characteristics of the collection. We have already considered some general questions which can be asked about a term vocabulary, and the fact that some terms in our test vocabulary occur frequently enough to justify special treatment in classification has been noted; we must, however, consider what can be described as the raw facts about our collection, terms, documents, requests and relevance judgements, if the results of our experiments are to be correctly understood.

It is not necessary here to go into the details of the way in which the

* Cleverdon's own full description of this material is to be found in *Factors* 1, 1, Chapters 3 and 4, with annotated lists in *Factors* 1, 2.
† For descriptions of the SMART project test collections see *ISR–12*, Chapter III, and *ISR–13*, Chapter I.

document keyword descriptions, request set, and relevance judgements were obtained by Cleverdon himself: these can be found in Cleverdon's own description. The only important point is the general one, namely that we are satisfied that these are as good as can be got for experimental purposes, without undue effort and expense. In particular, as mentioned earlier, we felt that we could regard the keyword descriptions as sufficiently sound for it to be unreasonable to attribute any failures in our experiments to their inadequacy. What we have to look at are the details of the collection as we were given it: the character of the initial document and request specifications necessarily influences the retrieval performance which can be obtained with the collection, irrespective of the way in which these specifications are modified by the use of different classificatory index languages or search rules. The object of a classification is, as we know, to remedy whatever the deficiencies of keyword specifications are; but it must be admitted that there is a limit to the extent to which effective changes can be made. The purpose of this chapter, therefore, is to indicate some of the more important features of the test data we have been working with, so that we can see how they affect our results, and can distinguish the consequences of these characteristics of our collection from the consequences of our use of a classification.

As far as the collection as a whole goes, the complete list of the 1400 documents is given in Appendix 3C in *Factors* 1, 2, and the specification of the subset of 200 appears as Subset 1 in Appendix 3E, p. 203; but the general character of the collection can be illustrated by some representative titles, as follows:

1311 PEARCEY, H. H., 'A method for predicting the onset of buffeting and other separation effects from wind tunnel tests on rigid models.' *NPL Aero.*, 358 (1958)

1509 ADAMS, W. E., 'A graphical approximation for temperatures and sublimation rates at surfaces subjected to small net and large gross heat transfer rates.' *J. Ae. Sc.,* **29**, 360 (1962)

1619 KING-HELE, D. G., 'Density of the upper atmosphere from analysis of satellite orbits: further results'. *Nature*, **184**, 1267 (1959)

1696 FALANGAN, R. A. and JANOS, J. J., 'Pressure loads produced on a flat plate by rocket jets exhausting in a spanwise direction below the wing and perpendicular to a free-stream flow of Mach Number 2.0'. *NASA TN. D*, 893 (1961)

The first point to be considered about the collection is the nature of the document descriptions and keyword vocabulary we were supplied with. The vocabulary contains a large number of technical words, such as 'mach', 'nacelle' and 'enthalpy', and many general words which are normally used in these documents but only in some technical sense, or perhaps senses, like 'drag' or 'buzz'. There is of course no explicit indication of the specific meaning of such a word, or indeed of the meaning of any word; but one object of using an overlapping classification, as we saw in

Chapter 2, is that in a classification a sense of a word is characterised by its appearance in a group with its contextual companions, and the different senses of a word are distinguished by the assignment of the word to different classes. It is interesting to note that Salton and Lesk, in examining methods of constructing manual thesauri, make it a rule that words should only be grouped according to the senses they actually have in the collection in question, irrespective of any other meanings they may have, which is particularly important where words with very many meanings are concerned. Classification procedures which are explicitly based on co-occurrences may achieve this automatically[1].

The document descriptions we actually began with were the complex ones containing several levels of analysis which Cleverdon originally formed, and we derived our keyword lists from these automatically. This has resulted (largely because of clerical errors in the original input) in differences of detail between our keyword lists and Cleverdon's, but these are trivial and can be ignored: for all material purposes our document descriptions are the same as Cleverdon's though any actual figures given below are of course derived from our particular descriptions.

Keywords and terms

The keyword vocabulary for the collection of 200 documents as a whole contains just over 1 500 different items, not including numerals or formulae, which are not common and have been disregarded throughout because they are awkward to handle; the document descriptions average about 35 words, and the average number of postings per keyword is 4 to 5. These figures are very rough, because the keyword lists themselves have never existed in a properly edited form. We decided to work with 'terms' rather than keywords, and we therefore extracted keywords from Cleverdon's original descriptions simply to obtain a keyword dictionary, from which a term dictionary could be derived. The only important point to notice about the keyword descriptions is that they are fairly exhaustive, which means that the term descriptions are also quite full. This clearly matters when the results of using a classification are evaluated: if the list of items characterising a document is replaced by a list of classes which is very skimpy, we cannot expect the classification to do too much to fill out the picture. It is of course the case that a classification increases the exhaustivity of a document description, because the list of items actually appearing in a document is supplemented by their class-mates; the object of the classification is precisely to bring in items which could well have characterised the document. But there is a limit to the extent to which this kind of supplementation can be used as a substitute for a fuller characterisation of a document in terms of items actually extracted from it. So that starting with a reasonably full list is very important.

We nevertheless decided, for a variety of reasons, to work with terms rather than keywords in our classification experiments, where a term is the representative of a set of morphologically related keywords, or, as they are sometimes described, of variant word forms; thus a series of keywords like a noun in its singular and plural forms, the related verb, and the corresponding adjectives, adverbs, and other derivatives, would be treated as one term. If we have the keywords 'convected', 'convecting', 'convection' and 'convective', for example, we can replace these by the single term 'convect-'. One reason for doing this is computational economy; but it is widely believed that it improves retrieval performance, and this has been clearly shown by both Cleverdon and Salton. It is, indeed, one of the few methods of processing keywords which Cleverdon found gave any improvement over keywords in his experiments[2]. Cleverdon regards this conflation of word forms as a minimal classification, and hence as a recall device, so that the replacement of extracted keywords by terms is one way of progressing beyond the minimal indexing language represented by keywords; but it is much more convenient to treat terms as the elementary units of the minimal indexing language, as if they were keywords, to which further processing is applied by the use of a thesaurus classification. This is generally Salton's practice, since he normally applies a suffix-stripping routine in the initial processing of his documents, which, in replacing keywords by their stems, produces the same result as an explicit grouping of different forms. This use of terms instead of keywords cannot, however, be regarded as a perversion of the simple idea of forming a thesaurus from extracted keywords: we could in principle hope to group variant forms of the same word, provided they were related semantically, with the classification procedures we hope to obtain groups of related but different words with; it is simply that conflating variants, either by suffix stripping or reference to a dictionary where different forms are replaced by terms, is preferable because it reduces the number of items to be handled by the actual classification program.

We in fact used dictionary lookup to substitute terms for keywords, rather than a suffix-stripping procedure; the marking of the groups of keywords to be represented by a single term was based on Cleverdon's list of variants[3], but this list represents a 'mechanical' conflation of forms of the kind which would be produced by a suffix routine, and does not reflect any semantic differences between the forms: thus 'block', 'blockage' and 'blocking' are replaced by a single term. For convenience we selected the alphabetically first member of such a group of keywords to serve as the term name: this occasionally results in somewhat unobvious representatives, including mis-spellings, which should be borne in mind when any examples of our term list or document descriptions, or later, of our classifications, are given.

We also decided to eliminate any term which occurred only once from the document descriptions, that is any keyword which was neither conflated nor occurred more than once. This was partly for computing reasons, because it reduced the size of the set of objects to be classified considerably, but it can also be justified from the classificatory point of view: terms which occur only once should not contribute to the information on which a classification is based because their co-occurrences and similarities are very unreliable. It is true that they may be valuable as document descriptors, and that their presence, as rare terms, in a class may lead to good request—document matches; but from another point of view, the presence of any number of such terms adds enormously to the total number of connections in the network from which the classification is derived, and these may simply confuse the overall picture. Such terms in fact represent a point where we have a deliberate choice to make in considering thesaurus classification, because retaining them, or rejecting them, leads to complementary gains and losses. For our particular data, however, we felt that we could afford to reject them in the interests of computational convenience, because the term lists for our documents, even after this deletion, were long enough to constitute adequate characterisations of the documents.

An additional reason for rejecting these terms was that the way we derived our keywords from Cleverdon's original material meant that they occurred not once in a document, but once in a document 'theme' or topic: each document was represented by several themes[4], and any keyword of importance would tend to occur in more than one theme; thus a term which occurred in one theme only, could really be regarded as insignificant. It is in fact the case that we originally intended to work with themes rather than documents, so that the co-occurrence of information on which our classification was based was more refined than that given by a simple document term list; but quite apart from the fact that we could not compare any retrieval results we obtained using themes instead of documents with Cleverdon's way, though the idea of theme retrieval in itself is a perfectly satisfactory one, we found that this approach led to association arrays and similarity matrices which were far too large to work with, and we were therefore obliged to abandon it. Unfortunately, hangovers from it are responsible for many of the details of our treatment of the document descriptions and term vocabulary.

As a result of these modifications, therefore, our initial vocabulary was reduced by over 400 items through conflation, and by nearly a further 400 through the elimination of 'once' items to give a final list of 712 terms, which was then used to generate further term descriptions for our original crude keyword ones. The character of the list can be illustrated by an example, as follows:

ablating	aircraft
absolute	airplane
accelerated	allmoveable
active	altitude

adiabatic	ambient
adjustable	amount
*aerodynamic	*analysis
*aerofoil	*angle
afterbody	apex
ahead	apogee
*air	

* = frequent term: see page 138)

Term distribution

We must look now at some of the properties of this vocabulary, given their effect on the way the terms characterise the documents, and hence influence retrieval performance. The number of postings per term, or term frequency, varies widely, one term, namely 'flow', occurring in as many as 144 documents out of the total of 200; 4 terms occur in more than a third of the collection, 89 out of the 712 in 20 or more documents, and 179, or about a quarter of the vocabulary, in 10 or more documents; on the other hand, some 228 terms occur in only 1 or 2 documents, and 422, or over half, occur in no more than 5 documents, so that the distribution of the terms follows the standard pattern, as shown in Figure 7.1*. The average number of postings, or average term frequency, is 8.8.

It is easy to see that the frequency properties of the terms characterising the documents in the collection must influence retrieval; at the most trivial level, if we are matching terms, and a request contains a particular term which occurs in 144 documents out of 200, we must necessarily retrieve this many documents if we search at all levels of coordination; and if we have two terms, one occurring 144 times and the other 82, we could not fail to retrieve at least 26 documents which match on both, and the chances are we would retrieve more. The effect when terms are replaced by their classes, if we are using a thesaurus, is more complex, but there will inevitably be some carry-over. If these two terms, for example, occur in the same class, and a request contains both, the effect will be the same as for the term match, though of course other documents for other terms contained in the same class may be retrieved as well: but this will be a match only at class level 1; if the terms occur in separate classes, we will get a class match at level 2, and probably more additional matches. These characteristics of the vocabulary in fact suggested the special treatment of these frequent terms in classification that we considered in Chapter 4. It is not merely that terms with very many connections present problems from the purely classificatory point of view: they present substantial problems in retrieval too, because their presence in a request, or in a class with a request term, inevitably leads

---

*The number of terms occurring only once is, of course, lower because eliminating terms which occurred once in themes also eliminated some occurring once in documents.

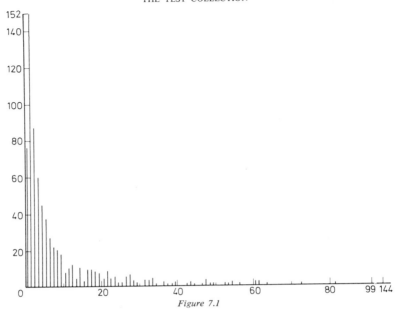

Figure 7.1

to the retrieval of a large number of documents. As already mentioned, one of Salton's rules for thesaurus construction is that the word groups in the thesaurus should not contain any frequent terms, precisely because once they appear in classes, the generally unwelcome consequences of their frequency are maximised rather than minimised. At the same time, we cannot reject frequent terms altogether, if we find that we need them to retrieve some relevant documents.

For our experiments, therefore, we set up the 'restricted' vocabulary referred to earlier, in which frequent terms were marked so that they were not permitted to enter the grouping process. Unfortunately, at the time when this vocabulary was set up, we were still working primarily with themes, and we decided to regard as frequent any terms occurring in more than 25 themes, rather than in more than a specified number of documents: a theme frequency of 25 does, however, correspond, roughly, to a document frequency of 20. Clearly an investigation of the effect of different frequency cutoffs was required, and some experiments for this purpose, though using document frequencies only, were carried out, as we shall see in Chapter 8; these incidentally served to establish that the theme frequency we selected corresponded to a sensible document frequency cutoff. The actual specification of frequent terms with which we worked in all our main experiments was, however, the one based on themes. The effect on the straightforward term vocabulary can be illustrated by the example given earlier (page 137), where frequent terms are marked with an asterisk, and for the vocabulary as a whole, 96 terms out of the 712, or 13 per cent, were defined as frequent.

Document and request descriptions

The fact that we have a real problem in our frequent terms is brought out if we look at the character of our term descriptions and requests. The overall effect on the document descriptions of replacing keywords by terms, and of deleting 'once' terms, was to reduce Cleverdon's keyword lists to term lists averaging 32 items. We have thus been working with document descriptions which can be illustrated by two examples as follows:

1316

aerofoil bound chord coefficient displaced distributed divergence edge flow height incidence layer lift mach onset position pressure reattachment recovery section separated shape shock span speed steady subsonic supersonic surface sweepback thick trailing two-dimensional upper vortex wing

1317

amount approximate body bow density dissociated excitation flow gas ideal infinite model newtonian node nonequilibrium normal position prediction pressure profile rotary shock sphere streamline temperature theoretical thin variable vibration wave

The variation in the length of document descriptions over the collection as a whole is considerable, ranging from a minimum of 7 terms to a maximum of 85, but these are exceptional: there are only 26 documents with less than 20 terms, and most of the documents are near the average. The fact that the real variation in the length of document descriptions is not great, and does not influence retrieval very much, is shown by the results obtained with the weighted Tanimoto similarity coefficient, which is intended to weight agreement in a document, for a pair of terms, by the length of the document, so that co-occurrence in a short list is regarded as more significant than co-occurrence in a long one: the results obtained with this coefficient did not differ markedly from those obtained with the unweighted coefficient, which presumably reflects the absence of substantial variation in list length.

The details of the way in which the test requests and their associated lists of relevant documents were obtained are given in Cleverdon's report, and complete lists of both are to be found there, in Appendices 3D and 3E (subset 2, page 201) and Appendix 3B in *Factors*, 1, 2. The general character of the requests can be illustrated by examples as follows, the search terms being italicised*.

---

* To avoid changing the character of the requests in our experiments, 'once' terms occurring in requests were retained as terms.

100 (2) How much is known about *boundary layer flow* along *non-circular cylinders*?

126 (9) What are *wind tunnel corrections* for a *two-dimensional aerofoil mounted off-centre* in a tunnel?

170 (20) Is there any information on how the addition of a *boattail affects* the *normal force* on the *body* of various *angles* of *incidence*?

The number of terms per request varies considerably. The average is 6.9, which can be regarded as, in principle, allowing a fairly precise topic specification for searching, but the range is from a minimum of 3 to a maximum of 11, with the overall distribution for the set of requests of Figure 7.2, and frequency distribution of Figure 7.3.

1	0000	22	000000000
2	0000	23	00000
3	0000000000	24	0000000
4	0000000000	25	0000000
5	0000000000	26	000000
6	000000	27	0000000
7	000000	28	00000
8	00000	29	00000000
9	000000	30	0000
10	000	31	000000
11	0000000	32	000000
12	0000000000	33	00000000
13	000000	34	0000
14	000000000	35	00000
15	0000000	36	000000
16	000000	37	00000000000
17	0000000000	38	00000
18	0000000	39	00000
19	00000000000	40	00000000
20	000000	41	0000000
21	0000000	42	000000000

Each 0 represents a term for the given request; each / shows that the term is a frequent one

Figure 7.2

1	
2	
3	0
4	0000
5	000000
6	0000000000
7	00000000
8	000
9	000
10	00000
11	00

Each 0 represents a request with the given number of starting terms

Figure 7.3

This shows that though a fair number of requests are near the average, there are several which do not contain many terms, which means either that they are not very discriminating, if the terms involved are frequent ones, or that they are unlikely to extract many documents, if the terms are rare ones, so that the chances are that relevant documents will be missed. The request terms are spread fairly well over the whole vocabulary: 166 terms appear at least once, so that the requests cover nearly a quarter of the vocabulary, which is important because it means that our results are unlikely to be unduly influenced by the idiosyncrasies of a few particular terms. 112 terms, that is nearly two-thirds of the set of request terms, occur only once, and only one term, namely 'flow' which is, as we have seen, the most frequent term in the entire vocabulary, occurs as many as 12 times. Again, the fact that the request terms appear in the requests with about the same frequency means that the retrieval performance we obtain for the requests is not likely to be distorted by the behaviour of individual terms.

On the other hand, both documents and requests exhibit one striking characteristic which must influence retrieval performance. This is the high proportion of frequent terms they contain. Though only just over one-seventh of the term vocabulary consists of frequent terms, and though a document description contains, on the average, as many as 32 terms, an average of 16 of these are frequent terms. Half of every document description, in other words, consists of frequent terms. The corresponding fact about the requests is even more striking: for out of an average of 7 terms, 4 are frequent ones. There are indeed two requests which consist entirely of frequent terms. Moreover, when we take into account the fact that while the average number of document occurrences for infrequent terms is only 4.8, that for frequent terms is 34, the consequences for retrieval of such a high proportion of frequent terms in the requests are evident. The distribution of frequent terms in the request is shown in detail in Figure 7.2.

In the context of information retrieval research as a whole, these details may seem so trivial that there is little point in going into them. However, the term properties of any test documents and requests have to be taken into account before we can attempt to predict what the effect of classifying our terms will be, and before we can evaluate the retrieval performance of any classification of these terms properly. The term characteristics of the test requests, and the relation between the term descriptions of their relevant documents and those of the non-relevant items in the collection, must determine the retrieval results we obtain as much as, or more than, any processing of the vocabulary itself does. Some comments on the features of our test material which give us the base term retrieval performance on which we hope to improve are therefore essential: we have already seen what the term retrieval performance curve looks like; we should now look more closely at the characteristics of the collection which are responsible for it.

Relevant documents

These primarily concern the relevant documents, and the relation between them and their requests. The first of the illustrative requests given earlier, for instance, has 4 relevant documents, where we can give the titles of these documents to indicate the kind of request-document match we are dealing with, as follows:

1785   Flow of fluid along cylinders
1786   The skin friction on infinite cylinders moving parallel to their length
1787   Rayleigh's problem for a cylinder of arbitrary shape
1788   An approximate boundary layer theory for semi-infinite cylinders of arbitrary cross-section

Altogether, we have 199 relevant documents, representing 153 different documents out of the 200, so that we can say that our test requests cover our document collection fairly well, as we said our requests covered our term vocabulary well. The number of relevant documents per request ranges

1	000	22	0000
2	0000	23	00
3	000000	24	0000000
4	00000	25	00
5	000000	26	00000
6	000	27	000000
7	00000	28	0000000
8	0000	29	00
9	00	30	0000000
10	0000	31	00000000
11	0000	32	0000
12	000000	33	00
13	000000	34	00000
14	0	35	00000
15	00000000000	36	0000
16	000000000	37	0000
17	00000	38	00000000
18	0000	39	00000
19	0000	40	00
20	00	41	00000
21	00	42	00000000

Each 0 represents a relevant document for the given request

Figure 7.4

from 1 to 12, with an average of 4.7 per request, the distribution being as shown in Figure 7.4, and frequency distribution as in Figure 7.5.

The important point, however, is the general character of the request-relevant document matches. How do the requests retrieve when they are simply treated as term lists? For this purpose it is not sufficient to look

1	0
2	00000000
3	00
4	0000000000
5	00000000
6	00000
7	000
8	000
9	0
10	
11	
12	0

Each 0 represents a request with the given number of relevant documents

Figure 7.5

simply at the overall recall/precision curve we considered earlier: we should look at the details of the matches more closely, if we are to obtain the understanding of what is happening that we need, before we can propose improvements. We can start, therefore, by considering the relation between the number of request terms we are given, and the number which actually

1	0000	22	000000000
2	0000	23	00000
3	0000000000	24	0000000
4	0000000000	25	0000000
5	0000000000	26	000000
6	000000	27	0000000
7	000000	28	00000
8	00000	29	00000000
9	000000	30	0000
10	000	31	000000
11	0000000	32	000000
12	0000000000	33	00000000
13	000000	34	0000
14	000000000	35	00000
15	0000000	36	000000
16	000000	37	00000000000
17	0000000000	38	00000
18	0000000	39	00000
19	00000000000	40	00000000
20	000000	41	0000000
21	0000000	42	000000000

0   starting terms
/   retrieving terms

Each 0 or / represents a starting or retrieving term for the given request

Figure 7.6

match when taken together, that is the relation between what Cleverdon calls the number of starting terms, and the number of retrieving terms, or the largest subset of the starting terms for which we obtain a document, whether this document is relevant or not. This relation between the maximum possible coordination level and the highest actual coordination level is shown in Figure 7.6, while the relative frequency distribution of starting and retrieving terms is given in Figure 7.7.

```
 1
 2
 3   0/////
 4   0000///////          0   starting terms
 5   000000//             /   retrieving terms
 6   0000000000//
 7   00000000         Each 0 or / represents a request with the given
 8   000              number of starting or retrieving terms
 9   000
10   00000
11   00
```

Figure 7.7

Term matching

From these figures it will be seen that there are only 7 requests out of the 42 for which the highest possible level is also the highest actual retrieving level, for the average number of retrieving terms is 5, where the average number of starting terms is nearly 7: the complete term specification cannot be matched for most of the requests, from which it follows that the reasonably precise topic specifications of the requests cannot be met, as they stand, even by the documents which are relevant to the requests. Further, only one request retrieves at the highest retrieving level, namely 9, and it even then selects a non-relevant document; and though 24, or over half the requests, retrieve at level 5 or above, the highest level reached by all the 42 requests is as low as 3. The average number of matching terms for the relevant documents retrieved is indeed only 3.6. These facts have repercussions when we consider the average performance for the set of requests, as we saw in Chapter 5: and indeed any results which we obtained above level 7 are based on such a small number of requests that they cannot be regarded as statistically reliable.

More important from the point of view of the retrieval performance we can obtain with terms are, however, some other features of the request collection matches. It is convenient to consider these against the background of the overall performance figures for terms for all the 42 requests, and though these will be given in their proper experimental context in Chapter 8, the relevant information can be repeated here. Thus Figure 7.8 gives (*a*) the total numbers of documents retrieved at each specific term coordination level, with the component totals for relevant and non-relevant documents retrieved respectively; and (*b*) the totals obtained by each level, that is for each level and those above it: in the first case, for instance, we find that 47 documents are retrieved at level 6, of which 23 are relevant, and in the second that 58 documents are retrieved for level 6 and above, of which 31 are relevant.

The striking feature of the retrieval performance obtainable with terms, at least for this request and document set, and it seems for others as well, is evident from these figures. This is that a substantial proportion of the relevant documents are only retrieved at low coordination levels at which a very large number of non-relevant documents are also obtained. More

(a)				(b)			
	R	−R	T		R	−R	T
1	25	2507	2532	1	192	4759	4951
2	29	1304	1333	2	167	2252	2419
3	45	633	678	3	138	948	1086
4	39	218	257	4	93	315	408
5	23	70	93	5	54	97	151
6	23	24	47	6	31	27	58
7	4	2	6	7	8	3	11
8	4	—	4	8	4	1	5
9	—	1	1	9	—	1	1

Figure 7.8

than half of the relevant documents can only be obtained at levels 3, 2 or 1, and indeed over an eighth only at level 1, at which over half of the non-relevant ones are pulled out. It is also worth noticing that 7 of the 199 relevant documents are not retrieved at all with terms. This relationship between relevant and non-relevant documents retrieved at the different

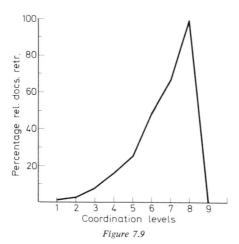

Figure 7.9

levels is illustrated more graphically in Figure 7.9, where the curve represents the percentage of relevant documents retrieved from the total number of documents retrieved at each coordination level. (The collapse at level 9 is of course due to the fact that only one 'non-relevant' document is pulled out at this level.)

From the human point of view, however, these facts are perhaps more striking if they are presented strictly in terms of the actual number of documents involved in a search, or rather which have to be inspected by the person who has made a request, to identify the relevant ones. If an exhaustive search on all coordination levels is carried out, an average of as many as 117.9 documents altogether are pulled out, to obtain an average of 4.6 relevant ones. Thus though nearly half of the relevant documents, i.e. an average of 2.2, from a total of 4.7 can be obtained from an inspection of only 9.7 documents retrieved altogether, the remaining ones can only be obtained if an additional 108.2 documents are inspected.

While it is true, in other words, that retrieval with terms at high levels is very good, in the sense that we do not have to inspect and discard many irrelevant documents to sort out some relevant ones, we are obliged to descend much lower to get a substantial proportion of the relevant ones to be found. If we are prepared to forgo a quarter of the relevant documents we require we can indeed avoid the really catastrophic increase in the numbers of irrelevant ones which appear at levels 2 and 1, and applying a cutoff of this kind may of course be the sensible thing to do in practice. We should concentrate, that is, on trying to maximise the number of relevant documents and minimise the number of irrelevant ones which are retrieved before we reach level 3; which means in practice that we should concentrate on improving retrieval performance in the middle levels of 6 to 3, say.

The relevance problem

The reasons for this level of performance when terms are used for searching are apparent when individual requests are studied in more detail. This clearly shows that the correspondence between requests and their relevant documents in terms of their verbal matches is not very close; or, to put the point another way, that the selective power of the requests is fairly poor. We are, indeed, up against the fundamental problem of relevance, that is, what is it that makes a document relevant to a request although they do not coincide verbally, where a document which is verbally closer to it is not relevant to the request? It is true that with a homogeneous collection of the kind with which we have been working, that is one which is very restricted in subject matter, it would be difficult to avoid false drops; but the way in which relevant documents fail to match requests at all closely is very striking. It is natural to attribute this to the primary deficiency of term descriptions, namely to the fact that they do not permit vocabulary variation; but this cannot be the only reason for results like those we are considering. The collection characteristics must play a part; we must, that is, expect to obtain a fair number of documents for any search through such a dense collection; and we must allow for the defective formulation of requests. But these results must chiefly be attributed to the much more fundamental fact that providing descriptions for documents which will enable us to distinguish relevant ones from non-relevant ones, and providing request specifications which will lead to correct matches, requires a much more sensitive treatment of both than one might suppose. This is indeed the basic indexing and retrieval problem, and we are squarely up against it. How much, therefore, can we hope to get round it by using a classification, given that this classification must be based on just these defective term descriptions? This is the question we have to try to answer.

The real nature of the problem is clear if we look at the results of a search for a typical single request. Thus request 190 (24), for instance, which is

190 (24) Has anyone *derived* simplified *pump equation* from the fundamental *three-dimensional* equations for *incompressible non-viscous flow*?

has 7 terms, given by the italicised words, but only 4 retrieving ones. The actual pattern of matches, on the separate levels, is as follows:

	Rel. retr.	*Non-rel. retr.*	*Total retr.*
level 1	2	103	105
level 2	1	37	38
level 3	1	8	9
level 4	3	1	4
Totals	7	149	156

The 7 relevant documents were all retrieved, but 2 matched on 1 term only. At the same time, a very large number of non-relevant documents were obtained. The reason for this is obvious, given the request terms: most of these do not occur in many documents, and so in principle constitute a good specification, especially in combination (though this is hard to match). At the same time, the request contains 2 frequently occurring terms: 1 occurs in 35 documents, and the other is the most frequent term in the vocabulary, namely 'flow', which will, as we know, by itself pull out 144 documents. When we look at the matching terms for the relevant documents, however, we find that this is the *only* matching term for 2 of them, and matches, with other terms, for the remaining 5, and so is partly responsible for their retrieval at higher levels. Thus this term, however disagreeable the consequences of its appearing in the request are in terms of false drops, is required for successful retrieval as well. Of the 5 non-frequent terms in the request, in fact, no more than 3 occur in any of the relevant documents, either singly or together, though 5 of the relevant documents do match on one of these at least, as well as on a frequent term. It will, however, be quite clear that the frequent terms in the request play an essential part in retrieving the relevant documents.

We can now consider the complementary picture, as it were, by looking at a particular document, say 1990, which is titled 'A rapid approximate method for determining velocity distribution on impeller blades of centrifugal compressors'. This has 27 terms altogether, including 'flow'. It is relevant to 2 requests, including the one just mentioned, but it is retrieved by 25 altogether. Virtually all of these matches are on 1 or 2 terms, which are also fairly frequently occurring ones. It matches request 24, to which

(*a*) Document 1990, relevant to requests 23 and 24.

Retrieved by request	1, matching on 1 keyword, i.e. on	1 frequent keyword
2	1	1
6	1	1
7	1	1
9	1	1
10	2	2
13	1	1
15	2	2
17	1	1
19	2	2
21	2	2
22	2	2
23	1	1
* 24	3	{ 2 non-frequent { 1 frequent
26	4	4 frequent
27	1	1
29	1	1
33	1	1
34	1	1
35	1	1
36	1	1
37	4	4
39	2	2
40	2	2
42	2	{ 1 non-frequent { 1 frequent

Total   25   Average   1.6

(*b*) Document 1990 retrieved at coordination level		No. requests	Relevant	Non-relevant
	1	14	1	13
	2	8	—	8
	3	1	1	—
	4	2	—	2
	Totals 25		2	23

Figure 7.10

it is relevant, on 3 terms, including 2 infrequent ones, but it matches request 23, to which it is also relevant, on 1 frequent term only. At the same time, it matches 2 other requests on 4 terms altogether (all frequent ones), and for 1 of these it matches at a higher level than any of the relevant documents concerned. The complete analysis is as in Figure 7.10. This shows again that we cannot distinguish those cases where the document is appropriately retrieved, from those where it is not, by saying that infrequent terms are responsible for the former, and frequent for the latter, or by any similar straightforward description of the difference in the relation between relevant documents and their requests, and between non-relevant documents and these requests.

This one request and one document are obviously not typical in all respects: there are some requests and documents for which the relation between the request and its relevant documents is more like what we would expect it to be, in that relevant documents are retrieved, on non-frequent word matches, at high coordination levels. But there are also cases which are even more discouraging than the one we have just considered, from the point of view of anyone trying to exploit some features of requests or documents to optimise retrieval performance. It is therefore very difficult to see how we can use a classification to obtain a better performance by systematically maximising the advantages of terms, and minimising their defects. One particular question we can naturally ask, for instance, is whether we are more likely to gain or lose by giving frequent terms special treatment, even to the extent of abolishing them altogether: we cannot afford to do this, it seems, when we are using terms alone, because we reduce our matching potential so much; but if we have a classification which is intended to widen the range of possible matches, we may be able to rely on this to retrieve the relevant documents we can only obtain with frequent terms if we are working with terms alone, without all the false drops that the latter bring with them. One of the objects of our experiments has indeed been to see whether this is possible.

In conclusion, then, the purpose of this chapter has been to exhibit some of the characteristic features of data we have been working with, both so that the account of the experiments we have carried out which follows is comprehensible, and so that the consequences of the use of a classification which is represented by these experiments can be properly evaluated. In the next chapter, the experiments themselves are presented: the conclusions which can be drawn from them are considered in Section III.

REFERENCES

1. *ISR–11*, Chapter 4
2. *Factors* 2, Chapters 4 and 5; *ISR–12*, Chapter III; *ISR–13*, Chapter VI
3. *Factors* 1, 2, Appendix 5.2, items numbered (2)
4. *Factors* 1, 1, Chapter 4, Figure 4.1

Chapter 8

Experimental Results

SUMMARY

In this chapter our experimental results are presented in a quite straightforward way, in terms of comparisons between the different values of test parameters, without any comment or analysis. The object of the chapter is to describe the tests we have carried out, that is to give a comprehensive picture of our experiments, rather than to consider what can be learnt from them: a summary of the results and the conclusions to be drawn from them are given in Section III, and those not wishing to consider the tests in detail should bypass this chapter: in the summary of the tests in Chapter 9, the necessary references back to the relevant points in this chapter are provided. The tests are described in terms of the experimental design mentioned in Chapter 5, that is in terms of a comparison between the different values of a given parameter in a base environment, with cross checks covering changes in the values of other parameters, though the latter are not exhaustive. The tests are, moreover, presented under four main headings, referring to alternative treatments of the term vocabulary, different choices of similarity coefficient, different classification procedures, and alternative search modes, respectively. Some repetition is unavoidable, in that a given test representing some combination of parameter values may appear in the context of experiments with different values for more than one parameter; we have in fact given the result explicitly in each case, in order to ensure that the presentation of the tests for each parameter is self-contained. The account thus follows a standard pattern: the alternatives to be investigated under each heading are listed, and the particular tests we have carried out for them are described; these are then summarised in tabular form, and are correlated with the recall/precision plots by which each test result is represented.

Experimental philosophy

In this chapter the experiments in automatic classification we have carried out to date are summarised, and the main results are presented in a standard form; the conclusions to be drawn from them will be considered in Chapter 9.

We have in fact carried out a large number of experiments, since this is necessary before reliable conclusions can be drawn about the utility of classification, but not all the comparisons we have made are of equal value, and so the reader who is prepared to take this detailed chapter on trust should go on to Chapters 9 and 10, in which the main conclusions are presented, and in which reference back to the relevant items in this chapter are given.

The general design of the experiments was discussed in Chapter 5, but it can usefully be recalled here: thus we are concerned with the effects of assigning different values to variables characterising the classification and class-using retrieval processes; we have grouped these variables for convenience under four heads based on our program system, namely those concerned with

(1) the specification of the term vocabulary to be classified,
(2) the formation of the term similarity matrix,
(3) the identification of term classes, and
(4) the use of these classes in searches;

and, as examining the effects of all the possible combinations of the values of these variables is impracticable, we have set up a base configuration of particular values for each which is used as a context to test changes in the value of an individual variable: we have, however, avoided over-dependence on the base configuration by carrying out cross checks so that the effect of changing the value of a given variable is studied not only in the base environment, but in at least one other environment, which can usually be regarded as a randomly-chosen one. This systematic organisation of our experiments means that our conclusions can generally be supported both by the actual results of some experiments, and by inferences as to the probable results of others which can be made because the consequences of changes in the values of different variables can be related through their having been tested in the common base environment. Our general principle can, in other words, be illustrated by an example as follows: if we have two alternative values for each of three parameters, say a or b, c or d, and e or f, we could in principle try a with c or d, with e, or with f, and test b in the same way, giving 8 test combinations altogether; but if we choose a, c and e as the base configuration and simply try the effect of substituting b for a, or d for c, or f for e, we get only 4 tests, though this will not mean we lose much information, because we should be able to infer what the effect of combining b and f would be. This is particularly the case if we carry out one cross check on each parameter, so that as well as trying e versus f in the base configuration we also try it in one other, say with b instead of a: this will increase the number of tests, but we still need not carry out some, such as, in this case, trying e or f with d instead of c.

I have described the principle on which our tests are based at some length, because it is clearly very important: we have to be able to show that our conclusions are well founded, given the practical impossibility of trying absolutely everything. We can now list all the variables, and the specific values for all of them, that we have tested, under our four main headings. The explanations of the various items are to be found in previous chapters; this list is simply a summary which is intended to introduce the account of the experiments. Thus under heading 1, VOCABULARY, we have four alternatives, namely the full vocabulary where all terms are classified, the restricted vocabulary where frequent terms are treated as unit classes, the remainder being grouped, and the frequent and infrequent vocabularies respectively, consisting of the two complementary subsets of the full vocabulary, all the terms in each being grouped. Under heading 2,

SIMILARITY, we have an initial choice of three similarity definitions, the unweighted and weighted Tanimoto, and the cosine correlation, with further choices of global threshold at two levels, one low and one high. Under heading 3, CLASSIFICATION, we have the four class types, strings, stars, cliques and clumps; both strings and stars are based only on the strongest connections, no other alternatives having been examined, while cliques are based on links above a specified threshold: one length of string has been tried and two different sizes of star, while under cliques two values of similarity threshold have been investigated; two clump definitions have been tested, namely the SAB[2] and 100/P, the latter with two values of P, and we have tried a gradient test with a particular combination of maximum and minimum levels under these definitions. Under heading 4, RETRIEVAL, we have two alternative modes of retrieval, the simple one using classes only, with a choice of whether we match only on classes or on class frequency as well; and the mixed one, using terms and classes, with a choice between the exclusive and inclusive procedures for setting up the class specification, and two alternative methods of incrementing term match levels for class matches. Some of the particular choices have of course been determined by the character of our material: thus the global threshold of 7 was chosen because it produced a matrix of reasonable size, of 19 because it seemed to be the highest which could be used without deleting all the connections of a term. No significance should therefore be attached to these particular choices: the important point is that we are investigating low and high level thresholds. The same holds true of the clique thresholds: the specific choices are of no general interest, though the fact that moderate and very high thresholds were investigated does matter. As an aid to clarity, the complete list of the alternatives we have examined, and their relationships, are given in tabular form in Table 8.1.

The configuration we decided to adopt as a base was determined largely by practical considerations: it is, for instance, much easier to find stars than cliques. But we also chose some parameter values because they seemed to give good results: there is, after all, no point in using a set of values which gives very inferior results; it is dreary to work with, and as we are interested primarily in good retrieval performance, we may as well work directly with a good configuration and make inferences about ones which work less well, rather than the other way round. The base configuration can, therefore, be specified as follows:

vocabulary: restricted;
similarity: unweighted Tanimoto, threshold level 7;
classification: stars, size 4;
retrieval: simple, class.

This is the base configuration for testing term classifications. We are, however, not only comparing one classification with another, but class retrieval with term retrieval. We thus have another configuration, namely that

152

Table 8.1

1 VOCABULARY

---

full
restricted
infrequent

---

2 SIMILARITY

Definition	Control	Level
unweighted Tanimoto weighted Tanimoto cosine correlation	threshold	7 19

---

3 CLASSIFICATION

Type	Definition	Specification
strings	strongest link	length 7
stars	strongest links	size $\begin{cases} 4 \\ 6 \end{cases}$
cliques	links above threshold	threshold $\begin{cases} 21 \\ 16 \end{cases}$
clumps	$\begin{cases} SAB^2 \\ 100/P \end{cases}$ $\begin{cases} P = \frac{1}{2} \\ P = 1 \end{cases}$	$\begin{cases} \text{no gradient test} \\ \text{gradient test, max 95 min 5} \end{cases}$

---

4 RETRIEVAL

Mode	Match	Modification
simple	$\begin{cases} \text{class} \\ \text{frequent class} \end{cases}$	
mixed	$\begin{cases} \text{exclusive} \\ \text{inclusive} \end{cases}$	$\begin{cases} +1 \\ +n \end{cases}$

---

associated with the use of unclassified terms, which is the one which produces the performance curve we are interested in as a standard of comparison for classes. This distinction is very important: the retrieval performance associated with the base configuration does not have any special status. The description of the configuration associated with single terms under the headings used for the class ones is, of course, rather unnatural; but it is worth doing because it serves to tie the term retrieval test into our overall experimental framework; we can use this description to pinpoint just those features of the retrieval process which characterise the use of classes. Thus if we imagine ourselves as importing alternatives, including null ones, where necessary in our list of variables, we can describe term retrieval as follows:

vocabulary: full/restricted (i.e. no distinction);
similarity: null;
classification: null;
retrieval: simple, term.

The following account of the experiments we have carried out is divided into four main sections dealing with tests of the variables falling under each heading. The general form of the description is the same in each case: the alternatives are noted, and an account of the comparisons made in the base configuration is given, followed by a description of the other configurations which have been used to make cross checks. In some cases several cross checks have been made, in which the values of a number of variables other than the test one are changed, especially if the parameters being tested are important ones; and it may also be the case that several different non-standard values can be assiged to one of these other variables. The effects of assigning different values to the given test variable may therefore be studied in a number of different environments, representing modifications to the base environment which are obtained by assigning other values to one or more of the system variables. In general, we can look at our experiments in two different ways. Any specific combination of variable values gives us one configuration, which can in principle be compared with any other; but it is more useful to concentrate specifically on individual variables, and to look at what happens when we give our parameters different values, from the point of view of this variable. Thus we obtain an initial set of configurations by trying alternative values for this parameter, while the other variables retain their base values; and we obtain one or more further sets, representing changes in the values of one or more other parameters. It will, however, be quite clear that any given test can be looked at from the point of view of more than one variable: if we study changes to parameter 1 in relation to changes in parameter 2, we can of course say that we are doing the reverse. But it makes for a much clearer presentation of the results if we consider one parameter at a time, though this will mean that the result of a retrieval test with a given configuration may be given under more than one head. The detailed description which follows is indeed repetitive in this way, in that the same result appears under more than one head, but the fact that the description of all the tests relevant to a given parameter is self-contained should hopefully make it easier to see what the implications of changes in a specific parameter are.

The description of tests is quite complicated, and we have therefore summarised the set carried out under each head in a table which also acts as a guide to the series of recall/precision curves which give the actual retrieval performance results obtained for the different configurations. These curves are standardised ones which have been derived from the raw recall/ precision graphs based on the retrieval program output using the procedure described in Chapter 5. The actual retrieval figures are, however, of some interest, and some selected ones are therefore given in Appendix 1. The fact that drawing more than at most half a dozen curves on one graph simply makes for confusion means that we have been obliged to display the curves representing tests on the variables under a particular heading in a series of graphs. This is really quite convenient because the tests themselves can be divided into sets representing the main set in which different values of the test variable are examined in the base environment, and check sets representing changes in other variables under the main heads. Thus the summarising tables give first the characterisation of the main set, leading to the major performance graph, and then characterisations, under as many of the four headings as are appropriate, of the other sets, where each characterisation generally leads to a group of curves on a single graph. This again may imply some repetition, but the significance of the changes in parameter values is much more clearly seen.

The tables and graphs have corresponding reference numbers, so that, for example, Table 8C1.2 matches Figure 8C1.2; the numbering system itself reflects the distinction between major and minor comparisons, but as in some cases several such sets may be involved under one overall heading, a more complicated system is followed. Thus if two major comparisons are involved, each with their appropriate cross checks, the former will be identified as, say, 8C2.1.1 and 8C2.2.1, with the respective cross checks as 8C2.1.2 and 8C2.2.2. Each item in a table representing a curve on the corresponding graph is numbered for identification on the graph; thus if three items are compared in Table 8C1.2, we will find the relevant curves numbered as 1, 2 and 3 in Figure 8C1.2. The abbreviated characterisations in the tables themselves should be clear enough if a reference is made to the overall description of the alternatives we have examined which is given in Table 8.1. In all graphs (except the first) term retrieval using the full vocabulary is represented by a broken curve, for comparative purposes.

Now it would in principle be nice if the cross checks on any variable could cover changes to some other variable under each of the three headings not associated with the primary variable, and further, if all the alternative values of such a secondary parameter were tried out. But this is impossible in practice, because it would involve too many tests. At the same time, we have frequently made more extensive checks in comparing some values of a primary variable, than we have made for the complete set of its values. It has often turned out that a few tests only have been sufficient to demonstrate that some alternatives are unrewarding, and we have therefore not pursued them any further, while we have carried out further tests on other values which are more promising. The experiments covering partial sets of values are thus often of interest, because they represent more important lines of investigation. In describing our experiments, therefore, we have concentrated on the results for the complete set of values for a given variable, but the results of additional experiments covering some of their values are also given, where they are appropriate. Some sets of results are also only partial ones, for another reason. Under some headings, especially 3, which refers to different classifications, we have several levels of parameters; we have, that is, a primary variable, the choice of a type of classification, and subsidiary ones, like that representing different methods of treating starting elements in the formation of a clump classification. For some of these subsidiary variables, there is little reason to make extensive cross checks, though we have usually tried to test the alternatives in at least one non-standard configuration.

The presentation of our test results is designed, then, both to present all the information we have obtained in our four main areas of investigation, and to exhibit the full range of our experiments. The important point which must be emphasised, however, is that we have throughout been interested in the comparison between the performance of any classification and that of unclassified terms. We have, moreover, carried out a number of term retrieval experiments connected with the different vocabularies we have listed. These are subsidiary tests, like those we have carried out using different thresholds to define frequent terms which will be described later; but tests like these are useful because they support our main investigations at important points. We have chosen to regard the performance obtainable with the full term list as our standard; but the retrieval consequences of using some other term sets are interesting, and I shall therefore preface the account of the classification experiments proper with a description of our test comparing term retrieval with different vocabularies: these can clearly be fitted into our main scheme, in the way in which we fitted the standard form of retrieval in, because the only difference is in the specification of the vocabulary. We can, moreover, say that tests with classifications using the different vocabularies constitute a kind of cross check on the comparison between term sets, so we can usefully illustrate our approach to the description of our experiments by presenting our results for terms in the standard way.

Term retrieval

In Chapter 4 we considered the properties of our term vocabulary from the classificatory point of view, and we decided that we could usefully distinguish the frequent and the non-frequent terms in the vocabulary. We could then decide whether to classify them all, but in two distinct ways, or to classify either frequent or infrequent terms only. If we are interested in term retrieval only, we cannot separate the first two of these, because what we have described as differences in vocabulary are really differences of classification; and we therefore have three term vocabularies to compare. The comparison between them was made in what can be described as the null version of the base environment, that is one with no similarity or classification choices, and with simple term matching, as given in Table 8T1.1. The resulting standard recall precision curves are given in Figure 8T1.1. The slightly unorthodox use of a classification comparison as a cross check is given by the substitution of unweighted Tanimoto similarities with a threshold of 7 (as in the base configuration) for null similarities, and stars of size 4 for null classes (again as in the base), as appears in Table 8T1.2, which matches Figure 8T1.2. This characterisation of the cross check indeed shows quite clearly the relation between term and class retrieval: it would be possible to regard the tests with terms as necessarily simultaneous changes in the base values of several of our variables.

We now come to the description of the classification tests proper, under their four headings.

1. *Vocabulary tests*

The reason for distinguishing the four vocabularies, it will be remembered, was the discovery that frequent terms, when they were permitted to appear in groups, degraded a classification, while it seemed that if they were controlled by being treated as unit classes, better results could be obtained. The attempt to understand the behaviour of different terms, when classified, then led us to set up the two other vocabularies consisting of the frequent and non-frequent subsets of the whole term list respectively. We have not, however, taken any further features of our term vocabulary into account, so that under this head we have only one parameter, with four values, to examine. Our primary comparison therefore contrasts the four vocabularies in the base environment, with unweighted Tanimoto similarities with threshold 7, stars of size 4, and the simple retrieval mode using straightforward class matches. The features of the test are summarised in Table 8C1.1, and the corresponding performance curves appear in Figure 8C1.1. The overall cross check is provided by the substitution of strings, with length 7, for stars, as given in Table 8C1.2 and Figure 8C1.2. Our main interest, however, has been in the relation between the two ways of treating the complete term list, which are represented by the full and restricted vocabularies, and we have therefore made further comparisons between these two. We have also felt that the choice of vocabulary is sufficiently important for us to try to check it against changes in the base values of the variables under each of the other three headings; and we have therefore carried out cross checks on the partial set of values of our vocabulary parameter represented by the two vocabularies, by comparing them in environments characterised by similarities based on the weighted Tanimoto definition, with the appropriate threshold of 5 (see below) instead of unweighted ones; classes consisting of cliques using a threshold of 21; and retrieval by the mixed mode, with exclusive class lists, adding 1 for one or more class matches above term matches. These substitutions for the base values of the relevant variables are summarised in Tables 8C1.3, 8C1.4 and 8C1.5, which are accompanied by Figures 8C1.3, 8C1.4 and 8C1.5.

2. Similarity tests

The tests here are rather more complicated, because several levels of parameter are involved, and even more, because these parameters are not independent of one another. Initially, we have a choice between the three simple definitions of similarity, namely the unweighted and weighted Tanimoto coefficients, and the cosine correlation coefficient. These definitions constitute the first variable. But we can also modify the matrices based on these definitions by suppressing unuseful similarities, by applying a global threshold, which deletes low similarities uniformly. The use of such a control constitutes a second variable, but clearly the choice of values for this variable is not independent of the choice of the similarity definition itself. We thus have a situation in which a comparison between the values of one of the parameters under the general heading, say the definition, cannot be carried out with identical values for the other internal parameters under the heading, as well as for parameters under other headings. If we have more than one internal parameter, as we have in this case because we have a choice of definition, and also one of level of control, we have to assign a value to each of them in any experiment; and our choice at a given point may be restricted by the choice we have made at another: thus the level of control depends on the method of control, but the level may differ according to the choice of definition. If we are comparing different choices at one point, therefore, we have the problem that we have assigned values to other parameters which cannot be identical, and which may therefore not be strictly comparable, though we have to try to show that they are. We can indeed assign the null value to some parameters, which will give us compatibility in principle, but this may be inconvenient for other reasons. Thus we can in principle apply no control to our matrix, which could be represented not by an alternative under the test parameter, but by the choice of a threshold of 1 for the global threshold, meaning that all non-zero similarities are accepted. Clearly, this is like suppressing the matrix test altogether; but quite apart from the fact that the null test may give an impossibly large matrix to work with, we cannot compare the tests themselves unless we give them positive values, and this is where the problem of ensuring that we have a legitimate comparison again arises. This kind of difficulty is not, however, a very serious one under this heading; it is, as we shall see, much more serious where our different classifications are concerned; but it imposed a constraint on our tests which must be borne in mind in the actual description of the various comparisons we have carried out which follows.

As far as the similarities go, the only criterion of comparability is whether the resulting matrices are of approximately the same size; thus, for example, a global threshold of 7 with the unweighted Tanimoto definition is equivalent to a threshold of 5 for the weighted one, and of 15 for the cosine correlation definition if the restricted vocabulary is used, and to 5 and 17 if the full one is used. For convenience in general discussions, however, remarks about threshold levels will refer to the actual levels used with the unweighted definition, the corresponding levels used with other definitions being understood: thus if we compare a low threshold of 7 with a high one of 19, though these are the actual values for the unweighted definition, the corresponding but different values for the other definitions are assumed.

The three similarity definitions we worked with have already been mentioned. We have worked with two real global thresholds, namely 7 and 19 (and their equivalents). The fact that we have several variables means that in theory we have quite complex tests, because we should consider different values of these variables in relation to one another, as well as in relation to variables falling under other headings; but we have only been able to make some of these comparisons, because too many tests would be involved if we were to go into them thoroughly. A further problem follows from the fact that the base configuration is not a suitable environment for making some of the necessary comparisons: stars depend strictly on the highest similarities in a matrix, and the consequences of using different methods of deleting low ones will not be apparent in their performance. The investigation of these different methods of handling the similarity of a pair of objects is really related to the use of clump-type class definitions, and some comparisons will therefore be made in this context, though the choice of different similarity definitions of course affects the other types of class. Our tests under this heading will therefore be represented by a more extended series of comparisons than were needed to contrast the different vocabularies: the fact that we have more than one variable to consider means that we have several sets of tests, where each is concerned with one variable and therefore represents a base comparison and cross checks for this variable, both against other values of the internal parameters, and against changes in the external ones. A more complicated numbering system is thus required to refer to the tables and graphs, and to exhibit their relationships clearly.

The first comparison is between the three similarity definitions in the base configuration. This test is summarised in Table 8C2.1.1, and the results are given in Figure 8C2.1.1. Cross checks are provided by the substitution of the full for the restricted vocabulary, of strings for stars, and of mixed, exclusive retrieval, adding 1, for simple class matches, as shown in Tables and Figures 8C2.1.2, 8C2.1.3 and 8C2.1.4.

To compare all the similarity definitions properly we have, as just mentioned, to use clump-type classes; and we have therefore made use of what can be called a modified base, referred to as 'base*', which is characterised by $100/P$ clumps with $P = 1$, and no gradient test. Thus, our main test of the three definitions was carried out in a base with the normal vocabulary and retrieval modes, but with 100/P clumps, and was designed to contrast the use of unweighted and weighted Tanimoto and cosine correlation matrices, with thresholds of 7 or its equivalents. This test is characterised by Table 8C2.2.1 and Figure 8C2.2.1. A simple cross check is provided by the substitution of the full vocabulary as shown in Table 8 and Figure 8C2.2.2. It is, however, also necessary to make an internal cross check to compare different values of the definition variable with another value or values of the threshold variable, as well as external checks against changes in variables under other headings. Such a check is provided by the substitution of a threshold of 19, or the corresponding 16 and 35, as shown in Table 8C2.2.3 and the corresponding graph.

We now come to the subsidiary comparisons between different global thresholds. The two values are contrasted in the modified base environment, with unweighted Tanimoto similarities and 100/P clumps, as given in Table and Figure 8C2.3.1. An external cross check substituting the full vocabulary appears in Table and Figure 8C2.3.2, and an internal one substituting weighted similarities is given in Table 8C2.3.3 and its graph.

3. Classification tests

Proper comparisons between the different possibilities under this heading are much more difficult to make than those under the previous one, partly because more variables are involved, but even more so because the different classifications are not defined by combinations of the same variables, with different values, but by different sets of variables. Under the similarity heading we were always concerned with the same three parameters, namely definition, control method and control level, though different values of these parameters could not be freely combined. Under the classification heading we have specific variables which cannot have a value in some cases: the different variables do not always form meaningful combinations. We have different values of some variables which cannot be freely combined, as for similarities, but the important point is that we also have some variables which cannot be combined. In fact, we have to look at the relation between the various alternatives in a slightly different way. We have one or more variables which always have a value, whatever the classification, and we have other variables which are only relevant or only have a value if certain values are assigned to the common parameters; we have, in other words, some variables which depend on others having specific values. If we have several of these dependent variables, therefore, we have to treat them as a group, when we compare one classification where they have a value with another where they do not. We can then say that a particular combination of values for such a set of dependent constitutes one value of a formal common parameter for which a specific combination of values for another dependent set, or the null value represented by an absence of these dependent parameters, are alternatives. We then have the situation which held

160

for similarities, namely that we have restrictions on the combinations of values of our different parameters: if we choose one value of one, we cannot freely combine it with any value of another internal parameter under the general classification heading; the only difference is that one of these parameters is a purely formal one.

Unfortunately, if we have several sets of dependent parameters, or several variables with several values in each, it means that we have a large number of alternative values for our formal parameter; and though these have in principle to be compared, making such a large number of comparisons presents considerable practical problems. A much more important point, however, is that the constraints on the combination of values of the different parameters means that we cannot guarantee that our comparisons are legitimate: if more than one of our parameters differs in value, how can we be sure that a comparison between the classifications concerned is a proper one. We have already encountered this problem in connection with similarities, where we were faced with a difficulty in comparing the effects of using two matrices, because they differed both in the method, by which they were formed, and in the levels of control which were used. This difficulty becomes more acute if we have more parameters, or more alternative values for them, or if we lack any external criteria which can be applied to show that a comparison is legitimate, like that of matrix size which we used to deal with this problem for similarities. One way of getting round the problem is by making exhaustive comparisons covering every possibility, but this is simply not practicable where the number of alternatives is large. Essentially, if the number of alternative combinations of the values of a set of dependent variables is too large, we have to choose one of them as representative, for comparison with another representative value, which gives us two values of our formal overall parameter for the sets to compare. The real difficulty about comparing combinations of values for our classificatory parameters is just the lack of any external criterion for the legitimacy of the comparison. It is of course the case that any difference in retrieval performance enables us to say that one of these alternative combinations gives better results than the other; the point is that we may not be able to ascribe this performance difference to any specific distinction in their individual parameter values: and though we are of course interested in performance, we also want to understand precisely what the effects of the individual components of the whole classification and retrieval process are.

Our problem, then, is that where we want to compare two values of a variable, and we have alternatives for their dependent variables, or variable sets, we have no real means of choosing the representative values for the dependent variables we need to limit our comparisons; we have no common ground on which to base our selection of the kind represented by matrix size for similarities. We cannot, at the same time, disregard the possible effects of alternative values in our dependent variables. The only possible method of dealing with this difficulty, in a finite number of comparisons, therefore, is to make proper cross comparisons over the range of classifications for those variables which have a genuine value in each case, where the choice of values for the subsidiary, non-general parameters is based on some arbitrary consideration, and to make further comparisons between different values of the latter only within the context supplied by the relevant values of the primary variables. The arbitrary base for the choice of representatives is in fact retrieval performance: we take that combination of values of dependent parameters which leads to the best performance for these parameters (where best is based crudely on a visual inspection of the recall/precision curves in question). The description of the comparisons is thus characterised by the disappearance, in some cases, of the base classification as an alternative being compared, and by the substitution of a given representative classification as a base.

Turning now to the actual variables and their values we have to consider, and to the actual comparisons we have made between them, it will be remembered that our first parameter is the type of class, where we have a choice of strings, stars, cliques and clumps. We then have a choice of definitions for a type, though under the first three we have examined only one alternative, namely the use of the strongest similarities for strings and stars, and of all similarities above a threshold for cliques; for clumps we have two alternative definitions, namely the SAB^2 and $100/P$ definitions. Our third parameter can be described as the specification parameter, which again has values depending on the choice of value for the type variable. For strings we have the length specification, under which we have only tried length 7, for stars the size, for which we have the two alternatives 4 and 6, and for cliques the threshold, namely 16 and 21; for clumps we have two alternative values for P for the third clump definition, $\frac{1}{2}$ and 1, and also a non-specialised choice between applying a gradient test or not, with a maximum of 95 and minimum 5, which may be used with any clump definition.

The main comparison is naturally that between types of class; and as we said earlier, the selection of representative classifications of this type for the comparison can only be based on retrieval performance. There is of course no choice under strings; for stars we obtain the classes of size 4 which in fact characterise the base configuration. For cliques we get the classes based on the higher threshold, and for clumps, those derived with the $100/P$ definition with $P = 1$, and no gradient test, that is the clumps we used for the modified base in the similarity comparisons. The comparison between these classifications in the base environment is shown in Table 8C3.1.1 and the matching graph. The use of the base environment as given is, however, not wholly satisfactory where comparisons between the types of class are concerned, for reasons like those which led to the substitution of clumps for stars in the base environment used for testing similarities. In this case the first three classifications are all based explicitly or implicitly on high similarities, while the clumps are not; the use of the similarity threshold of 7 is 'unfair' to the clump classification. For this reason, the curve for $100/P$

clumps based on a threshold of 19, which are better suited to the comparison with the other classifications, has been added to the graph. Cross checks using the full vocabulary, weighted similarities and the mixed exclusive mode of retrieval incrementing by 1, are shown in Tables and Figures 8C3.1.2, 8C3.1.3 and 8C3.1.4 respectively.

If we now proceed to the comparisons between different classifications of a given type, we have of course no comparison for strings; and the comparison between different star classifications is confined to two alternatives, sizes 4 and 6, as shown for the base environment in Table and Figure 8C3.2.1. We feel that the comparisons between classifications based on the different definitions are sufficiently important, though they are restricted, to rate more cross checks than is usual for the subsidiary parameters under a given heading, and we have therefore made them where possible. Thus cross checks for stars with the full vocabulary, weighted similarities, and retrieval by the mixed mode are shown in Tables 8C3.2.2, 8C3.2.3 and 8C3.2.4 and the associated graphs.

With cliques, we again have a comparison between two alternatives, based on thresholds of 16 and 21, as shown for the base in Table and Figure 8C3.3.1. Cross checks with the full vocabulary, weighted similarities and mixed retrieval with exclusive matches adding 1, are given in Tables and Figures 8C3.3.2, 8C3.3.3 and 8C3.3.4.

We now come to the comparisons between different clump classifications. These are more complex, because more variables are involved, and some selection from the possible range has necessarily been made; in particular we have been obliged to take classifications based on one value of P for the 100/P definition as representative in comparisons involving the different definitions, for the reason mentioned earlier. We thus have an initial comparison between SAB^2 and 100/P clumps, with no gradient test, P being set $= 1$ for the latter. This comparison in the base environment is shown in Table 8C3.4.1 and Figure 8C3.4.1; cross checks using the full vocabulary, weighted similarities and mixed retrieval, as before, are given in Tables and Figures 8C3.4.2, 8C3.4.3a and 8C3.4.4. As the use of different control levels seems to affect clump performance considerably, a second cross check under the similarity heading using a high threshold of 19 is given in Table and Figure 8C3.4.3b. An internal cross check using the gradient test with a maximum of 95 as minimum of 5 is shown in Table and Figure 8C3.4.5.

The next comparison is between the two values of P, as shown in Table and Figure 8C3.5.1, with the external cross check using weighted similarities and the internal one using the gradient test given in Tables 8C3.5.2 and 8C3.5.3 and their graphs respectively.

The final comparison is between the gradient test choices, namely either disregarding the test or using it—in our case in only one way, with a maximum level of 95 and a minimum of 5 (as opposed to a null maximum of 100 and a minimum of 5, say). This is shown for the base in Table and Figure 8C3.6.1, and an external cross check using the full vocabulary and an internal one using SAB^2 clumps are shown in Tables and Figures 8C3.6.2 and 8C3.6.3.

4. Retrieval tests

Under this heading, the comparisons become much simpler again. We have in fact not pursued some of the possibilities very far because they do not appear promising, though, as we shall see later, the reasons for this are not clear. Our first choice (considering retrieval involving classes in some way, and not only terms) is between the simple and mixed modes of retrieval, that is between the straightforward substitution of class specifications for term lists and their combination. Under the first option we have a subsequent choice of whether simply to look for a matching class in searching, or whether we require the class frequency for a document to be at least as great as its frequency for the request, that is between what we can describe as class and frequent class matches respectively. Under the second mode we again have two alternatives, according to whether we have an exclusive or inclusive class specification for matching beyond terms; we can, that is, either form a class list from our term list, and then delete classes associated with matching terms, so that class matches are only obtained for the remainder; or we can form a class list for only non-matching terms. In either case we have a further modifying variable, according to whether we supplement our term retrieval levels by 1, for any number of additional class matches, or by n, for the number of such matches. We thus have two overall variables, the retrieval mode and the match definition, though their values cannot be freely combined, and a dependent modifying variable associated with some options. This means that we again have the problem of choosing representatives that we have already encountered, but in a very mild form. We decided, in fact, to make our main comparison between the two modes of retrieval, simple and mixed, using the class and exclusive match definitions respectively, with the $+1$ modification for the latter. This comparison, in the base environment, is shown in Table 8C4.1.1 and Figure 8C4.1.1. Cross checks using the full vocabulary, weighted similarities, and strings for classes are shown in Tables and Figures 8C4.1.2, 8C4.1.3 and 8C4.1.4 respectively. The use of the frequent class as opposed to the plain class match, again in the base environment, is shown in Table 8C4.2.1 and its graph, and a cross check substituting $100/P$ clumps is shown in Table and Figure 8C4.2.2. The comparison between the two mixed modes, both with $+1$, for the base environment, appears in Table 8C4.3.1 and its associated graph, with a cross check with weighted similarities in Table and Figure 8C4.3.2. The final comparison is between the two forms of modifying the mixed mode of retrieval, $+1$ and $+n$; this was unfortunately not completed, for independent reasons: the single result, using strings instead of stars, in the base environment, is given in Table and Figure 8C4.4.1.

164

Supporting tests

Apart from the main body of tests described above, we have carried out a number of subsidiary tests which are needed to justify some of the particular decisions we have taken. The most important of these are concerned with the separation of frequent from non-frequent terms: we clearly need to investigate the use of a given cutoff for selecting frequent terms for treatment as unit classes. Giving frequent terms special treatment seems to pay dividends; but an examination of the effects of different cutoffs is clearly needed, both to show that we were working with a sensible cutoff in our experiments with a certain collection, and, more generally, to show that we can hope to identify a suitable cutoff without much difficulty, for any collection. It would be unfortunate if the value of a cutoff depended on the correct identification of one particular level, because a disagreeable amount of experiment might be required to find it. It would be much more satisfactory in practice if it could be shown that any cutoffs within an area, which would be more readily identified than one specific level, would produce comparable results, so that an effectively arbitrary choice of level could be made without unfortunate consequences.

We decided to examine this question for our test collection by making four alternative cutoffs, so that we treated terms which occurred only in more than 30 documents out of 200 as unit classes, or in more than 25, or in more than 20, or in more than 15. We then compared the star classifications for these four term sets, that is the classifications grouping the remaining terms and taking the selected terms as single-member classes, in the base environment, along with the star classification for a null cutoff, that is one for the full vocabulary in which no terms are treated as unit classes. This comparison is shown in Table and Figure 8F1.

Table 8T1 COMPARISON OF TERM VOCABULARIES

		Vocab	Sim	Class	Retr	Figure
Base	1	full/restr	null	null	simple, term	T1.1
	2	freq				
	3	infreq				
Cross checks	1	full	unwTan, 7	stars, 4	simple, class	T1.2
	2	freq				
	3	infreq				

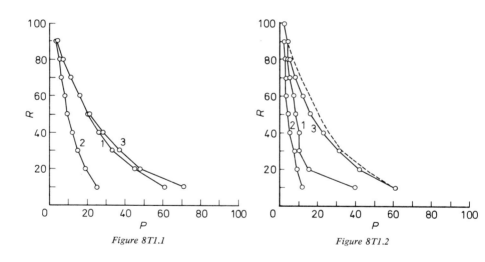

Figure 8T1.1 *Figure 8T1.2*

Table 8C1 COMPARISON OF VOCABULARIES

		Vocab	Sim	Class	Retr	Figure
Base	1	full	unwTan, 7	stars, 4	simple, class	C1.1
	2	restr				
	3	freq				
	4	infreq				
Cross checks	1	full	unwTan, 7	strings, 7	simple, class	C1.2
complete	2	restr				
	3	freq				
	4	infreq				
partial	1	full	wTan, 5	stars, 4	simple, class	C1.3
	2	restr				
	1	full	unwTan, 7	cliques, 21	simple, class	C1.4
	2	restr				
	1	full	unwTan, 7	stars, 4	mixed, excl, +1	C1.5
	2	restr				

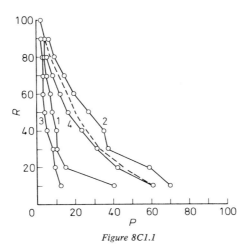

Figure 8C1.1

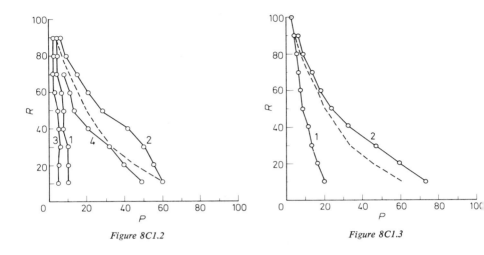

Figure 8C1.2

Figure 8C1.3

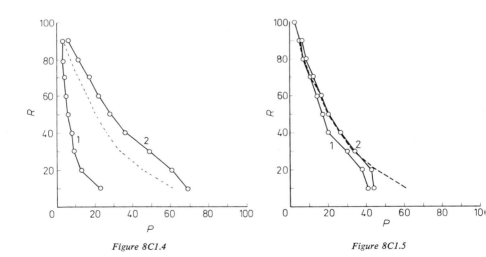

Figure 8C1.4

Figure 8C1.5

Table 8C2 COMPARISON OF SIMILARITIES

		Vocab Sim		Class	Retr	Figure
Base	1	restr	unwTan, 7	stars, 4	simple, class	C2.1.1
	2		wTan, 5			
	3		coscor, 15			
Cross checks	1	full	unwTan, 7	stars, 4	simple, class	C2.1.2
	2		wTan, 5			
	3		coscor, 17			
	1	restr	unwTan, 7	strings, 7	simple, class	C2.1.3
	2		wTan, 5			
	3		coscor, 15			
	1	restr	unwTan, 7	stars, 4	mixed, excl, + 1	C2.1.4
	2		wTan, 5			
	3		coscor, 15			
*Base**	1	restr	unwTan, 7	clumps, 100/P	simple, class	C2.2.1
	2		wTan, 5	P = 1, no grad		
	3		coscor, 15			
Cross checks	1	full	unwTan, 7	clumps, 100/P	simple, class	C2.2.2
	2		wTan, 5	P = 1, no grad		
	3		coscor, 17			
	1	restr	unwTan, 19	clumps, 100/P	simple, class	C2.2.3
	2		wTan, 16	P = 1, no grad		
	3		coscor, 35			
*Base**	1	restr	unwTan, 7	clumps, 100/P	simple, class	C2.3.1
	2		unwTan, 19	P = 1, no grad		
Cross checks	1	full	unwTan, 7	clumps, 100/P	simple, class	C2.3.2
	2		unwTan, 19	P = 1, no grad		
	1	restr	wTan, 5	clumps, 100/P	simple, class	C2.3.3
	2		wTan, 15	P = 1, no grad		

169

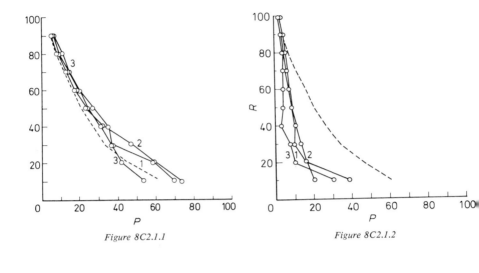

Figure 8C2.1.1

Figure 8C2.1.2

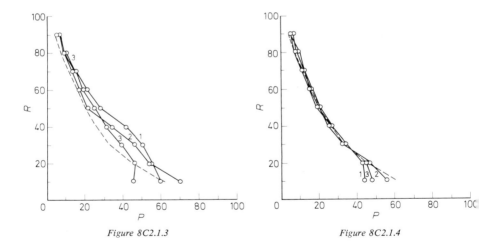

Figure 8C2.1.3

Figure 8C2.1.4

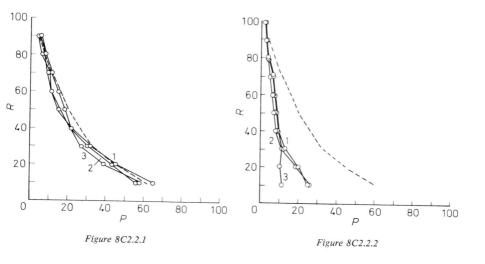

Figure 8C2.2.1

Figure 8C2.2.2

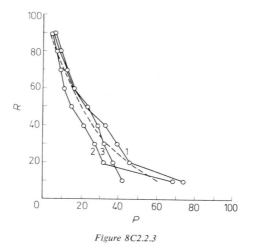

Figure 8C2.2.3

171

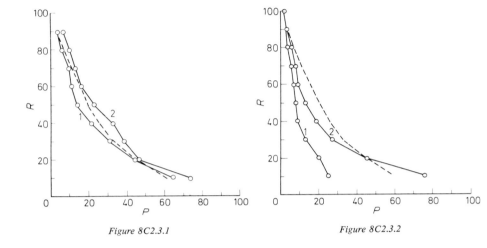

Figure 8C2.3.1   *Figure 8C2.3.2*

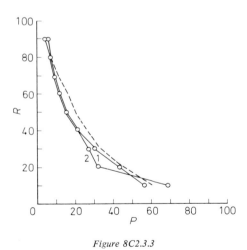

Figure 8C2.3.3

Table 8C3 COMPARISON OF CLASSIFICATIONS

		Vocab Sim		Class	Retr	Figure
Base	1	restr	unwTan, 7	strings, 7	simple, class	C3.1.1
	2			stars, 4		
	3			cliques, 21		
	4			clumps, 100/P		
				P = 1, no grad		
	5		unwTan, 19	clumps, 100/P		
				P = 1, no grad		
Cross checks	1	full	unwTan, 7	strings, 7	simple, class	C3.1.2
	2			stars, 4		
	3			cliques, 21		
	4		unwTan, 19	clumps, 100/P		
				P = 1, no grad		
	1	restr	wTan, 5	strings, 7	simple, class	C3.1.3
	2			stars, 4		
	3			cliques, 21		
	4		wTan, 15	clumps, 100/P		
				P = 1, no grad		
	1	restr	unwTan, 7	strings, 7	mixed, excl, + 1	C3.1.4
	2			stars, 4		
	3			cliques, 21		
	4		unwTan, 19	clumps, 100/P		
				P = 1, no grad		
Base	1	restr	unwTan, 7	stars, 4	simple, class	C3.2.1
	2			stars, 6		
Cross checks	1	full	unwTan, 7	stars, 4	simple, class	C3.2.2
	2			stars, 6		
	1	restr	wTan, 5	stars, 4	simple, class	C3.2.3
	2			stars, 6		
	1	restr	unwTan, 7	stars, 4	mixed, excl, + 1	C3.2.4
	2			stars, 6		
Base	1	restr	unwTan, 7	cliques, 21	simple, class	C3.3.1
	2			cliques, 16		
Cross checks	1	full	unwTan, 7	cliques, 21	simple, class	C3.3.2
	2			cliques, 16		
	1	restr	wTan, 5	cliques, 21	simple, class	C3.3.3
	2			cliques, 16		
	1	restr	unwTan, 7	cliques, 21	mixed, excl, + 1	C3.3.4
	2			cliques, 16		
Base	1	restr	unwTan, 7	clumps, SAB[2]	simple, class	C3.4.1
				no grad		
	2			clumps, 100/P		
				P = 1, no grad		

Table 8C3 (*contd*)

		Vocab	Sim	Class	Retr	Figure
Cross checks	1	full	unwTan, 7	clumps, SAB[2] no grad	simple, class	C3.4.2
	2			clumps, 100/P $P = 1$, no grad		
	1	restr	wTan, 5	clumps, SAB[2] no grad	simple, class	C3.4.3a
	2			clumps, 100/P $P = 1$, no grad		
	1	restr	unwTan, 19	clumps, SAB[2] no grad	simple, class	C3.4.3b
	2			clumps, 100/P $P = 1$, no grad		
	1	restr	unwTan, 7	clumps, SAB[2] no grad	mixed, excl, $+1$	C3.4.4
	2			clumps, 100/P $P = 1$, no grad		
	1	restr	unwTan, 7	clumps, SAB[2] grad 95/5	simple, class	C3.4.5
	2			clumps, 100/P $P = 1$, grad 95/5		
Base	1	restr	unwTan, 7	clumps, 100/P $P = 1$, no grad	simple, class	C3.5.1
	2			clumps, 100/P $P = \frac{1}{2}$, no grad		
Cross checks	1	restr	wTan, 5	clumps, 100/P $P = 1$, no grad	simple, class	C3.5.2
	2			clumps, 100/P $P = \frac{1}{2}$, no grad		
	1	restr	unwTan, 7	clumps, 100/P $P = 1$, grad 95/5	simple, class	C3.5.3
	2			clumps, 100/P $P = \frac{1}{2}$, grad 95/5		
Base	1	restr	unwTan, 7	clumps, 100/P $P = 1$, no grad	simple, class	C3.6.1
	2			clumps, 100/P $P = 1$, grad 95/5		
Cross checks	1	full	unwTan, 7	clumps, 100/P $P = 1$, no grad	simple, class	C3.6.2
	2			clumps, 100/P $P = 1$, grad 95/5		
	1	restr	unwTan, 7	clumps, SAB[2] no grad	simple, class	C3.6.3
	2			clumps, SAB[2] grad 95/5		

174

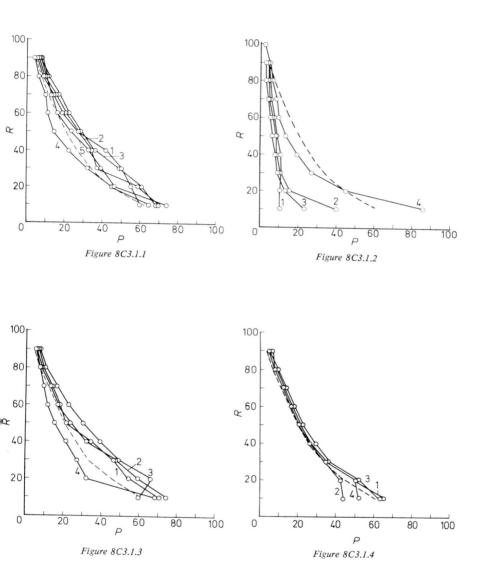

Figure 8C3.1.1

Figure 8C3.1.2

Figure 8C3.1.3

Figure 8C3.1.4

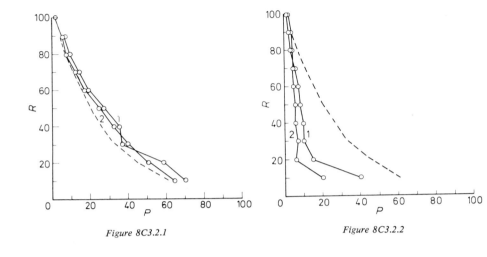

Figure 8C3.2.1

Figure 8C3.2.2

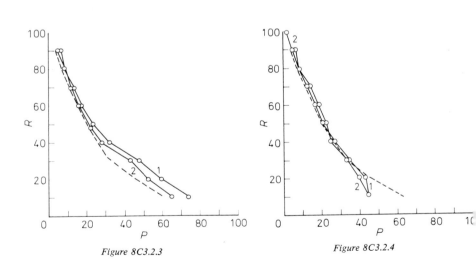

Figure 8C3.2.3

Figure 8C3.2.4

176

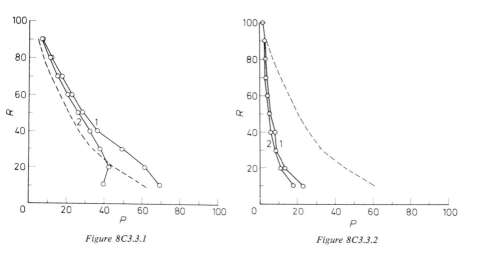

Figure 8C3.3.1   Figure 8C3.3.2

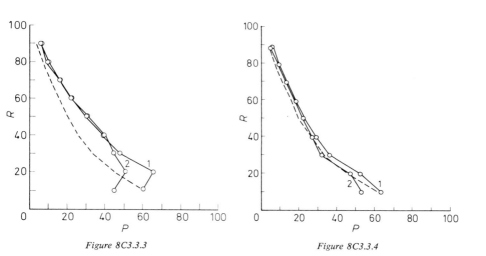

Figure 8C3.3.3   Figure 8C3.3.4

177

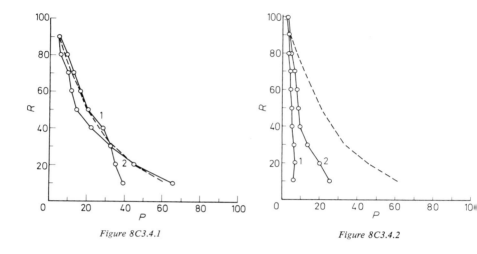

Figure 8C3.4.1

Figure 8C3.4.2

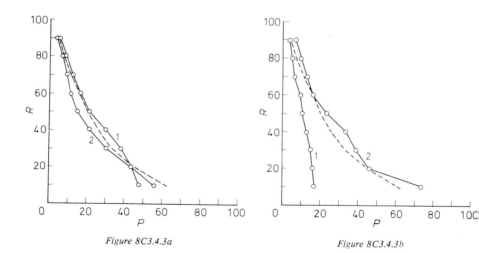

Figure 8C3.4.3a

Figure 8C3.4.3b

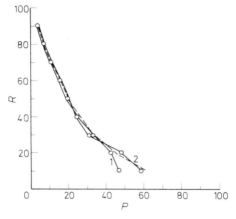

Figure 8C3.4.4

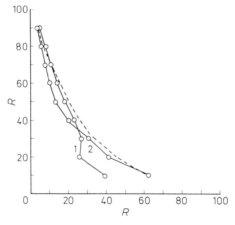

Figure 8C3.4.5

179

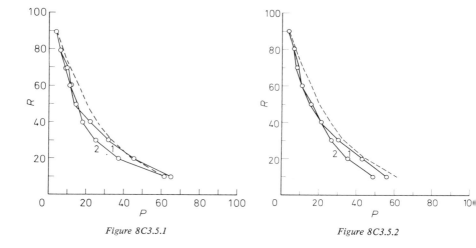

Figure 8C3.5.1   *Figure 8C3.5.2*

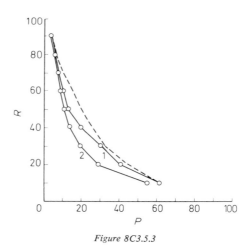

Figure 8C3.5.3

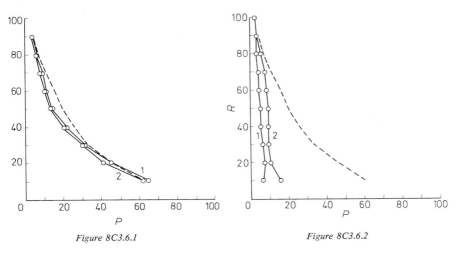

Figure 8C3.6.1   *Figure 8C3.6.2*

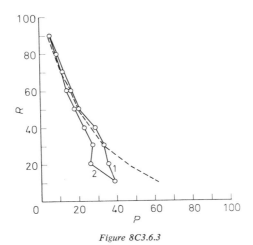

Figure 8C3.6.3

Table 8C4 COMPARISON OF RETRIEVAL MODES

		Vocab	*Sim*	*Class*	*Retr*	*Figure*
Base	1	restr	unwTan, 7	stars, 4	simple, class	C4.1.1
	2				mixed, excl, +1	
Cross checks	1	full	unwTan, 7	stars, 4	simple, class	C4.1.2
	2				mixed, excl, +1	
	1	restr	wTan, 5	stars, 4	simple, class	C4.1.3
	2				mixed, excl, +1	
	1	restr	unwTan, 7	strings	simple, class	C4.1.4
	2				mixed, excl, +1	
Base	1	restr	unwTan, 7	stars, 4	simple, class	C4.2.1
	2				simple, freq	
Cross checks	1	restr	unwTan, 7	clumps, 100/P P = 1, no grad	simple, class	C4.2.2
	2				class, freq	
Base	1	restr	unwTan, 7	stars, 4	mixed, excl, +1	C4.3.1
	2				mixed, incl, +1	
Cross checks	1	restr	wTan, 5	stars, 4	mixed, excl, +1	C4.3.2
	2				mixed, incl, +1	
Base	1	restr	unwTan, 7	strings	mixed, excl, +1	C4.4.1
	2				mixed, excl, $+n$	

182

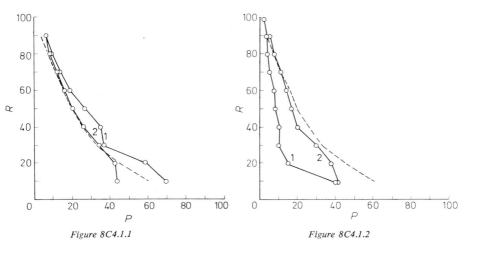

Figure 8C4.1.1   Figure 8C4.1.2

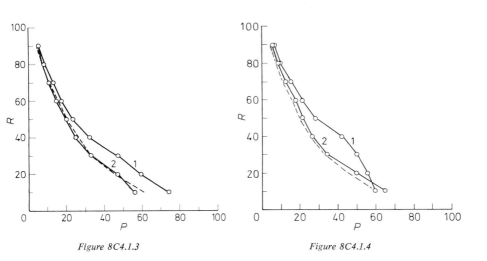

Figure 8C4.1.3   Figure 8C4.1.4

183

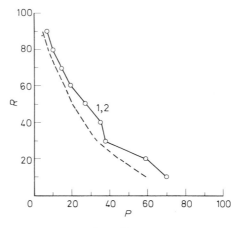

Figure 8C4.2.1

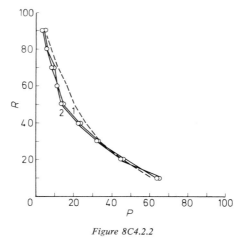

Figure 8C4.2.2

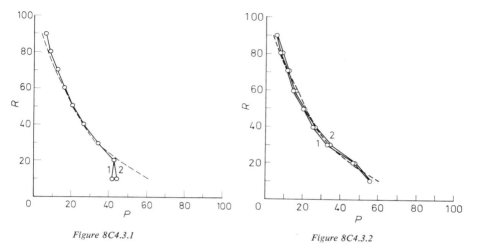

Figure 8C4.3.1

Figure 8C4.3.2

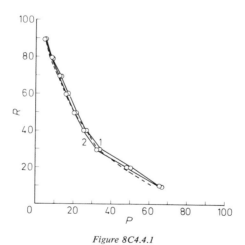

Figure 8C4.4.1

185

Table 8F1 COMPARISON OF TERM FREQUENCY CUTOFFS

	Vocab	Sim	Class	Retr	Figure
1	full	unwTan, 7	stars, 4	simple, class	F1
2	30+				
3	25+				
4	20+				
5	15+				

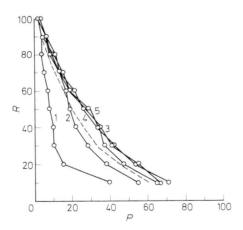

Figure 8F1

Chapter 8

Appendix 1

Table A1 TERMS, ALL

Level	Recall	Precision	Total	Non-rel. Retrieved	Rel. Retrieved
1	96	3	4951	4759	192
2	83	6	2419	2252	167
3	69	12	1086	948	138
4	46	22	408	315	93
5	27	35	151	97	54
6	15	53	58	27	31
7	4	72	11	3	8
8	2	80	5	1	4
9	0	0	1	1	0

Table A2 TERMS, FREQUENT

Level	Recall	Precision	Total	Non-rel. Retrieved	Rel. Retrieved
1	91	3	4698	4515	183
2	72	6	2139	1994	145
3	46	10	868	776	92
4	24	17	276	227	49
5	11	23	94	72	22
6	4	38	21	13	8
7	0	50	2	1	1

Table A3 TERMS, INFREQUENT

Level	Recall	Precision	Total	Non-rel. Retrieved	Rel. Retrieved
1	59	13	860	741	119
2	22	44	99	55	44
3	10	71	28	8	20
4	2	80	5	1	4

Table A4 STARS, FULL; UNWTAN, 7; 4; SIMPLE CLASS

Level	Recall	Precision	Total	Non-rel. Retrieved	Rel. Retrieved
1	100	2	7818	7619	199
2	99	2	7072	6874	198
3	98	3	6512	6315	197
4	98	3	6006	5810	196
5	95	3	5612	5420	192
6	94	3	5225	5036	189
7	93	3	4850	4663	187
8	92	4	4517	4333	184
9	88	4	4217	4041	176
10	85	4	3973	3803	170
11	83	4	3730	3564	166
12	75	4	3504	3348	156
13	74	4	3188	3039	149
14	73	5	2855	2709	146
15	71	5	2493	2350	143
16	69	6	2194	2056	138
17	68	7	1883	1747	136
18	62	7	1620	1496	124
19	58	8	1402	1286	116
20	49	8	1221	1122	99
21	47	8	1046	952	94
22	44	9	883	795	88
23	39	10	726	648	78
24	31	10	581	519	62
25	27	11	484	429	55
26	26	12	406	354	52
27	22	13	332	287	45
28	20	15	265	225	40
29	18	17	208	171	37
30	16	20	158	126	32
31	14	21	129	101	28
32	12	24	101	76	25
33	12	32	76	51	25
34	10	40	49	29	20
35	7	42	35	20	15
36	7	53	26	12	14
37	5	55	20	9	11
38	3	46	15	8	7
39	2	36	11	7	4
40	1	50	6	3	3
41	1	50	6	3	3
42	1	40	5	3	2
43	1	66	3	1	2
44	1	100	2	0	2
45	1	100	2	0	2

Table A5 STARS, RESTRICTED; UNWTAN, 7; 4; SIMPLE, CLASS

Level	Recall	Precision	Total	Non-rel. Retrieved	Rel. Retrieved
1	99	3	6217	6019	198
2	95	4	3988	3797	191
3	89	7	2517	2339	178
4	78	10	1474	1317	157
5	68	14	930	793	137
6	60	19	613	493	120
7	50	26	384	283	101
8	41	33	250	167	83
9	32	34	184	120	64
10	26	44	117	65	52
11	22	50	87	43	44
12	17	57	61	26	35
13	15	64	48	17	31
14	12	64	39	14	25
15	10	68	29	9	20
16	7	65	23	8	15
17	7	68	22	7	15
18	6	75	16	4	12
19	4	81	11	2	9
20	4	80	10	2	8
21	3	100	6	0	6
22	1	100	3	0	3
23	0	100	1	0	1

Table A6 STARS, FREQUENT; UNWTAN, 7; 4; SIMPLE, CLASS

Level	Recall	Precision	Total	Non-rel. Retrieved	Rel. Retrieved
1	97	2	7784	7589	195
2	94	2	7037	6848	189
3	94	2	6483	6295	188
4	88	2	5892	5716	176
5	87	3	5480	5306	174
6	86	3	5076	4904	172
7	82	3	4705	4540	165
8	76	3	4383	4231	152
9	68	3	4086	3950	136
10	64	3	3837	3709	128
11	60	3	3546	3425	121
12	60	3	3353	3232	121
13	57	3	3149	3034	115
14	54	3	2836	2728	108
15	50	4	2452	2352	100
16	48	4	2182	2085	97
17	46	4	1923	1830	93
18	43	5	1665	1578	87
19	40	5	1462	1381	81
20	39	6	1266	1187	79
21	38	6	1105	1029	76
22	36	7	956	884	72
23	33	8	781	714	67
24	25	8	627	576	51
25	21	8	512	469	43
26	19	9	412	373	39
27	16	9	340	308	32
28	15	11	275	244	31
29	14	13	215	187	28
30	9	12	141	123	18
31	7	15	98	83	15
32	5	16	66	55	11
33	2	12	33	29	4
34	2	18	22	18	4
35	2	30	13	9	4
36	1	42	7	4	3
37	1	75	4	1	3
38	1	75	4	1	3
39	0	100	1	0	1

Table A7 STARS, INFREQUENT; UNWTAN, 7; 4; SIMPLE, CLASS

Level	Recall	Precision	Total	Non-rel. Retrieved	Rel. Retrieved
1	83	4	3651	3485	166
2	72	7	1976	1831	145
3	63	10	1242	1115	127
4	54	15	709	601	108
5	43	19	436	349	87
6	36	28	259	186	73
7	29	31	187	129	58
8	23	35	132	85	47
9	19	44	85	47	38
10	17	51	66	32	34
11	15	60	50	20	30
12	12	65	38	13	25
13	7	56	25	11	14
14	7	63	22	8	14
15	5	61	18	7	11
16	3	63	11	4	7
17	3	66	9	3	6
18	3	85	7	1	6
19	3	100	6	0	6
20	1	100	2	0	2
21	0	100	1	0	1

Table A8 STRINGS, RESTRICTED; UNWTAN, 7; SIMPLE, CLASS

Level	Recall	Precision	Total	Non-rel. Retrieved	Rel. Retrieved
1	97	3	5315	5121	194
2	89	6	2934	2756	178
3	78	10	1484	1327	157
4	64	18	687	559	128
5	47	30	312	218	94
6	38	45	170	93	77
7	22	54	83	38	45
8	17	57	61	26	35
9	12	61	39	15	24
10	8	58	29	12	17
11	5	61	18	7	11
12	4	61	13	5	8
13	1	50	6	3	3
14	1	50	6	3	3
15	1	40	5	3	2
16	0	33	3	2	1
17	0	50	2	1	1
18	0	100	1	0	1

Table A9 CLIQUES, RESTRICTED; UNWTAN, 7; 21; SIMPLE, CLASS

Level	Recall	Precision	Total	Non-rel. Retrieved	Rel. Retrieved
1	97	3	5318	5124	194
2	91	6	2856	2674	182
3	80	11	1405	1244	161
4	65	20	644	513	131
5	46	30	308	215	93
6	35	41	171	100	71
7	24	59	81	33	48
8	14	64	45	16	29
9	11	67	34	11	23
10	8	72	22	6	16
11	2	55	9	4	5
12	1	75	4	1	3
13	0	50	2	1	1
14	0	100	1	0	1

Table A10 CLUMPS, RESTRICTED; UNWTAN, 19; 100/P, P = 1, NO GRAD; SIMPLE, CLASS

Level	Recall	Precision	Total	Non-rel. Retrieved	Rel. Retrieved
1	97	3	5435	5240	195
2	92	6	2989	2805	184
3	79	10	1563	1404	159
4	61	15	794	671	123
5	48	24	389	292	97
6	37	36	201	127	74
7	24	41	119	70	49
8	16	52	63	30	33
9	11	67	34	11	23
10	9	82	23	4	19
11	3	87	8	1	7
12	2	100	5	0	5
13	1	100	3	0	3
14	0	100	1	0	1

SECTION III

Analysis

Chapter 9

Test Conclusions

SUMMARY

This chapter presents the conclusions to be drawn from the comparisons detailed in Chapter 8 about the various aspects of keyword classification we have examined in our experiments. Using the four headings under which the experiments were categorised, we can say, first, that as far as the different vocabularies go, the restricted one in which frequent terms are treated as unit classes while non-frequent ones are grouped, gives unequivocally better results than the alternatives; second, that there is not much difference between the results given by the various similarity definitions, but that confining the classification process to strongly connected items only, by applying a matrix threshold, say, leads to a noticeable improvement in performance; third, that the different approaches to grouping can generate classifications which lead to the same retrieval performance, though differences in the performance both of classifications of different types, and of different classifications of the same type, are apparent: it is in fact the case that for a given type, those classifications which are restricted to strongly connected items are most successful, and that the best classifications of each type are very comparable; fourth, that the simple mode of retrieval is sometimes better, and sometimes worse, than the mixed one. From these separate points it then follows that if the combination of parameter values under the four headings which are individually associated with the best results is adopted, we can obtain not merely good results in retrieval, but a better performance than that derived from keywords alone.

Conclusions on the vocabulary tests

We have so far presented the results of individual experiments, and of comparisons between the different values of a given parameter, without comment. This section will be devoted to an analysis of these results, and to a discussion of their wider implications. In considering the conclusions to be drawn from our experiments, therefore, I shall start with a detailed discussion of the experiments themselves, that is with the specific statements that can be made about the particular approaches to the construction and use of keyword classifications we have examined; and I shall go on to consider the conclusions about the use of automatically obtained keyword classifications in general that can be drawn from these results, and from work on the same problems which has been done elsewhere.

It is convenient, in considering the results of our experiments themselves, to discuss them under the four main headings we used to present them. We can start, that is, by looking at the consequences of the different treatments of the term vocabulary we have investigated, and then proceed to those of the different ways of setting up the similarity matrix, of forming classes and of using them in searches, that we have studied; we can then consider what the combined effects of these choices are, and in particular what combina-

195

tions seem to be effective, before going on to see why they are effective. These points will be illustrated with standardised graphs of the kind described in Chapter 5, representing selections from the complete set given in Chapter 8, to which references for supporting evidence will be made.

First, vocabularies. As far as these go, there is little doubt that the restricted vocabulary, in which all the terms are included, but grouping is confined to non-frequent terms only, gives by far the best retrieval performance compared with any of the others, the differences being consistent for changes in other parameters. It must, however, be admitted that we considered the two sub-vocabularies consisting respectively of frequent and non-frequent terms only chiefly as controls: we did not expect them to perform really well, and studied them mainly to see how they behave in retrieval. We looked in particular at the performance of the unclassified sets of terms, to get a lead on how these sets should be treated when classification of the full vocabulary is envisaged. The results in this respect are indeed quite interesting as they were not what we expected. As Figure 8T1 shows, when we look at the term retrieval performance of the full, frequent and non-frequent sets of terms respectively, we find that the non-frequent terms do nearly as well as the full set, apart from the fact that they have a lower recall ceiling (though this is actually 59 per cent, and not the 50 per cent to which it is somewhat misleadingly reduced by the standardising procedure), while the frequent terms do very much worse. The interesting point about the term performance is indeed that the non-frequent terms do so well, compared with the full set; the only advantage of the latter is that recall is better at low coordination levels*. Using a classification, exemplified by stars, improves recall for non-frequent terms, but does not effect an overall improvement in retrieval performance, and if anything marginally degrades it; the performance of a star classification for frequent terms, on the other hand, is worse than that of the frequent terms alone; while for the complete set of terms, a full classification does worse than terms alone, while the restricted star classification does better. These relationships are all exhibited in Figure 8C1.1; and from this figure we can draw the inference which is supported by Figure 8C1.2, namely that the restricted vocabulary, in which all the terms appear but grouping is confined to the non-frequent ones, the frequent terms being treated as unit classes, can give a retrieval performance which is superior not merely to that of the other vocabularies when classified, but to any of the unclassified sets of terms. The persistent difference between the performance which is typically obtained for the restricted vocabulary and the full vocabulary, whatever classification procedure is adopted, is particularly striking.

The experiments with the two sub-vocabularies were somewhat limited, and further studies of the effects of classification here are really required, to show whether grouping in either case in general improves or degrades per-

---

* The significance test discussed earlier is not applicable in a straightforward way here, since the curves do not cover the same recall range.

formance compared with that obtainable for the two sets of terms alone, and also to show what their systematic relationships with the complete set of terms and the full and restricted vocabularies representing different ways of classifying this complete set are. It is difficult to believe, however, that any improvement in performance which might be obtained by classifying either of these two subsets of terms would be so marked that we would prefer either of these to the complete one, or in other words, that we could find some way of processing either subset in classification which would give better results than any way of handling the complete set. The important point is the treatment of the complete set of terms. Here we have carried out a fairly extensive range of experiments, one way and another, but they all support the general conclusion given earlier, to the effect that the full vocabulary in which all terms are grouped generally performs less well, not merely than restricted vocabulary, but than the corresponding complete set of terms, while the restricted vocabulary does better than either. There is no doubt, moreover, that it is the restriction which confines frequent terms to unit classes, which is responsible for this improvement: if they are allowed to appear in classes, the unwanted documents which are retrieved as a result far outweigh the wanted ones. This is borne out, in particular, by a comparison between the performance of the classified full and frequent vocabularies on the one hand and that of the restricted and non-frequent vocabularies on the other. The former are worse than the latter, and this difference must be ascribed to the occurrence of frequent terms in classes in these cases, though the absence of non-frequent terms where the frequent vocabulary is concerned must also affect its performance. The actual numbers of documents retrieved in each case show what is happening very clearly: thus we find that for the four star classifications concerned, the total numbers finally retrieved by level one are:

full		restr		freq		infreq	
R	−R	R	−R	R	−R	R	−R
199	7 619	198	6 019	195	7 589	166	3 485

and if we look at individual requests, the effect of permitting frequent terms to appear in classes is obvious. For example for requests 16 and 33 respectively we get:

full		restr		freq		infreq		
R	−R	R	−R	R	−R	R	−R	
9	170	9	104	9	165	8	90	(req 16)
2	198	2	149	2	193	2	119	(req 33)

At the same time, it is clear that the inclusion of frequent terms as unit classes, to permit direct request document matches on these terms, is of value, because the restricted vocabulary works better than the non-frequent one. Though this is not surprising, if we remember how many of the request terms are frequent ones: throwing them away altogether reduces the request specification too much, as will be apparent if we refer to the examples in Chapter 7; the frequent terms, if we consider term retrieval only, are responsible to a considerable extent for the retrieval of relevant documents, as we saw.

Our experiments thus provide some actual support for the suggestions, about the appropriate way of handling any vocabulary which is to be classified, that we put forward in Chapter 4; for, as noted earlier, this result about the relative merits of the restricted vocabulary is well established, in the sense that they are still apparent, whatever changes are made in the values of other parameters: the result holds for different similarity definitions, and different approaches to classification, though it is true that the difference between the full and restricted vocabularies is not so obvious when changes

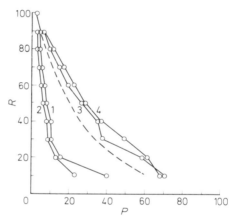

Figure 9.1 Vocabularies

1	full	unwtan, 7	stars, 4	simple, class
2			cliques, 21	
3	restr		stars, 4	
4			cliques, 21	

are made in the retrieval parameters, for reasons which will be apparent later. This conclusion is illustrated in Figure 9.1.

In this context, the experiments with different frequency cutoffs can also be referred to, although their primary object was the rather different one of establishing that our test cutoff was well chosen: for the different results obtained with the different cutoffs also show how important the restriction of grouping for frequent terms is. Thus as the results obtained with a star classification which are given in Figure 8F1 show, if the cutoff is very high a comparatively poor performance is obtained, presumably because many relatively frequent terms are still grouped, while if it is very low, so few terms are grouped that not enough of the benefits of classification are obtained.

Conclusions on the similarity tests

Our next set of choices was for similarities; and it will be remembered that we tested a more complex series of alternatives on several levels here, including different definitions of similarity itself, and, for one method of controlling the formation of a matrix, a choice of different levels of control. As far as the actual definitions themselves go, it seems on the whole to be the case that there is no difference in the performance to be obtained with the unweighted and weighted definitions, whatever values are assigned to other parameters, as is apparent in Figures 8C2.1.1–C2.2.3: weighting the similarity between a pair of terms by the lengths of the document descriptions in which they co-occur or occur does not, in other words, help, though this is not surprising because, as we saw in Chapter 7, though there is considerable variation in document length, most descriptions are near the average. When these two coefficients are compared with the cosine coefficient, we find, if we again refer to the figures mentioned, that the cosine coefficient seems to work less well, though not very much less well.

It is difficult to get a very clear picture of the consequences of using these different definitions, because the different classification procedures we have examined do not exploit the information contained in a similarity matrix in the same way: the contrast between clump-type class definitions and those of the other three types is particularly important in this respect. Thus if we want to check the consequences of using the various similarity definitions against different class definitions, we have as we saw to use a high explicit threshold on the matrix for any clump-type class definition; otherwise, we can only compare all the different similarity definitions for clumps. The general characteristics of the various similarity definitions can, however, be illustrated by their effect on clump classifications, as shown in Figures 8C2.2.1–C2.2.3, and it must be emphasised that the relations between them hold through changes in other parameters, like the vocabulary one, for example. Similar difficulties appear in evaluating the effect of the method of control, and the level at which this control is imposed: it really only applies to clumps. In the context of these type 4 classifications, however, we tried two threshold levels, and as Figures 8C2.3.1–C2.3.3 show, the effects of different choices here are very marked. A high threshold, that is, leads to a very substantial improvement in performance for clumps, irrespective of, for instance, the choice of clump definition, and of the choice of values for the other parameters under the other main headings.

The overall conclusions we can draw about the treatment of similarities, therefore, are that we have no good grounds for preferring one of the unweighted or weighted definitions to the other, so that we may as well choose the former because it is easier to apply, though the evidence that we have suggests that both of these give better results than the cosine coefficient. As far as the method of control goes, on the other hand, it is apparent that

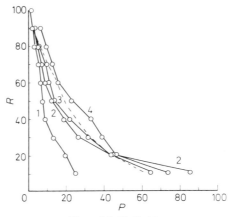

Figure 9.2 Similarities

1	full	unwTan, 7	clumps, 100/P	simple, class
			P = 1, no grad	
2		unwTan, 19		
3	restr	unwTan, 7		
4		unwTan, 19		

changes in the threshold level have very marked effects on the forms of classification for which they are appropriate, with conspicuous improvements in retrieval performance accompanying higher thresholds. These points are illustrated by some representative performance curves in Figure 9.2.

The reasons why these different alternatives lead to these conclusions are clear enough. As just mentioned, the character of the document descriptions is such that the unweighted and weighted Tanimoto definitions would be unlikely to produce different results. The cosine coefficient, on the other hand, is not really suited to binary incidence data of the kind with which we are dealing: it is more appropriately used as a matching coefficient, with weighted index terms, in the manner described by Keen[1]. (It has been extensively used for this purpose by the SMART project, since it has been found to give much better results in this context than other correlation coefficients[2].) The explanation for the fact that a much better performance is achieved when a high global threshold is used, as opposed to a low one, is more conveniently discussed in connection with our actual classification experiments, and I shall therefore return to it when we consider the conclusions we can draw from these.

200

Conclusions on the classification tests

Our main results, indeed, concern the actual approaches to the formation of the term classification itself that we have investigated. It will be remembered that the comparisons here were the most complicated ones, and we have therefore to be careful about the conclusions we draw from them, though the main points are solid enough. Thus we have to consider the alternative types of classification, the consequences of different definitions for some of these types, of different specifications for the definitions, and also of control value for one clump definition. We can, however, identify the more important consequences of different choices of values for these variables.

If we first consider the four types of classification, strings, stars, cliques and clumps, taking as representatives the choices of definition and so on which worked best in each case, so that we have strings, small stars, high-threshold cliques and also 100/P clumps formed from a similarity matrix to which a high global threshold had been applied (for compatibility), the only conclusion we can arrive at is that there is no really striking difference between these classifications. The relevant reference for Chapter 8 is to Figure 8C3.1.1 but since this can be described as the main conclusion concerning our classifications, the performance curves are reproduced in Figure 9.3 here. This conclusion about the relative merits of the four types is, moreover, borne out by the performances obtained in other tests in which values of variables under other headings were changed, as shown in Figures 8C3.1.2–C3.1.4. We have not, for purely practical reasons, been able to make completely exhaustive tests in this area, but those we have carried out are sufficiently varied to show that the result is a genuine one.

Looking now at the alternatives of each type, it will be remembered that we did not try more than one string classification, because the definition using the most strongly connected elements seemed, if not the most sensible, at least as sensible as the alternative involving elements with connections greater than a specified threshold; and there was no point in trying another length specification because most of the strings found terminated naturally after one or two elements: there was thus no reason for looking for longer strings than those permitted, and there equally seemed little point in looking for still shorter ones. Under stars we again worked with only one definition, for similar reasons, but we actually tested two different sizes. The experiments with these, which are illustrated in Figures 8C3.2.1–C3.2.4, show that classes based on the smaller size specification, that is limited to 4 as opposed to 6 members (or more if equal connections occur), give consistently better results in retrieval, irrespective of the values assigned to other parameters. For cliques the situation is very similar: here again we worked with only one definition, and two specifications of threshold, namely 21 and 16; and we found that cliques based on the higher threshold lead to a better retrieval performance, as we can see in Figures 8C3.3.1–C3.3.4.

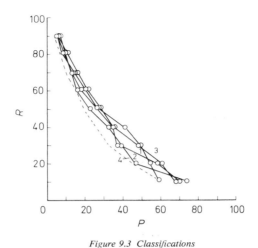

Figure 9.3 Classifications

1	restr	unwTan, 7	strings, 7	simple, class
2			stars, 4	
3			cliques, 21	
4		unwTan, 19	clumps, 100/P	
			P = 1, no grad	

The tests for clump-type classifications were more complex, but we can still draw some useful general conclusions from them. Here we tried two alternative definitions, with a choice of two subsidiary specifications for the 100/P definition; and if we again take the better of the latter, and compare the results obtained for the different definitions, keeping the controls constant, we find that clumps based on the 100/P definition generally give more satisfactory results, and that this is true if changes in the values of other parameters like those under the similarity heading, which affect the performance of clump classifications considerably, are made, or if different options are exercised in the controls on the formation of this kind of classification. This is apparent in Figures 8C3.4.1–C3.4.5; but as the investigation of clump classifications has a historic importance for our project, some selected curves are given here in Figure 9.3a. This result is not really surprising; as we saw in Chapter 3, the poor performance obtained with SAB[2] clumps was responsible for the extension of our research in classification for retrieval purposes in general; and though an improved performance may be expected if a high similarity threshold is used, these definitions do not work very well. At the same time, it is of interest that the 100/P definition does give a performance which is competitive with that of the best classification of other types, so that we cannot say that clump-type classifications are in principle inappropriate. As far as the subsidiary choices under this head are concerned, it seems to be the case that setting P = 1 for

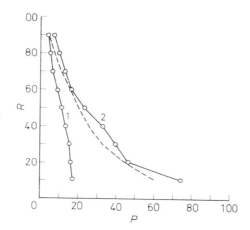

Figure 9.3a Comparison of clump classifications

1	restr	unwTan, 19	clumps, SAB²	simple, class
2			no grad	
			clumps, 100/P	
			P = 1, no grad	

the 100/P definition gives consistently better results, as shown in Figures 8C3.5.1–C3.5.3. The gradient test, on the other hand, does not behave in a consistent way: its effect is sometimes quite marked, though the relative merit of the null and genuine test is not always the same, while in other cases there is no real difference between the two. The marked differences are, however, associated with the use of SAB² clumps, and clumps of this kind are so eccentric (as we saw in Chapter 3) that the random behaviour of the test is not surprising. Otherwise, in so far as there is any difference between the null and genuine tests, it is in favour of the former. So we can definitely conclude that there is no point in using the test; and it is indeed a good example of the classificatory refinements we have consistently found are necessary.

The general conclusion to be drawn about the alternative approaches to classification we have investigated, therefore, is that any class definition of the four types which selects very strongly connected sets of elements is to be preferred, because the resulting classifications will give a better retrieval performance than those containing less well-connected or diffused classes. As far as the range of alternatives under the heading of clumps go, it is clearly the case that the 100/P definition works better than the SAB², though the alternative subsidiary choices do not have marked effects.

The reasons for these results seem to be quite clear. The implications of the most important one, namely the lack of difference between the performances of the best classifications of each type, will be more fully considered later; but there is little doubt that the reason for this lack of difference is that these classifications are essentially much the same. In confining grouping to items which are very strongly connected only, as these successful classifications do, the same connections tend to be picked up. The emphasis on strong connections is explicit where strings and cliques and the best clumps are concerned, but stars based on a comparatively small size specification are of course similarly restricted. As far as the differences in performance for the alternative definitions of each type are concerned, the reason why the smaller-size stars and high-threshold cliques worked best is that in both cases sets of more strongly connected elements are selected: again, the implications of this will be considered later. For clumps, the reasons for the superiority of the 100/P clumps were really given earlier: thus the SAB^2 clumps were defective because terms were somewhat randomly grouped, the definition being rather unstable in the sense that changes at other points, say in the matrix threshold, can influence the formation of clumps in a very striking way. The differences following the two specifications of P can be explained by the fact that where P $= 1$ the internal coherence of a clump is emphasised at the expense of its external separateness; where P $= \frac{1}{2}$ the emphasis on the internal coherence is less. Thus where the 100/P definition is used with P $= 1$, we are again obtaining classes confined to strongly connected elements.

Conclusions on the retrieval tests

When we look at the effect of the different retrieval modes we have examined, the situation is more complicated, or at least the results are less easily explained. Thus if we start with the two modes of retrieval, namely substituting classes for terms, and combining them, and again take the best alternative under each head, we find that the plain class match, representing the former, works very much better than the exclusive term and class match, representing the latter, in some cases, but this difference is not impervious to changes in the other parameters, as we can see in Figures 8C4.1.1–C4.1.4. The performance obtained with the best simple definition varies very widely, according to the vocabulary used, and the classification, while the performance given by the mixed definition varies very little. This is because the latter is effectively the same as that for terms alone, being neither markedly better nor markedly worse, so that the relation between the two search procedures is, therefore, hardly surprisingly, not a constant one: with some classifications we do better with simple class matches than we do with terms, and with others we do less well, while the mixed match performance is always close to that for terms. Some illustrative results are reproduced in Figure 9.4. With respect to the different methods of carrying out retrieval in the simple mode, it seems that the frequency definition,

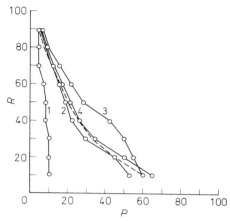

Figure 9.4 Retrieval modes

1	full	unwTan, 7	strings, 7	simple, class
2				mixed, excl, +1
3	restr			simple, class
4				mixed, excl, +1

which can be regarded as a more sophisticated version of the plain class match, has no effect: the results are the same, whatever other changes are made. The same applies to the various methods of using the mixed mode: there is no difference to speak of between the performance obtained with the exclusive definition and the inclusive one, or between upgrading documents selected through additional class matches by one level or by as many levels as there are such additional matches.

The overall conclusions to be drawn from our experiments with this parameter, therefore, are that the substitution of classes for terms in request and document specifications can be much more effective than their combination, and that as effective results can be obtained if this is done with straightforward class matches as with matches controlled by class frequencies. The reasons for the difference between the two modes are not clear: the effect of the term matches is clearly outweighing that of the classes in mixed matches, but it is not obvious why this should happen, given that the same classes may be very effective if they are used on their own, though the fact that retrieval performance for the mixed mode is primarily determined by terms explains the absence of any real differences between the various ways of manipulating this sort of match. This question will, however, be considered more fully in the general discussion of our investigations in Chapter 10. The absence of any improvement in performance for the frequency version of the simple mode seems to be due to the fact, that the numbers of classes characterising documents is so much larger than the numbers characterising requests, that no selection is made. It is also possible that the fact that terms may occur in more than one class, combined with the fact the numbers of classes in which elements occur are very variable, and are apparently lacking in significance, may mean that we cannot use frequency matches as we want to use them, in a discriminating way.

Summary of conclusions

Given this detailed analysis of our experimental results, we can now summarise our main conclusions about the four sets of parameters we have examined, as follows:

(1) The distributional characteristics of the vocabulary which is being classified are important, and it is necessary to take them into account in the formation of the classification; more specifically, suppressing the grouping possibilities of frequent terms so that they have to be matched explicitly, and not by substitution, leads to a better retrieval performance than that which is obtained when all the terms in the vocabulary are grouped, irrespective of the choices which are made at other points in the classification and retrieval process.

(2) The choice of similarity definition, within broad limits, does not affect retrieval performance very much. So the unweighted similarity definition can be recommended as both easy to work with and logically sound.

(3) The choice of a class type from the set we have considered need not matter, in the sense that we can obtain equally good results with classifications of each type. That of a class definition and specification is, however, very important, because different choices can lead to wide variations in performance in general, irrespective of the values assigned to other variables. Thus strings, small stars, high threshold cliques and 100P clumps, with $P = 1$ and a matrix to which a high global threshold has previously been applied, though a gradient test is unnecessary, give the best results.

(4) The use of simple modes of retrieval where terms are replaced by classes, as opposed to mixed modes in which the two are combined, will give a much better retrieval performance, provided that the correct selections under the other headings have been made.

It will of course be clear from this list that we cannot altogether behave as if we can assign values to the different system variables in isolation. While it is generally true, in other words, that the same consequences follow the assignment of alternative values to a given variable, whatever values are assigned to other parameters, so that one value gives a better performance than another, it is also true that this may not be the best retrieval performance that we can obtain, or even a better performance than that of unclassified terms. We may find, for instance, that small stars consistently work better than large ones, but the performance we obtain with small stars can vary very much according to the other parameter values involved; so that, for instance, small stars based on the restricted vocabulary not merely work better than unclassified terms, but as well as any other classification, while this is not true of small stars and the full vocabulary, though with either vocabulary, smaller stars work better than larger ones. While the relative merits of different choices of value for a given parameter may be consistent, their absolute merits may vary according to the values assigned to other parameters. So what we are particularly interested in are those combinations of values which give an absolutely good performance, that is which give the best performance for classifications, and which also give a better performance than unclassified terms. For the question we have to answer explicitly now is whether any of our classifications do work better than unclassified terms, and if so, which these are. We can then go on to see why these classifications work, and whether they have any common features which explain their success.

Suppose, then, that we put together the options under each of our four headings that we have found are individually preferable. This means that we should take the restricted vocabulary, because this works better than the others, either the unweighted or weighted similarity definitions, so say the unweighted, with a global matrix threshold of 19 if we want to form a clump-type classification, strings, stars 4, cliques T21 or 100/P clumps (with $P = 1$ and no gradient test) as class definitions, and retrieval by simple substitution and matching. In all of these four cases we obtain a retrieval performance curve which is (but for one point) wholly to the right of, and hence on the preferred side of, the unclassified term performance curve. We obtain, that is, recall/precision curves which have the characteristics we required of our classificatory curves in Chapter 2, as shown in Figure 9.3 above. And if we apply our very crude significance test, we find that all these curves are significantly better than the term curve. It is also the case,

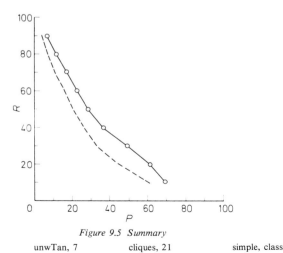

Figure 9.5 Summary

restr   unwTan, 7   cliques, 21   simple, class

as the detailed results and previous discussion will have made clear, that none of the other combinations or parameter values consistently approach this level of performance.

Thus the overall conclusion we can draw from our series of experiments is that for this test collection at least, using an automatically obtained term classification in a certain way does enable us to obtain a better retrieval performance than we obtain with the unclassified terms alone, as we can see from the representative example of our final Summary Figure 9.5. So the questions we have to turn to now are firstly, why can we achieve this result; and secondly, given the apparent differences between the techniques used to obtain them, what is it about the four best classifications just listed which means that they give the same results? Presumably, whatever they have in common will be responsible for their similar performances, and we should therefore ask what their common properties are. We can then go on to consider these results in relation to the conclusions reached by other projects, and what the prognostications are for automatic classification for retrieval in general.

REFERENCE

1. *ISR–13*, Chapter III
2. *ISR–12*, Chapter III

Chapter 10

Interpretations, Predictions and Comparisons

SUMMARY

This chapter is devoted to an analysis of the conclusions drawn in Chapter 9, with a view to showing what features of the collection and ways of describing it by classificatory index languages are responsible for the results obtained. In particular an attempt is made to characterise the effect of the best classifications on retrieval. Thus the discussion of a simple model shows that the improvement in performance given by these classifications, over that of keywords, must be primarily attributed to the 'promotional' effect of the classes, in the sense that the classes strengthen the matches between relevant documents and requests, without correspondingly strengthening that of non-relevant ones. For a given notional matching level, that is, using classes leads to the retrieval at that level of relevant documents which are only pulled out at lower levels by terms, without an equal promotion of non-relevant documents. The improvement in recall at the given level thus leads to an improvement in precision as well, which accounts for the characteristic relation between the term recall/precision curve and that of a good classification. On this basis, the different performances of the vocabularies can be accounted for, in terms of their capacity for discrimination as opposed to their sheer capacity to retrieve documents: with the frequent terms grouped, for instance, the number of documents retrieved is so great that this must lead to the retrieval of non-relevant documents whenever relevant ones are promoted by class matches. An alternative way of looking at the effects of the vocabularies and classifications is by referring to some general hypotheses, and the way in which an individual classificatory indexing language reconciles them. Thus the Relevance Hypothesis states that the closer the match between a document and a request, the more chance there is of the document being relevant to the request; and the Classification Hypothesis states that co-occurrence in documents is a good base for providing sets of inter-substitutible terms which will strengthen matches; but the Frequency Hypothesis states that since the minimum number of documents retrieved by a class is determined by the most frequently occurring term in the class, if the number of relevant documents to be retrieved is very small in relation to the size of the collection, then enlarging the scope of matches by including frequent terms in classes will tend to promote the retrieval of non-relevant documents as much as, or more than, relevant ones. Thus the problem is to reconcile these features of description and retrieval, and the reason why the restricted vocabulary and classes confined to strongly connected terms only are more successful than the alternatives, is because they balance these factors best. The next question is why superficially different classifications work equally well. The answer is that on the one hand, the underlying sets of class-mates for a term are similar, though their distributions differ, and on the other that the remaining differences cancel one another out. This last point leads indeed to a fundamental one, namely that it is possible that we cannot expect a given permitted substitution to be of value on all occasions. If we have two similar but not identical classifications, they are of value in so far as their common groupings represent substitutions which are generally helpful, while their variations in grouping represent substitutions which are sometimes helpful, so that one classification works in one case, and the other in another. The chapter concludes with some comparisons between our project and others, followed by a discussion of some future lines of research, with a reference to possible practical implications.

Reasons for the test results

In the previous chapter we presented the main conclusion we can draw from our experiments, which is that when a term classification is formed and used in a certain way, it gives noticeably better results than unclassified keywords, at least for our test collection. The important question we now have to consider is why we obtained this result, and what light it throws on the ideas about the value of a retrieval thesaurus, and the character it should have, with which we started. Do the successful classifications satisfy our demand for a device which improves both precision and recall, for example? What are their linguistic, classificatory and retrieval properties? Can we make any predictions, using our test results, about the general value and general characteristics of term classifications for other collections?

The reasons for our result will to some extent be apparent, given the points made in the last chapter about the various component parameters of the kind of retrieval system with which we have been working: the object of this chapter is to look at these points in more detail, in an attempt to see exactly what features of the successful classificatory languages are responsible for their performance, and how the improvement over unclassified keywords is obtained.

To start with, we saw in Chapter 9 that the restricted vocabulary works better than the others, and we have discussed the reasons for the differences in performance of the various vocabularies, and for the superior performance of the restricted vocabulary, given the character of the test requests and documents, at some length. Essentially, the point seems to be that the frequent terms must be retained because, for these requests at any rate, they promote recall; but as they introduce too much noise if they are grouped, the best course is to include them in the classification as unit classes. The non-frequent terms, on the other hand, are primarily precision aids, in the sense that they retrieve relevant documents rather than non-relevant ones. So that the vocabulary which contains both frequent terms and non-frequent ones is more effective than the vocabularies depending only on one or the other. The question then is, what does classifying the non-frequent terms only do for us? It seems to be the case with the full vocabulary that grouping the frequent terms degrades performance so much that any benefits to be obtained by grouping non-frequent terms, whatever they are, are lost: this is shown by the fact that the full vocabulary performance is worse than that of the corresponding complete set of terms, while the performance of the restricted vocabulary is better, the difference between the two vocabularies being precisely in the treatment of frequent terms. But if the restricted vocabulary performance is better, not only than that of the full vocabulary, but than that of the complete set of terms, why is it better? When non-frequent terms only are grouped in the non-frequent vocabulary, the resulting performance curve is worse than that of the corresponding set of terms.

Problems of comparison

The difficulty which arises in discussing these questions is that of making detailed comparisons between performance curves. We can indeed look at the standardised graphs we have used, and make *some* remarks about them. Thus if we take the graphs for the different term sets of Figure 8T1.1, and star classifications for the different vocabularies of Figure 8T1.2, which are reproduced in Figure 10.1 for convenience, we can say, for example, that the curves for the complete set of terms and full vocabulary stars differ in that, though they are effectively the same at high recall, they differ substantially at low recall, precision for the latter being much lower than precision for the former; there is a gradual divergence so that there is a noticeable difference between the middles of the curves too. But can we make any more precise remarks than this? We would like to be able to, so that we can make specific statements about the reasons for the differences between performance curves. It is true that with any standardised or normalised curves we can make further remarks, of the kind which can be illustrated by saying that at a recall level of 50 per cent the two curves just referred to have a precision of 20 per cent and 8 per cent respectively; if a ranked search output is used, analogous remarks can be made about performance up to a certain cutoff point. But can we do more?

What we would really like, is to be able to make remarks of the following kind: if we have retrieved a relevant document on a specific coordination level using terms, we find that in substituting classes for terms, we have retrieved it on the next higher level, say. To study the effects of a classification compared with terms, that is, we would like to be able to make precise statements about the consequences of the substitution, in terms of changes in the levels at which documents are retrieved. Now it is true in wanting information about the behaviour of individual requests or documents, we are wanting something which cannot be obtained from overall performance curves of the kind we have been working with hitherto. But this is not the real problem. We could equally ask for information of the same kind about sets of requests. We could, that is, ask what the effects of substituting classes for terms are for the sets of documents obtained for a set of requests. In either case we want to say that at a given level we have obtained x relevant documents and y non-relevant ones with classes, where we obtained p relevant documents and q non-relevant ones with terms; or, alternatively, that we have changed the recall and precision ratios for the given level in such and such ways. If we can make statements of this kind about individual levels, we can also make remarks about the total effects over all levels: for example, we can say that using a classification promotes relevant documents, if we can see that the recall ceiling of 100 per cent is reached at level 3 with classes, where it was reached only at level 1 with terms. Whether we are interested in performance for sets of requests or individual requests, and for sets of documents or individual documents, we want to be able to say the same kind of thing; so that deciding to go behind the set results and look at individual performance is entirely a matter of choice.

In the present context, the sort of thing we would like to be able to do is use the results—recall/precision curves or retrieved document figures—for the two subsets of terms, and sub-vocabularies, to throw some light on the performance we obtain for the complete set and full and restricted vocabularies; but these results are not comparable in the required way, because the numbers of coordination levels involved are different. And the same difficulty arises if we want to compare the performance for a given term set, and the corresponding vocabulary, because there is in general no correspondence between the numbers of terms specifying requests or documents and the numbers of classes. We have in fact already encountered this problem, because it arises, as we saw in Chapter 5, in averaging over requests, and indeed in standardising to obtain comparable curves. We are simply approaching it from a different angle now. The point which matters here, however, is that though standardising (whether properly done or by our *ad hoc* graph-based method) makes it possible to compare different retrieval performance results correctly, the comparisons we can make are limited in kind, and we cannot make the detailed remarks we would like to make about the effects of replacing one retrieval method by another. With our crude standardised curves we can only make either overall remarks about their comparable shape, or statements about precision values for given recall levels; we cannot, however, connect these at all with the actual pattern of document retrieval. With a procedure where standardisation is pushed further back, as it were, as in cases where a ranked output is used, we can compare the positions at which documents are retrieved; but in this case, the fact that the request-document match function is not the simple coordination one, makes it very difficult to correlate changes in position with changes in document and request specifications, where what we would really like to be able to say is precisely that, for example, the effect of replacing terms by classes is that of adding a matching term to a given number of matching terms.

Given, then, that we have to content ourselves with relatively general and informal remarks, can we provide some explanations for our results? Here it must be recognised that we can say more in some cases than in others. We can make some useful informal comparisons between different ways of treating the complete set of terms and its subsets in classification, but we cannot say very much about the reasons for the differences between the complete set of terms and the classified frequent terms, for example, because these languages differ in more than one respect: they differ, that is, both in the presence and absence of terms, and in the presence and absence of classes. We cannot, therefore, attribute any performance differences between them unequivocally either to the difference between them with respect to terms, or to the difference with respect to the use of a classification. We can really only compare term sets and vocabularies which differ only in one respect, whether this concerns terms or classes. Thus we can make a series of paired comparisons, as follows:

frequent terms	all terms
non-frequent terms	all terms
frequent terms	frequent classes
non-frequent terms	non-frequent classes
all terms	full classes
all terms	restricted classes
full classes	restricted classes

but we cannot compare

frequent terms	full classes
frequent terms	restricted classes
non-frequent terms	full classes
non-frequent terms	restricted classes
all terms	frequent classes
all terms	non-frequent classes

In these cases we can only put forward rather tentative explanations for performance differences, because the languages concerned differ in more than one respect, and we cannot certainly identify the specific features of the languages which are responsible for given performance differences: we can only attempt to do this indirectly, and therefore uncertainly, by references to any explanations we can provide for differences between pairs in the first set.

The retrieval effect of classes compared with terms

After these preliminaries, we can start to consider our main problem, namely the effect of using a classification, and especially the successful classifications of the restricted vocabulary, by comparing the term vocabularies represented in Figure 10.1: these comparisons will supply us with some background information for the term/class comparisons which are really important, though they can only, as we have seen, be either of the informal kind we first considered, or of the somewhat more precise but still inadequate kind based on specific standardised recall levels. The main points about the term sets are in fact quite simple: namely that the performance of the frequent set of terms, compared with the complete one, is characterised by a recall ceiling which is almost as high as that reached by the complete set (which is in turn almost 100 per cent), but that precision falls away towards the higher coordination levels. The non-frequent set of terms, on the other hand, produces a performance curve which is very close to that of the complete set for high to medium precision and low to medium recall, but the recall ceiling is very much lower. Thus there is little doubt that for the complete set, the frequent terms are primarily responsible for recall, and the

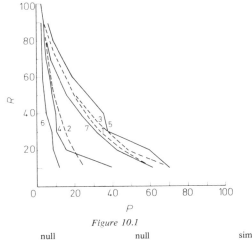

Figure 10.1

1	full/restr	null	null	simple, term
2	freq			
3	infreq			
4	full	unwTan, 7	stars, 4	simple, class
5	restr			
6	freq			
7	infreq			

non-frequent ones for precision. This is not surprising. What we cannot, however, do is identify the relative contributions, at a given point on the performance curve for the complete set, of the two components; this is because combining the frequent and non-frequent request and document specifications to form the complete ones changes their character in a not necessarily simple way, and this in turn means that the performance of the combined set is most unlikely to be simply related to that of the two components.

But now, what happens with a classification? It is true that we cannot demonstrate that a classification has certain effects in given retrieval situations, for the reasons we considered earlier; but we can make some inferences about what is happening in general, from our performance curves and figures. The best way of attacking the problem, however, is via an illustration where we do have the same number of coordination levels for the languages being compared, so that we can make the specific remarks we cannot make in real life. This example should provide us with information about the reasons for performance differences, though we may only be able to say that they are responsible for the differences between our real results in a broad rather than specific way. Suppose, then, that we have a request containing 3 terms. We will imagine that this retrieves, using term matches, at coordination level 3, as follows:

R (relevant documents)	$-R$ (non-relevant documents)
2	2

Thus if we assume that we have 3 relevant documents altogether for the request, we get a recall value of 67 per cent and a precisión ratio of 50 per cent. Now suppose that in this hypothetical example, we have one and only one term class for each term, and none of the terms co-occur in a class with one another: this means that replacing terms by classes will lead to matches on the same number of levels. So that if we now substitute classes for terms, retrieval on term level 3 is replaced by retrieval on class level 3. Clearly, in this case, whatever is retrieved on term level 3 is necessarily also retrieved on class level 3. Thus on class level 3, we must retrieve at least those relevant documents that we retrieved on term level 3. The important fact about using classes in this situation, in other words, is that we cannot lower recall: if we retrieved 2 relevant documents before, we will still retrieve 2 relevant documents, at this same level. If we retrieve more documents without retrieving more relevant documents, on the other hand, this will lower precision; thus if we say that we retrieve 2 more non-relevant documents, so that the picture is

$$
\begin{array}{cc}
R & -R \\
2 & 4
\end{array}
$$

we have a recall ratio of 67 per cent as before, but a precision ratio of only 33 per cent, as opposed to the previous 50 per cent.

But though we cannot lower recall, we can, if we still assume that we retrieve more documents than we did with terms, raise recall. Thus if we imagine that using classes pulls out the remaining relevant document at this level, this will give us a recall ratio of 100 per cent. As far as precision in this case is concerned, however, we may either improve it, or keep it the same, or lower it, according to whether we retrieve any additional non-relevant documents or not, and according to how many of these there are if we do retrieve any. Thus if we retrieve the extra relevant document without retrieving any extra non-relevant ones, compared with terms, we will get

$$
\begin{array}{cc}
R & -R \\
3 & 2
\end{array}
$$

so that precision is now 60 per cent instead of 50 per cent; but if we retrieve one extra non-relevant document with the relevant one, we get

$$
\begin{array}{cc}
R & -R \\
3 & 3
\end{array}
$$

which means that precision is the same as before, namely 50 per cent, though recall has increased; while if we get more non-relevant documents, say 4, so that we have

$$
\begin{array}{cc}
R & -R \\
3 & 6
\end{array}
$$

this gives us a precision ratio of 33 per cent, compared with 50 per cent, for the increase in recall. Thus retrieving extra relevant documents through classes may or may not improve precision, but it must improve recall. The range of possibilities compared with the initial term retrieval results, and assuming that extra documents are pulled out with classes, can be illustrated by the table which follows, in which the changes in recall and precision values effected by using classes as opposed to terms are indicated, along with the actual values:

	R	$-R$	$R\%$	$P\%$	Change to	
					R	P
terms 1.	2	2	67	50		
classes 2.	2	4	67	33	0	−
3.	3	2	100	60	+	+
4.	3	3	100	50	+	0
5.	3	6	100	33	+	−

If we now plot the positions of these recall/precision pairs we get the results shown in Figure 10.2.

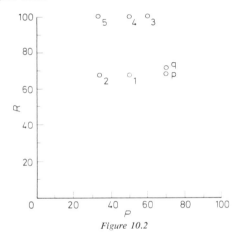

Figure 10.2

But now if we look at the example we see one very important fact, namely that we cannot improve precision without improving recall; we cannot, that is, obtain the point p instead of 1. For we cannot reduce the number of relevant documents retrieved, and the only way of improving precision without improving recall would be in this way. By definition, we must re-trieve as many documents, both relevant and non-relevant, as we did with terms. The only way of improving the ratio of relevant to non-relevant documents is by increasing the number of relevant documents without increasing the number of non-relevant ones, which give us point 3, and not point p. (Though it must be remembered that for large sets of requests we might get the point q, which is very near p; it is, however, above p, and this means an increase in recall as well as one in precision.) We cannot, in

216

this model, move the point representing retrieval performance for a given level only to the right, and not up as well; and we cannot, of course, move it downwards in any direction.

Clearly, if we imagine ourselves making consistent changes of this kind for every request and every coordination level, we get the kind of performance curve displacement we originally considered in Chapter 2; thus if we have a curve 1, and displace it to match the point changes of the previous plot, in a consistent way, we get the set of curves of Figure 10.3.

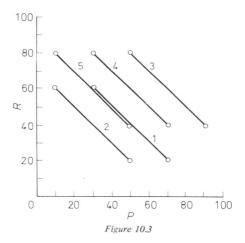

Figure 10.3

Now if we in fact have a situation where we cannot set up correspondences between specific points, representing individual levels, we can still compare curves as whole. Thus take the two curves of Figure 10.4:

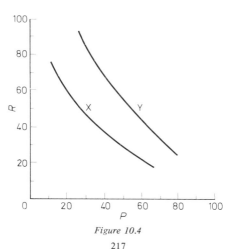

Figure 10.4

217

we cannot connect any point on X (other than the ends of course) with any point on Y, though we at least know that the point cannot be linked with a point at lower recall on Y. But we can make the kind of remark about the relationship of the one curve to the other that we made in the previous case about the relationship between points.

Relevant document promotion

If we now return to the real performance curves, what can we say about them on this basis? Looking back to the term performance we considered earlier, we can display their relationships, taking the complete set of terms as the standard, as follows:

	R	P	
all terms	0	0	
frequent terms	0	—	(difference increasing towards higher matching levels)
non-frequent terms	—	0	(difference increasing towards lower matching levels)

In considering the classifications, we shall take the star classifications as representatives, as before, primarily because the star groups for the restricted vocabulary were among those giving a good performance, but also because we have not tested other classifications exhaustively across all the vocabularies. If we first compare the vocabularies and corresponding term sets we get

	R	P	
frequent terms	0	0	
frequent classes	0	—	(difference increasing towards higher levels)
non-frequent terms	0	0	
non-frequent classes	+	—	(R difference increasing towards lower levels, P difference towards lower levels)
all terms	0	0	
full classes	0	—	(difference increasing towards higher levels)
restricted classes	+	+	(difference at middle levels)

In the last case, in other words, which is the one we are most interested in, we can conclude, using the previous example, that we must have an improvement in both recall and precision, because we would otherwise not get the relative positioning of the two curves that we have. And the question now is exactly how this increase is achieved. Clearly, it must be the result of an increase in the retrieval of relevant documents at comparable matching levels, without a corresponding retrieval of non-relevant documents, so that the more favourable precision ratio accompanies a better recall ratio. What we have, in other words, is a promotion of relevant documents; we can only

218

get a shift in the position of the curve of the kind we have got, if in fact a relevant document which was previously retrieved at level x is now retrieved at a level comparable with some higher level $x + n$. We have to put the change in this way, because we of course do not have actual corresponding levels. In the earlier illustration, we could say that if a new relevant document was retrieved at level 3, it must have been promoted from a lower level, say 2; with our real classifications we do not, as we have seen, have the same number of levels, so we have to assume that there are comparable levels, without knowing which these are: we cannot say that class level 8, for example, corresponds with term level 4, but there must be some class level which matches term level 4.

Thus the use of the restricted classification promotes the retrieval of relevant documents more than that of non-relevant ones, or rather, which is more important, promotes them at the middle and higher levels where the concurrent gain in precision is most noticeable. This point is brought out in another way if we look at the number of documents retrieved in total (we cannot, unfortunately, of course, consider the numbers at higher levels). The relevant figures for terms and classes, with percentage increases for the latter over the former are as follows:

	Terms		Classes		% increase	
	R	−R	R	−R	R	−R
all terms, full classes	192	4 759	199	7 619	3.6	60.1
all terms, restricted classes	192	4 759	198	6 019	3.1	26.5
frequent terms, frequent classes	183	4 515	195	7 589	6.6	68.1
non-frequent terms, non-frequent classes	119	741	166	3 485	39.5	370.3

It is quite clear here that the generally substantial increase in the numbers of non-relevant documents retrieved with classes, assuming they are evenly distributed over all levels, means that though there is also an increase in the numbers of relevant documents retrieved, we cannot expect an improvement in precision; and this is borne out by the results for the frequent and full classes. The decline in precision in these cases must be due to the wide distribution of frequent terms, and their enhanced retrieving power when grouped, which must lead to many false drops. With the restricted vocabulary the total number of non-relevant documents retrieved is lower, but the increase is still quite large, and the better curve in this case must be due to the fact that the non-relevant documents are predominantly retrieved at low levels. This is supported by the result for the non-frequent vocabulary, where precision is almost maintained, with a considerable improvement in recall; in this case the total number of non-relevant documents retrieved is smaller than that for the restricted vocabulary, but it is still quite large, and represents an enormous increase over the corresponding total for the non-frequent terms. The fact that the overall performance is still quite good must be due to the substantial increase in the number of relevant documents retrieved, even though the total is not as high as for the restricted vocabulary; at the same time, the fact that the non-frequent class curve does not represent an overall improvement over the corresponding term curve, in spite of the gain in relevant documents, must be due, not so much to the percentage increase in non-relevant documents, or even to the total number retrieved, as to their distribution over all the levels.

With the restricted vocabulary we must thus have a situation where we are retrieving proportionately more relevant documents, and hence improving precision, in the sense that we are promoting relevant documents more than non-relevant ones through the increased matching potential of classes, as opposed to terms; and this must be attributable solely to the fact that the non-frequent terms are being classified: these produce more matches than terms alone, and are more likely to produce relevant matches than classes containing frequent terms; but we need the frequent terms themselves to maintain adequate request and document specifications. The non-frequent classes do a great deal to overcome the limited matching potential of the non-frequent term specifications, but clearly we will do better if we start with the fuller specifications provided by the complete set of terms. It is a general rule that increasing the number of items characterising a request (up to a point we are nowhere near reaching) increases its specificity, so the more terms we have to substitute classes for, the better off we shall be; at the same time classes increase exhaustivity, that is the range of possible alternative matching items. The effectiveness of the classes for the non-frequent terms only in the restricted vocabulary therefore comes from the fact that they make requests more exhaustive, in, so to speak, the right direction: they permit the substitution of non-frequent terms for one another, which, because of their comparative rarity, are more likely to appear only in documents which are relevant to requests characterised by the original terms.

Analysis of one request

Perhaps the best way of driving all these points home is to look at a concrete example.

Consider Request 34, for instance. It concerns 'Work on flow in channels at low Reynolds (numbers)', which gives us the 4 terms

65	channel
298	low
642	flow
679	Reynolds

220

65 and 298 being non-frequent terms, and 642 and 679 frequent, the actual numbers of documents for the terms being

65	5
298	17
642	144
679	27

If we now take the 5 relevant documents, we find that the request terms match them as follows:

65	1 351			1 966	
298					
642	1 351	1 964	1 965	1 966	1 967
679	1 351	1 964	1 965		

and when we take the request and match it against the whole collection containing 200 documents, we find that this gives us relevant and non-relevant documents containing 1, 2, 3 and 4 of the request terms respectively, as follows:

	R	$-R$	T
1	1	105	106
2	3	25	28
3	1	8	9
4		1	

we retrieve 144 documents altogether, that is, of which 5 are relevant. Of the 5 relevant documents, 1 is retrieved by matching 3 terms, 3 by matches on 2 terms, and 1 by 1 term; more importantly, in all cases one of the matching terms is the most frequent term, 642; and to obtain the last relevant document which matches only on this one term, we have to accept another 106 non-relevant ones as well. A further point of interest is that all the documents in which the other terms, 65, 298, and 679, occur contain 642 as well.

If we now look at the effects of classification for the full, restricted, frequent and non-frequent vocabularies respectively, using the 'standard' stars of size 4 given earlier as an example, we get the following stars for each of the request terms, the frequency of occurrence of the terms involved being given below:

full vocabulary

65	65	193	370	374	382	412	520
	5	18	7	1	2	1	17
298	298	593	679	708			
	17	9	27	26			
642	634	642	661	674			
	82	144	64	99			
679	669	679	707	708			
	47	27	29	26			

restricted vocabulary

65	65	193	370	374	382	412	520
	5	18	7	1	2	1	17
298	53	123	298	443	593		
	5	13	17	10	9		

frequent vocabulary

642	634	642	661	674
	82	144	64	99
679	669	679	707	708
	47	27	29	26

infrequent vocabulary: as restricted

But these are only the stars initiated by the request terms: the terms may also occur in other classes, along with other terms, and it is the over-all set of class-mates for the request terms which determine their retrieval performance. Inspection of the lists of classes in which each request term occurs in the four classifications therefore gives additional classes as follows:

full	65	+4
	298	—
	642	+11
	679	+5
restricted	65	+4
	298	—
frequent	642	+11
	679	+5
infrequent	65	+4
	298	—

Clearly, however, what matters is the numbers of class-mates generated for the request terms by these classes, and the frequency of occurrence of these terms, and their co-occurrences, in documents. Thus if we look at the first two vocabularies, as being of primary interest, we find that the set of class-mates for all the request terms taken together totals 42, with an average document frequency of 32, while for the restricted vocabulary we get a total of 16, with an average frequency of 10. In general, therefore, we find that with the full vocabulary, we expand the request specification to include a large number of predominantly frequent terms, which is not true of the restricted classes.

The effect on retrieval of this addition of frequent terms to classes, and hence to request specifications, is predictable. For this request, it can be introduced by comparisons between the numbers of relevant and non-relevant documents retrieved for the corresponding term and class versions of the request, as follows:

full				*restricted*				*frequent*				*non-frequent*			
T		*C*		*T*		*C*		*T*		*C*		*T*		*C*	
R	−R	R	−R	R	−R	R	−R	R	−R	R	−R	R	−R	R	−R
5	139	5	185	5	139	5	158	5	139	5	189	2	19	5	94

But the real situation is more complicated than that suggested by these simple totals. In particular, if we consider the retrieving power of the full and restricted vocabulary classes, based on the document distribution of the terms involved, we find that the number of extra non-relevant documents retrieved by the class-mates of the request terms for the restricted vocabulary is not large, while the matches with the relevant documents are reinforced by further term matches, though no additional relevant documents are retrieved. Thus if we inspect the class-mates of the two non-frequent terms in the restricted vocabulary classes, we find that the classes add 16 new terms to the request specification, with an average of 10 document occurrences each. These terms retrieve a further 19 documents (not including any new relevant ones). The important point about retrieval in this case, however, is that when the class retrieval performance is analysed out in terms of the actual numbers of term matches involved, we get a picture as follows (the original term retrieval performance being given as well for comparison):

	Class retrieval (as term matching)			*Term retrieval*	
	R	−R		R	−R
1.		103	1.	1	105
2.		24	2.	3	25
3.		14	3.	1	8
4.	3	9	4.		1
5.	1	2			
6.	1	3			
7.		1			
8.					
9.		1			
10.					
11.		1			

We find, in other words, that along with a general increase for class retrieval in the numbers of matching items for all the documents, from an average of 1.3 to one of 1.9, we obtain a much greater increase in the score for relevant documents, from an average of 2 to one of 4.6; and a striking feature of the results is that whereas, with terms alone, we had to retrieve all 144 documents to pull out the 5 relevant ones, with the classes we have to retrieve only 22 documents altogether to get the relevant ones: i.e. for a recall of 100 per cent we obtain a precision value of 11.7 per cent as opposed to one of 3.5 per cent. The last relevant document, which was only obtained through the frequent term 642 in term matching, is retrieved through 4 matches altogether with the classes. The promotional effect of the restricted vocabulary classes—that is, their ability, given an overall raising of the matching level, to ensure relatively more matches for relevant documents than non-relevant ones—is quite clear. In terms of the earlier discussion, therefore, we are improving recall, and with it precision.

The corresponding analysis for the full classes is tedious to carry out, but it is not difficult to see what the effect of the large number of frequently occurring items in expanded request term lists will be. They on the one hand lead to the retrieval of more documents altogether, but it is the extent to which terms co-occur in documents which is really critical: and it is apparent that with so many terms occurring so frequently, though the numbers of matching items for relevant documents will increase, the chances are high that there will be an equal, or even greater, increase in the number of matches for non-relevant documents, so that the relevant documents are not promoted.

The Relevance, Classification and Frequency Hypotheses

The way different features of the term sets and classes interact can also be looked at from another point of view, in terms of certain general hypotheses. Thus retrieval in general is based on what can be described as the Relevance Hypothesis, to the effect that the larger the number of matching descriptive items, for a request and document, the more likely the document is to be relevant to the request. This is obviously connected with the point about specificity we considered earlier. This hypothesis applies to any descriptive units, but it is convenient to connect it, in the present instance, with terms and classes. Now if we make use of a keyword thesaurus, we are also invoking what can be described as the Retrieval Classification Hypothesis, to the effect that co-occurrence as a basis for grouping makes for good swops, i.e. permits substitutions which retrieve relevant rather than irrelevant documents. This hypothesis has indeed been the basis of our work, and we encountered it as such in Chapter 1. As permitting more swops, moreover, makes for matches on more items, the conclusion which follows is that substituting a co-occurrence classification for terms should promote the retrieval of relevant documents. The general effect of substituting classes for terms in this way is well illustrated by specifications of requests and documents in terms of Boolean functions. Thus if items linked by 'and' represent a treatment of request specifications which promotes precision, while linking by 'or' promotes recall, when we substitute classes for terms we get a mixture of the two. For example, if we have two terms which we will imagine for simplicity's sake are replaced by unit classes, and a third term for which using classes provides one substitute, this means that the term request specification $a \cap b \cap c$ becomes the class specification $(a) \cap (b) \cap (c) \cup (d)$. This serves to bring out the fact that though substitution is primarily regarded as a recall device, so that permitting d as a substitute for c could retrieve more relevant documents, we are still combining d with a and b, so that we get a more precise specification of our request than we would if we only used a and b, because c did not match.

But as we have seen, swopping does not always lead to the preferential promotion of relevant documents, for example with the full vocabulary; and this can only be attributed to facts about the requests and documents concerned which are covered by what can be called the Frequency Hypothesis, though 'hypothesis' is perhaps a slightly misleading label in this case. This hypothesis concerns the retrieving power of descriptors; essentially it states that if we replace one set of descriptors by another with greater retrieving power, it is probable that in any case where the maximum number of relevant documents for a request is both very small in relation to the size of the collection, and most of these were obtained by the previous form of the request, we will mainly retrieve non-relevant documents with the new form, so that any benefits of the change are likely to be outweighed. Thus if we take the example just given, and find that the descriptor $(c \cup d)$ does match where c did not, we may obtain so many non-relevant documents that the fact that a relevant document containing d has been retrieved is not very noticeable.

Here in fact we have to do with hard statistics about our descriptive units. Suppose we have two terms which each occur m and n times respectively: clearly, if they are both used in a request, there are some documents we can expect to obtain purely on a statistical basis, irrespective of their relevance to the request; each descriptor—in this case each term—has some retrieving power, and we can in consequence expect to obtain a minimum number of documents on purely statistical grounds. Now if we have not a single term as a descriptor, but a class of terms, we will clearly expect in general that our class descriptor has a greater retrieving power than its source term descriptor (though the precise increase is not easy to specify); for although grouping terms as classes is justified by their tendency to co-occur, it is not usually true that all the members of a class co-occur in all and only the same documents. The total number of documents we can retrieve using the class will therefore be at least the number in which the most frequently occurring member of the class appears (which in itself may be more than the number in which the source term appears), and may well be more still. It then follows that if the number of relevant documents to be retrieved for the request is very small in relation to the size of the collection, as it usually is, nearly all the increase in the number of documents retrieved when the change from one type of descriptor to another is made will be due to the extra false drops which are pulled out by descriptors with a wider scope. And this is especially likely if the total number of relevant documents retrieved for a request or set of requests cannot be enlarged by the change, so that the object of the change can only be to promote relevant documents. The Frequency Hypothesis, then, conflicts with the Relevance and Classification Hypotheses: the latter in principle lead to an improvement in retrieval, because they increase the chances of relevant documents being retrieved; but if the classes are designed so that they have enormously greater retrieving power than the terms they have replaced, any gains which could be made on these grounds are counteracted by the losses due to the greater retrieving power of the classes, which must mostly be taken up by non-relevant documents. Thus if we put frequently occurring terms in classes, we will necessarily obtain many non-relevant documents, so that any useful documents obtained with the classes will as it were be swamped by the useless ones. But with the restricted vocabulary, on the contrary, we only classify non-frequent terms, and so do not get descriptors with a greater retrieving power which is not in fact counteracted by the greater effectiveness of retrieval which comes from permitting useful substitutions.

Characteristics of the good classifications

But though we have shown why the restricted vocabulary works well, compared with the others, and also incidentally, why classification and retrieval by substitution are useful, we have still to see why the particular classifications and retrieval procedures which worked well were effective; we have, that is, to carry the analysis of the other components of the successful options further, though there is no real need to consider the question of similarity definitions in more detail that we did in Chapter 9.

Strong term connections

The common feature of the successful classifications, it will be remembered, is that the classes in each consist of very strongly connected terms. Thus the strings (which looped), the smaller stars selecting the most strongly connected items, the higher-threshold cliques, and the 100/P clumps derived from a heavily thresholded matrix, work best. What we have to consider here, therefore, is why these classifications work best, and also why they work equally well, given that they both appear different and are based on quite different class definitions, though they share the one common property of being confined to strong connections.

If we consider the first question, the answer is in a sense obvious: the classes depending on the strongest connections must be those containing terms which are most likely to co-occur; and clearly, the more terms co-occur, the better they are as substitutes. This is indeed obvious; but the point of some surprise is the extent to which terms must co-occur before substituting them for one another as members of the same class is really useful. The results we have obtained seem to show that substitutions which are not based on extensive co-occurrences among the members of the class determining the substitutions, are likely to produce more non-relevant documents than relevant ones, though we should allow that some substitutions not generated by strong co-occurrences can be helpful. It is after all the case that we can substitute two members of a class for one another, once the class has been set up, though they may not be strongly connected, because the connection between them was not inspected when the class was set up: this could obviously happen with stars, for instance, though not with cliques. In general, however, we should expect fairly strong connections between any members of a class in one of the successful classifications, either because the connections were used explicitly to form the class, or for the reason we shall consider in a moment, and strong connections can only be based on extensive co-occurrences. Thus if we consider the 100/P clump classification based on a global matrix threshold of 19, for instance, this means that any pair of terms which are represented as co-occurring at all in the matrix must co-occur at least once for every five distinct occurrences of one or the other; this is the minimum: many of the connections in this matrix are stronger than this.

The important point is, however, rather different. Suppose that we have a star based, say, on element x, so that the structure of the star as it is found is

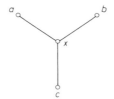

Now we know that the individual connections between x and a, x and b, and x and c, are strong ones (i.e. they are relatively strong, if not absolutely so: the star depends on the strongest connections of x, but these may of course not be very strong); but the point of interest is that the chances are very high that the elements a, b and c will be connected, if not very strongly, at least noticeably, with each other. Though we cannot infer, in general, that if p is very similar to q, and q is very similar to r, that p is very similar to r, in real life there is a strong possibility not merely that p and r will be directly connected, but that if the similarities of each to q are very strong, the similarity between them will also be fairly strong, or at least not negligible*. When we have formed a class like a star, we abandon the

---

* Of course if the connections between p and q, and q and r, respectively, are strong enough, we must expect a non-zero connection between p and r on purely statistical grounds.

information about the connection pattern we used to set it up: the star just given becomes the simple class $abcx$, where each member is regarded as a substitute or swop for all the others; intersubstitutibility among the members of a class means precisely that a and b, a and c, and a and x, and b and c, b and x, and c and x, are all regarded as swops, whatever their relationship before the class was set up.

If it is the case, therefore, that when we make such substitutions in using our classes in retrieval, the results are of value, this must generally be because the real document relationships between the terms in question support the substitutions, that is that the presumed substitutibility is founded on co-occurrence, though the connection depending on this may not have been used explicitly in the formation of the class. Of course we must allow that in some cases two terms may be substituted for one another to good effect, though they are not strongly related by co-occurrences, or even do not co-occur at all; but in general substitution must have something to do with the common document distribution of the terms in question or it would not be valuable. (We can at least say that it would be very surprising if helpful relations between documents had nothing to do with document distribution, though we must accept that not all useful relations are reflected in the document distribution of the terms in question.) The only point is that in using a class definition like that represented by stars, we allow for the occasional absence of document co-occurrences for a pair of terms which it pays to allow to substitute for one another, because the link between them is provided by their indirect co-occurrence, through co-occurrence with a common term or terms.

With cliques, of course, the connection structure on which the formation of a class is based is also the actual structure: the members of a clique are not linked by any extra connections, because all their connections to one another are used in the formation of the clique. It is this strong requirement about the connections between terms in a clique, however, which is in principle objectionable, just because it may not be satisfied by sets of usefully substitutible terms which are well connected, but not maximally connected. One of the original reasons for working with clumps was to avoid this problem, and stars and strings have the same advantage. We thus have a situation in which classes like stars, or string or clumps, seem to be of value because they approximate to cliques in terms of their real connections; while cliques seem to be objectionable because they make such heavy demands on connections, that there may be sets of object which, though they are strongly enough connected for it to be likely that they would permit substitutions of value, do not satisfy the clique definition.

This apparent paradox is explained, however, by an important feature of the classifications. This is that in all of them, there is a heavy class overlap. Suppose, that is, that we have a star $abcd$, but a clique containing only a, b and c: the chances are that at least some of the connections between d and a, b and c which are represented in the star are represented by the occurrence of d with one or more of $\bar{a}$, b and c in one or more other cliques. In general, that is, if we have a given set of connections, we may find that they are, if not completely, at least substantially represented in all our classifications, though in terms of a different class distribution of the elements. This necessarily only applies to overlapping classes, but a substantial overlap in terms of the appearance of given term pair connections in some class or other, is visible in the successful classifications. For example, if we take the star based on element 2, we find that it consists of the elements 2 423 463 584; while the clique generated from 2 consists only of 2 423 584. But there is another clique containing 2, namely one consisting of 2 463 584, so that all the connections for 2 represented in the star are covered by one clique or the other. It follows, then, that the use of cliques may be less restrictive than it appears to be, and that there is more coincidence, and hence less conflict, between the classifications based on different definitions, than there appears to be.

The comparable success of these different classifications must also be due to another fact about them which has to do with the retrieving power of the classes, in the sense considered earlier. We saw that we can in general expect the retrieving power of a class which is substituted for a term to be greater than that of the term. But clearly, the more strongly connected the members of a class are, the more they will co-occur, and the less the increase in the retrieving power of the class will be. This is obvious if we look at an example. If we have term a occurring in 3 documents, say, and we now replace it by a class abc, if a is strongly connected with b and c, and also $\bar{b}$ with c, this means that b and c cannot occur in many documents in which a does not occur, so that the increase in the number of documents which are necessarily retrieved as a result of the replacement of the term a by its class cannot be very large. It is certainly true that the more strongly connected classes work better than the less connected ones, and while this may in part, or even mainly, be attributed to their weaker linguistic rationale, so to speak, this purely formal consequence of the character of the classes in each must affect their retrieval performance too: for the less strongly connected classes can be expected to have a greater retrieving power. The fact that the tightest classes for the restricted vocabulary, in which infrequent terms only are grouped, works absolutely best, is then explained by the comparatively small numbers of occurrences of the items concerned, combined with the formal character of the classes: even though strongly connected frequent terms will overlap in document distribution, the total number of documents classes containing them will retrieve must exceed the total number pulled out by classes which consist not merely of strongly connected terms, but also of non-frequent ones.

Differences between the good classifications

But though we can account for the comparable success of the good classifications by the fact that they share certain general properties, the question of interest which arises now is why do they give effectively the same performance when there are obvious differences between them? It is true that there is more underlying resemblance between them than there may appear to be, because the same term connections appear in different guises, so to speak, but there are still differences between them; not only are there surface differences in the numbers and sizes of classes, and so on, but we do not always find the same connections appearing in some class or another.

To start with, the superficial differences between the classifications are quite marked. As we have already seen, if we take the classes based on some specific element in the string, star and clique classifications (though not the clump one, because the starting object does not have the same status), we find that though they typically contain some common elements, they are generally not identical, or even very similar. For example, for element 6 we get

string	6 137 510
star	6 137 510 610
clique	6 32 297

These specific differences are, moreover, reflected in overall differences. Thus the average size of class (leaving out the frequent term unit classes) is different, and also the number of classes in which an element appears; the total numbers of classes differ, and the relationships between the classifications and the documents are different. This is suggested even by the information about a single element, like 6, which appears in classes in the four 'standard' classifications (clumps now being included) as follows:

strings	a	6 137 510
stars	b	6 137 510 610
	c	6 32 153 393
	d	6 137 410 420 510 610
cliques	e	6 32 297
	f	6 137 226 410 420 510 610
clumps	g	6 32 137 226 393 410 420 510 610
	h	6 137 182 226 348 410 420 510 597 610
	i	6 32 137 226 410 420 510
	j	6 32 137 226 410 420 610

Summarising the different facts about the classes in which element 6 occurs then gives us the following:

	strings	stars	cliques	clumps
number of classes for 6	1	3	2	4
average size of class	3	4.7	5	8.3
number of documents for class set of 6	2	5	8	15

If the relevant figures or averages for the four classifications as wholes are compared, moreover, striking differences are apparent, as follows*:

	strings	stars	cliques	clumps
Number of classes	494	547	376	372
average number of objects per class	3	5.2	3.7	4.7
average number of classes per object	3	4.5	2.8	2
average number of documents per class	6.2	12.2	10	9.9
average number of classes per document	18.3	35.8	18.7	18.3
average number of class-mates per object	4.8	17.2	7.1	6.8

It seems, therefore, that substitution in one case in one classification will lead to quite different results from substitution in another; but if so, why does this not affect their performance more? Presumably, if one classification permits the helpful substitution of *b* for *a*, and this is not permitted by another, we can expect a performance loss at this point for the second.

Resemblances between the classifications

This is where we have to look at an aspect of a classification which is not represented by the figures and averages just given. This is what the 'class-mates' of a term are. If we have a term *a*, say, which occurs in three classes, for example

abc
acdef
agh

the class-mates of *a* are *b, c, d, e, f, g,* and *h*; and the important point about the class-mates of a term is that they are its substitutes in retrieval, irrespective of how they are distributed in the classes, if we adopt the simple term-class replacement scheme of the successful experiments. Thus we have the same class-mates for *a* if we have two classes, say *abcdefg* and *ah*, or seven,

*These figures are based on hand averaging over the first fifty items in each case, and so will not match up in detail.

say *ab, ac, ad, ae, af, ag,* and *ah.* It will be evident, therefore, that classifications which are apparently quite different in terms of the average size of class and so on, can lead to the same set of class-mates for a given term: averages in an overlapping classification may be inflated by the recurrence of the same set of objects in different classes, but these repetitions do not affect class-mates.

This point about the class-mates of a term is very important, in that it may explain the fact that the different classifications we used gave very similar performances: if the class-mates for a term are the same throughout, this is what we would expect. Or at least it would be a partial explanation, because the actual differences between the distribution of terms in classes must matter too; the actual matches in retrieval are on classes, and the distribution in classes will affect the numbers of matching items, and hence level at which a document is retrieved. If we refer back to the original discussion in Chapter 2 of the retrieval function of a classification too, and to the point that non-exclusive classifications not only permit distinctions between the senses of words, but permit class weighting, both of which are precision devices, it is obvious that if we have classifications which differ in the respects represented in the table, they will differ in the consequences of these differences for precision. But it seems clear that it is the substitutions which good classifications permit which are really effective, and it is here that the character of the sets of class-mates for terms in classifications is important.

This discussion is of course only taking the earlier point about the fact that strong connections between terms will tend to be picked up in some class or other in a classification further: it is not simply that individual strong connections will be represented in some class or another in different classifications, though not in matching classes, but that the set of connections for a given term, and hence sets of connections for terms, are largely represented in all the classifications. The question we have to ask now, therefore, is: are the sets of class-mates for terms in the different classifications at least similar, if they are not the same? And the answer seems to be that there is a considerable overlap. This can be shown by some examples, as follows:

term 12

strings	12	57	82	225	277		313	347	
stars	12	57	82	225	277	305	313	347	549
cliques	12	57			277				
clumps	12	57			277				

term 290

strings				148			290		350							
stars	17	25	93	148		246	290	340	350			385			474	
cliques	17	25	93	148			290		350		361	385	386	466		
clumps	17	25	93	133	148	176	246	290	340	350	352	361	385	386	466	474 511

term 541

strings		227	330		541 583
stars	48 49 50	227 237	293 324 330 405 448	497	541 583
cliques	49	174 227	330		541 583
clumps	49	73 174 227 237 250	330	488	502 541 583

term 552

strings		354		534 552	
stars	223 224 225 277 301 354 364 376 380			534 543 552 553	
cliques	224	354		552	
clumps	224	354	376	381	552

Effects of the differences and resemblances on substitution

These comparisons show that though there is considerable overlap between the class-mate sets for the different classifications, there are still some differences. Why, then, do these not affect performance more? For it must be the case that they do not, given that the differences in performance are not really significant. It cannot be the case that one classification is better than another: they must be equally good, or equally bad; and it is at the same time hard to believe that the substitutions which are common to them all are the only good ones, and that the others represent different random selections of bad ones. This suggestion should perhaps be tested experimentally: for clearly, on this hypothesis, selecting the common class-mates only would lead to a retrieval performance which was at least as good, and perhaps better, than that for the current classifications. It is, however, doubtful whether this is the explanation, because the class-mates which are common to all the classifications are comparatively few: the sets of class-mates themselves form an overlapping classification. An alternative hypothesis is required.

The alternative hypothesis that can be put forward is best presented in terms of a general proposition about term substitutions, namely that a given substitution may not always be valuable, though it is more often useful than not. We encounter here, in other words, the basic question that can be asked about term thesauri, namely whether substitution is really helpful. This is even more fundamental than the question the Classification Hypothesis is intended to answer, which is that substitution classes based on co-occurrences lead to good swops: it is assumed that substitution in itself may be a good thing, and this Substitution Hypothesis is what we are now concerned with. Essentially, we have two questions to consider here; these are

(1) whether substitution in a single request can improve the retrieval performance for the request; and

(2) whether substitutions which improve performance for one request also improve performance for others, so that substitutions are of value over sets of requests.

From the point of view of research in classification, the crucial question is clearly the second: but it is also true that unless we can answer both (1) and (2) affirmatively, we cannot proceed to further questions about the best way of forming classes of substitutible terms. We cannot, in particular, go on to ask whether classes of useful substitutes can be obtained automatically unless we have answered (1) and (2) affirmatively.

Investigating these two problems in a careful and critical way would involve an enormous amount of work: we would have to test individual substitutions and combinations of substitutions for their effect for every individual request and every term in the vocabulary. We are indeed hoping to go into this question to some extent, to see what happens in detail; but in general, if classifications work better than terms, it must follow that substitution is helpful: the question of interest is how helpful can we expect them to be? Suppose, however, that we accept that some substitutions are of value in retrieval, that is over sets of requests and not simply for individual requests; what does this imply? The important point is that what it almost certainly implies is that while individual substitutions may generally be of value, it is quite likely to be the case that they are not always of value. A given substitution works in most cases, but not all; but we accept it just because it is of value in the majority of cases, and are prepared to allow that it may be unhelpful in the minority, especially if we can rely on other features of our requests or documents, like the presence of other terms, to counteract the bad consequences of inappropriate substitutions. It is hard to believe, given the variety of requests and documents even in a homogeneous collection, that any substitutions would *always* give better results than we would obtain without allowing the substitutions.

What follows from this, however? What follows is a possible further explanation for both the success of some of our classifications, and the fact that classifications that differ to some extent give effectively the same performance. The classifications are successful because they permit substitutions which are generally valuable; and the fact that their differences do not matter can be explained by the hypothesis that different substitution pairs have complementary effects. For example, if classification A permits the (helpful) substitution of q for p, which is not permitted by classification B, this may not mean that the performance of classification B is worse than that of classification A, as long as B permits some other substitution, say of r for p, which acts as an alternative way of retrieving the relevant documents obtained by the qp substitution. In this case, different substitutions can lead to the retrieval of the same documents, and *ipso facto* of the same relevant ones as well as non-relevant ones. The different classification may work in the same way, either because they permit the same substitutions, or because they permit alternative ones with the same or similar effects. That this is possible is shown by the earlier example on page 223, in which expanding the request term set does not lead to the retrieval of many more documents: i.e. alternative terms may retrieve the same documents.

A more interesting suggestion is that it may be the case that over a set of requests, if a substitution like that of *q* for *p* is helpful in some cases and not in others, there is another substitution, say of *r* for *p*, which is helpful perhaps in just those cases where the first substitution is unhelpful, and vice versa; so that in one case we get some good effects and some associated bad ones, and in the other the reverse, so that the net effect overall of the substitutions is the same. Presumably, it follows from this that a classification which permitted both substitutions would maximise the benefits to be obtained, which gives us a suggestion about the use of classifications which is the complement of the earlier one about selecting the common features of classifications only: in this case we would be forming the union of several classifications, as opposed to identifying their intersection. A potential disadvantage of this approach, however, might well be that the resulting classes would be so large that their retrieving power would become excessive, which is, equally, the complementary defect to that of the selective classification. This suggestion is nevertheless one which should be investigated further, like the other one, if only so that we learn more about the way classifications work.

Thus the different classifications work equally well for several reasons: they have a substantial overlap, so that the effects of many substitutions are the same for all—and these are perhaps, because they are common to the classifications, the central or most valuable ones—while the remaining different substitutions are alternatives or complementary. In particular, the common substitutions probably represent the strongest connections, which can be expected to be most valuable.

Finally, we come to the point that the mode of retrieval (or strictly, indexing language) in which terms are simply replaced by classes, works better than the more complex mode, involving term and class combinations. The explanation here seems to be one which is in tune with those we have given for the other facets of the successful retrieval systems: this is that as the difference between the performance curves for the successful classifications and the base term retrieval can be characterised by saying that the former are promoting relevant documents, i.e. increasing recall and *ipso facto* increasing precision, the most important feature of the classifications is that they allow substitutions which do this. The way in which the classifications contribute to retrieval is by allowing substitution, and it then follows that the various ways in which this is modified in the modes of retrieval other than the simple class one are too restrictive; they simply inhibit useful substitutions.

Retrieval, classificatory and linguistic properties of the good classifications

Given, now, that we can make these remarks about our results, so that we can say not merely that automatic keyword classification proved of value for our test collection, but that it could be of value in other cases, what light does this discussion throw on our original views on the nature of retrieval thesauri? To start with, our first question was about the purpose of a retrieval thesaurus; and it will be remembered that we argued that to obtain a genuine improvement over terms, we would need a classification which acted both as a recall device and as a precision device. The result we have obtained shows that this requirement was reasonable, and can be satisfied, though not in the way we originally expected. But what about the linguistic, classificatory and retrieval properties of the successful classifications, compared with our original specifications? As far as the last two properties are concerned, it will be remembered that we originally thought that our classes should be loosely connected ones of the kind associated in general with clump definitions; and that the classes should be designed to have considerable retrieving power, i.e. should be extractive or exhaustive, rather than selective. It will be clear now that the actual properties of the successful classifications are rather different. In particular we have found that it is essential to make the classes selective, to avoid swamping the relevant documents retrieved with non-relevant ones. As far as the classificatory properties are concerned, it will be evident that we are interested in much 'tighter' classes than we were originally, though we do not go so far as to *require* a really solid structure of the kind given by clique definitions. In this connection it is useful to distinguish the actual strength of the individual connections between the members of a class from the numbers of connections: our original specification was for classes which permitted both weak connections between individuals and an irregular pattern of connections over the class as a whole; we have found that we must have strong connections between individuals, but that we can permit an irregular pattern, not only of explicit connections used in class formation, but of implicit ones.

What we have not said anything about so far, however, is the linguistic character of the classes we have obtained. This is best illustrated by examples. Thus if we look at some random groups chosen from each of the successful classifications we get:

strings	aspect delta rectangular
	asymptotic criterion cycles
	interplanetary manœuvre
	band grain technique
stars	asymptotic criterion cycles problem
	entering planet probe tumbling
	gust indicial penetrating sharp
	channel circular fluid steady
cliques	criterion cycles estimate lyapunov
	ablating capacity shield teflon
	entering planet probe
	direct elevon lateral rudder sideslip
	aspect delta
	equilibrium specific thermal

clumps   ablating capacity shield teflon
fuel methane miles nautical
contracting distance eccentricity lifetime
oblate orbit perigee period satellite
aspect central chord planform sweep
circular fluid incompressible steady
kirchoff navier stokes

At first sight, some of these sets look very unobvious. But two points are relevant here*. One is that words which may, so to speak, give semantic body to a class, or may bind it together by supplying linguistic or conceptual connections between members, may either appear with the same terms in other classes, or may be frequent terms which are excluded by definition. The effect of these on the semantic obviousness of the classes is shown if we compare the cliques, say, for the restricted vocabulary with those for the full vocabulary, for example as follows:

restricted: dependent time
full: dependent perigee period time

restricted: aspect delta
full: aspect delta lift wing

restricted: diameter discharge
full: diameter discharge nozzle throat

It will nevertheless be obvious that the classes do not in general illustrate regular groupings in the sense that they do not consist of sets we would normally, as ordinary English speakers, regard as conceptually related. They do, on the other hand, consist to a large extent of sets of words which are recognised as related by anyone familar with the special subject matter of the collection: many individual collocations are of this kind, as we can see from examples like

blasius problem threepoint
entering planet probe tumbling
ablating capacity shield teflon

or as the connections are more obvious in classes for the full vocabulary, from examples like

mach test tunnel wind
angle attack lift mach

a particularly good instance is

band between grain technique

where the collocational structure of the class is clearly exhibited. So the classes are satisfactory if we accept the arguments advanced in Chapter 1

* Also the trivial point that the written form of the term is the alphabetically first of the group of keywords—which may not be the most obvious form in the context.

to the effect that it is these collection-oriented classes that we really need. The sets of words are brought together by their subject connections, and not by any systematic semantic relations like synonymy. In this case, therefore, our results are in accord with our initial hypotheses.

External comparisons

We have to turn now to the comparison between our results and those obtained elsewhere. Given that we can say that our results are satisfactory, because they support the arguments for a keyword thesaurus, what does the comparison between these results and those of other projects suggest? To start with, we have to recognise that the number of really useful comparisons we can make is not large. It is true, as we saw in Chapter 1, that a variety of methods for constructing thesauri and also associative pseudo-classifications automatically have been proposed, and that a variety of experiments have been carried out. The first suggestions were put forward in the late fifties when work in this and the complementary area of automatic document classification was begun by Baker, Borko, Doyle, Giuliano, Needham and Stiles in particular[1]. This research was surveyed by Stevens in 1964[2], and the two major difficulties of the field are apparent in her account of the different projects: these are the scale problem which is peculiar to automatic classification, and the general problem of retrieval testing; and it is unfortunately the case that the exhaustive tests and comparisons which are required to demonstrate that an automatically obtained keyword classification is (*a*) of some value, i.e. is better than unclassified terms, and (*b*) works better than any manually-constructed ones which themselves work well, have still not been carried out. Our own experiments represent only a beginning in this direction. Moreover, even where experiments have been carried out, it is very difficult to make any comparisons other than the most general ones, especially if, for instance, the details of the way performance is measured are different. It will also be evident by now that such points as the use of terms taken from abstracts as opposed to whole texts, and the average length of the initial term lists for the documents, as well as differences in collection size and so on, can all interfere with straightforward comparisons. In general, it seems to be the case that after being initially adopted with enthusiasm, the idea of using an automatic term thesaurus for retrieval has been largely disregarded, presumably mainly because of the daunting problems which appear when any attempt is made to investigate it fully[3].

For one reason or another, therefore, the only results which are immediately relevant to our own are those which have been obtained by Cleverdon himself, and by the SMART project. Cleverdon's own experiments with manual thesauri only showed that, for the Cranfield collection, keywords, or rather terms, worked as well as, or better than, the manual thesauri he

Bibliography

This bibliography is not intended to be exhaustive. It covers (a) items cited in the text; (b) relatively accessible works on automatic classification for information retrieval; and (c) salient publications in related areas, specifically classification, and retrieval testing and evaluation.

ABRAHAM, C. T., 'Techniques for Thesaurus Organisation and Evaluation', *Parameters of Information Science, Proc. A.D.I.*, **1**, 485 (1964)

ABRAHAM, C. T., 'Graph-Theoretic Techniques for the Organisation of Linked Data' in *Some Problems in Information Science* (Ed. Kochen), New York, Scarecrow Press (1965)

ABRAHAM, C. T., 'Techniques for Thesaurus Organisation and Evaluation' in *Some Problems in Information Science* (Ed. Kochen), New York, Scarecrow Press (1965)

ATHERTON, P. A. (Ed.), *Classification Research: Proceedings of the Second International Study Conference*, Copenhagen, Munksgaard (1965)

ATHERTON, P. and BORKO, H., 'A Test of the Factor-Analytically Derived Automated Classification Method Applied to Descriptions of Work and Search Requests of Nuclear Physicists', American Institute of Physics, New York (1965)

BAKER, F. B., 'Information Retrieval Based Upon Latent Class Analysis', *J. Ass. Comput. Mach.*, **9**, 512 (1962)

BAKER, F. B., 'Latent Class Analysis as an Association Model for Information Retrieval' in *Statistical Association Methods for Mechanised Documentation* (Ed. Stevens et al.), National Bureau of Standards, Washington D.C. (1965)

BALL, G. H., 'Data Analysis in the Social Sciences', *Proceedings of the 1965 Fall Joint Computer Conference; AFIPS Conference Proceedings*, Vol. 27, Part 1, 533 (1965)

BAXENDALE, P. B., 'Content Analysis, Specification and Control' in *Annual Review of Information Science and Technology* (Ed Cuadra), Vol. 1, New York, Interscience (1966)

BONNER, R. E., 'On Some Clustering Techniques', *IBM J. Res. Dev.*, **8**, 22 (1964)

BORKO, H., 'The Construction of an Empirically-Based Mathematically-Derived Classification System', *Proceedings of the 1962 Spring Joint Computer Conference; AFIPS Conference Proceedings*, Vol. 21, 279 (1962)

BORKO, H. and BERNICK, M. D., 'Automatic Document Classification', *J. Ass. Comput. Mach.*, **10**, 151 (1963)

BORKO, H. and BERNICK, M. D., 'Automatic Document Classification, Part II—Additional Experiments', *J. Ass. Comput. Mach.*, **11**, 138 (1964)

BORKO, H., 'Measuring the Reliability of Subject Classification by Men and Machines', *Am. Docum.*, **15**, 268 (1964)

BORKO, H., 'Research in Computer Based Classification Systems' in *Classification Research: Proceedings of the Second International Study Conference* (Ed. Atherton), Copenhagen, Munksgaard (1965)

BORKO, H., 'Studies on the Reliability and Validity of Factor-Analytically Derived Classification Categories' in *Statistical Association Methods for Mechanised Documentation* (Ed. Stevens et al.), National Bureau of Standards, Washington D.C. (1965)

BORKO, H., 'Indexing and Classification' in *Automated Language Processing* (Ed. Borko), New York, John Wiley (1967)

CHIEN, R. T. and PREPARATA, F. P., 'Search Strategy and File Organisation in Computerised Information Retrieval Systems with Mass Memory' in *Mechanised Information Storage, Retrieval and Dissemination* (Ed. Samuelson), Amsterdam, North-Holland (1968)

CLEVERDON, C. W., MILLS, J. and KEEN, M., *Factors Determining the Performance of Indexing Systems*, Aslib Cranfield Project, Cranfield, Vol. 1, Design (Parts 1 and 2), Vol. 2, Test Results (Cleverdon and Keen) (1966)

BIBLIOGRAPHY

CLEVERDON, C. W., 'Evaluation Tests of Information Retrieval Systems', *J. Docum.*, **26**, 55 (1970)

CURTICE, R. M., 'Experiments in Associative Retrieval', *Progress in Information Science and Technology, Proc. A.D.I.*, **3**, 373 (1966)

CURTICE, R. M. and JONES, P. E., 'Distributional Constraints and the Automatic Selection of an Indexing Vocabulary', *Proc. A.D.I.*, **4**, 152 (1967)

DALE, A. G. and DALE, N., 'Some Clumping Experiments for Associative Document Retrieval', *Am. Docum.*, **16**, 5 (1965)

DALE, A. G. and DALE, N., 'Clumping Techniques and Associative Retrieval' in *Statistical Association Methods for Mechanised Documentation* (Ed. Stevens *et al.*), National Bureau of Standards, Washington D.C. (1965)

DATTOLA, R. T. and MURRAY, D. M., 'An Experiment in Automatic Thesaurus Construction' in *Information Storage and Retrieval*, Report No. *ISR–13*, Department of Computer Science, Cornell University (1967)

DATTOLA, R. T., 'A Fast Algorithm for Automatic Classification, in *Information Storage and Retrieval*, Report No. *ISR–14*, Department of Computer Science, Cornell University (1968)

DENNIS, S. F., 'The Construction of a Thesaurus Automatically from a Sample of Text' in *Statistical Association Methods for Mechanised Documentation* (Ed. Stevens *et al.*), National Bureau of Standards, Washington D.C. (1965)

DENNIS, S. F., 'The Design and Testing of a Fully Automated Indexing–Searching System for Documents Consisting of Expository Text' in *Information Retrieval—A Critical View* (Ed. Schechter), Washington D.C., Thompson (1967)

DOYLE, L. B., 'Semantic Road Maps for Literature Searching', *J. Ass. Comput. Mach.*, **8**, 553 (1961)

DOYLE, L. B., 'Indexing and Abstracting by Association', *Am. Docum.*, **13**, 378 (1962)

DOYLE, L. B., 'The Microstatistics of Text', *Inf. Storage & Retriev.*, **1**, 189 (1963)

DOYLE, L. B., 'Is Automatic Classification a Reasonable Application of Statistical Analysis of Text?', *J. Ass. Comput. Mach.*, **12**, 473 (1965)

DOYLE, L. B., 'Some Compromises Between Word Grouping and Document Grouping' in *Statistical Association Methods for Mechanised Documentation* (Ed. Stevens *et al.*), National Bureau of Standards, Washington D.C. (1965)

DOYLE, L. B. and BLANKENSHIP, D. A., 'Technical Advances in Automatic Classification' *Progress in Information Science and Technology, Proc. A.D.I.*, **3**, 63 (1966)

FAIRTHORNE, R. A., 'The Mathematics of Classification' in his own *Towards Information Retrieval*, London, Butterworths (1961)

FAIRTHORNE, R. A., 'Content Analysis, Specification and Control' in *Annual Review of Information Science and Technology* (Ed. Cuadra), Vol. 4, Chicago, Encyclopedia Britannica (1969)

GIULIANO, V. E. and JONES, P. E., 'Linear Associative Information Retrieval' in *Vistas in Information Handling* (Ed. Howerton and Weeks), Vol. 1, Washington D.C. (1963)

GIULIANO, V. E. (Project Director), *Centralisation and Documentation*, Arthur D. Little, Inc., Cambridge, Mass., 1st edn (1963), 2nd edn, revised (1964)

GIULIANO, V. E., 'The Interpretation of Word Associations' in *Statistical Association Methods for Mechanised Documentation* (Ed. Stevens *et al.*). National Bureau of Standards, Washington D.C. (1965)

GIULIANO, V. E. and JONES, P. E., *Study and Test of a Methodology for Laboratory Evaluation of Message Retrieval Systems*, Arthur D. Little, Inc., Cambridge, Mass. (1966)

GOFFMAN, W. and NEWILL, V. A., 'A Methodology for Test and Evaluation of Information Systems', *Inf. Storage & Retriev.*, **3**, 19 (1966)

GOODMAN, L. A. and KRUSKAL, W. H., 'Measures of Association for Cross Classification II: Further Discussion and References', *J. Am. Statist. Ass.*, **54**, 123 (1959)

GOTLIEB, C. C. and KUMAR, S., 'Semantic Clustering of Index Terms', *J. Ass. Comput. Mach.*, **15**, 493 (1968)

HARPER, K. E, 'Some Combinatorial Properties of Russian Nouns', The Rand Corporation, Santa Monica, Calif. (1966)

HAYES, R. M., 'Mathematical Models for Information Retrieval' in *Natural Language and the Computer* (Ed. Garvin), New York, McGraw-Hill (1963)

HILL, D. R., 'A Vector Clustering Technique' in *Mechanised Information Storage, Retrieval and Dissemination* (Ed. Samuelson), Amsterdam, North-Holland (1968)

HILLMAN, D. J., 'Mathematical Classification Techniques for Non-Static Document Collections, with particular reference to the problem of relevance' in *Classification Research: Proceedings of the Second International Study Conference* (Ed. Atherton), Copenhagen, Munksgaard (1965)

IVIE, E. L., *Search Procedures based on Measures of Relatedness between Documents*, Massachusetts Institute of Technology, Cambridge, Mass. (1966) (Thesis MAC–TR–29)

JACKSON, D. M., 'A Note on a Set of Functions for Information Retrieval', *Inf. Storage & Retriev.*, **5**, 27 (1969)

JACKSON, D. M., 'Comparison of Classifications' in *Numerical Taxonomy* (Ed. Cole), London, Academic Press (1969)

JACKSON, D. M., *Automatic classification and Information Retrieval*, Ph.D. Thesis, University of Cambridge (1969)

JARDINE, C. J., JARDINE, N. and SIBSON, R., 'The Structure and Construction of Taxonomic Hierarchies', *Mathematical Biosciences*, **1**, 173 (1967)

JARDINE, N. and SIBSON, R., 'The Construction of Hierarchical and Non-hierarchical Classifications', *Comput. J.*, **11**, 177 (1968)

JARDINE, N. and SIBSON, R., 'A Model for Taxonomy', *Mathematical Biosciences*, **2**, 465 (1968)

JONES, P. E., 'Historical Foundations of Research on Statistical Association Techniques for Mechanised Documentation' in *Statistical Association Methods for Mechanised Documentation* (Ed. Stevens *et al.*), National Bureau of Standards, Washington D.C. (1965)

JONES, P. E. and CURTICE, R. M., 'A Framework for Comparing Term Association Measures', *Am. Docum.*, **18**, 153 (1967)

JONES, P. E., GIULIANO, V. E., CURTICE, R. M., *Papers on Automatic Language Processing*, Arthur D. Little, Inc., Cambridge, Mass. (1967)
3 vols: 1. Selected Collection Statistics and Data Analyses; 2. Linear Models for Associative Retrieval; 3. Development of String Indexing Techniques

KEEN, E. M., 'Evaluation Parameters' in *Information Storage and Retrieval*, Report No. *ISR–13*, Department of Computer Science, Cornell University (1967)

KEEN, E. M., 'Thesaurus, Phrase and Hierarchy Dictionaries' in *Information Storage and Retrieval*, Report No. *ISR–13*, Department of Computer Science, Cornell University (1967)

KEEN, E. M., 'Suffix Dictionaries' in *Information Storage and Retrieval*, Report No. *ISR–13*, Department of Computer Science, Cornell University (1967)

KING, D. W., 'Design and Evaluation of Information Systems' in *Annual Review of Information Science and Technology* (Ed. Cuadra), Vol. 3, Chicago, Encyclopedia Britannica (1968)

KUHNS, J. L., 'The Continuum of Coefficients of Association' in *Statistical Association Methods for Mechanised Documentation* (Ed. Stevens *et al.*), National Bureau of Standards, Washington D.C. (1965)

LANCASTER, F. W., *Evaluation of the Medlars Demand Search System*, National Library of Medicine, Bethesda, Md. (1968)

LANCASTER, F. W., *Information Retrieval Systems: Characteristics, Testing and Evaluation*, New York, John Wiley (1968)

LANCE, G. N. and WILLIAMS, W. T., 'A General Theory of Classificatory Sorting Strategies. I, Hierarchical Systems', *Comput. J.*, **9**, 373 (1967)

LANCE, G. N. and WILLIAMS, W. T., 'A General Theory of Classificatory Sorting Systems II, Clustering Systems', *Comput. J.*, **10**, 271 (1967)

LEFKOWITZ, D., *Automatic Stratification of Descriptors*, Doctoral Dissertation, University of Pennsylvania (1964)

LESK, M. E., 'Performance of Automatic Information Systems', *Inf. Storage & Retriev.*, **4**, 219 (1968)

LESK, M. E. and SALTON, G., 'Relevance Assessments and Retrieval System Evaluation', *Inf. Storage & Retriev.*, **4**, 343 (1969)

LESK, M. E., 'Word–Word Associations in Document Retrieval Systems', *Am. Docum.*, **20**, 27 (1969)

LEWIS, P. A. W., BAXENDALE, P. B. and BENNETT, J. L., 'Statistical Discrimination of the Synonymy/Antonymy Relationship Between Words', *J. Ass. Comput. Mach.*, **14**, 20 (1967)

ARTHUR D. LITTLE, INC., *Automatic Message Retrieval: Studies for the Design of an English Command and Control Language System*, Arthur D. Little, Inc., Cambridge, Mass. (1963)

LUHN, H. P., 'A Statistical Approach to the Mechanised Encoding and Searching of Literary Information', *IBM J. Res. Dev.*, **1**, 309 (1957)

MACNAUGHTON-SMITH, P., *Some Statistical and Other Numerical Techniques for Classifying Individuals*, London, H.M.S.O. (1965)

MARON, M. E. and KUHNS, J. L., 'On Relevance, Probabilistic Indexing and Information Retrieval', *J. Ass. Comput. Mach.*, **7**, 216 (1960)

MARON, M. E., 'Automatic Indexing: An Experimental Enquiry', *J. Ass. Comput. Mach.*, **8**, 404 (1961)

NEEDHAM, R. M. and JOYCE, T., 'The Thesaurus Approach to Information Retrieval', *Am Docum.*, **9**, 192 (1958)

NEEDHAM, R. M. and PARKER RHODES, A. R., 'The Theory of Clumps', Cambridge Language Research Unit, Cambridge, England (1960)

NEEDHAM, R. M., 'The Theory of Clumps II', Cambridge Language Research Unit, Cambridge, England (1961)

NEEDHAM, R. M., *Research on Information Retrieval, Classification and Grouping*, 1957–61, Ph.D. Thesis, University of Cambridge (1961)

NEEDHAM, R. M., 'A Method for Using Computers in Information Classification', *Information Processing 62, Proceedings of IFIP Congress 1962* (Ed. Popplewell), Amsterdam, North-Holland, 284 (1963)

NEEDHAM, R. M. and SPARCK JONES, K., 'Keywords and Clumps', *J. Docum.*, **20**, 5 (1964)

NEEDHAM, R. M., 'Applications of the Theory of Clumps', *Mech. Transl.*, **8**, 113 (1965)

NEEDHAM, R. M., 'Automatic Classification in Linguistics', *The Statistician*, **17**, 45 (1967)

O'CONNOR, J., 'Mechanised Indexing Methods and Their Testing', *J. Ass. Comput. Mech.*, **11**, 437 (1964)

PARKER-RHODES, A. F., 'Contributions to the Theory of Clumps', Cambridge Language Research Unit, Cambridge, England (1961)

PRICE, N. and SCHIMINOVICH, S., 'A Clustering Experiment: First Steps towards a Computer-Generated Classification Scheme', *Inf. Storage & Retriev.*, **4**, 271 (1968)

RAMO WOOLDRIDGE, INC., *Automatic Thesaurus Compilation*, Thompson Ramo Wooldridge, Inc., Canoga Park, Calif. (1963)

REES, A. M. and SCHULTZ, D. G., *A Field Experimental Approach to the Study of Relevance Assessments in Relation to Document Searching*, Final Report, Center for Documentation and Communication Research, Western Reserve University (1967)

REES, A. M., 'Evaluation of Information Systems and Services' in *Annual Review of Information Science and Technology* (Ed. Cuadra), Vol. 2, New York, Interscience (1967)

ROBERTSON, S. E., 'The Parametric Description of Retrieval Tests; Part 1: The Basic Parameters', *J. Docum.*, **25**, 1 (1969)

ROBERTSON, S. E., 'The Parametric Description of Retrieval Tests; Part 2: Overall Measures', *J. Docum.*, **25**, 93 (1969)

ROCCHIO, J. J., 'Document Retrieval Systems-Optimisation and Evaluation' in *Information Storage and Retrieval*, Report No. ISR–10, The Computation Laboratory, Harvard University, 1966 (Doctoral Thesis, Harvard University (1965))

RUBINOFF, M. and STONE, D. C., 'Semantic Tools in Information Retrieval', *Proc. A.D.I.*, **4**, 169 (1967)

RUDIN, B., 'Some Approaches to Automatic Indexing' in *Computer and Information Sciences II* (Ed. Tou), New York, Academic Press (1967)

SALTON, G. (Project Director), Scientific Reports on *Information Storage and Retrieval*, Nos. *ISR–1–9*, The Computation Laboratory, Harvard University (1961–65); Nos. *ISR–11–17*, Department of Computer Science, Cornell University (1966–69)

SALTON, G., 'Some Experiments in the Generation of Word and Document Associations', *Proceedings of the 1962 Fall Joint Computer Conference*; *AFIPS Conference Proceedings*, Vol. 22, 234 (1962)

SALTON, G., 'Associative Retrieval Techniques using Bibliographic Information', *J. Ass. Comput. Mach.*, **10**, 440 (1963)

SALTON, G., 'An Evaluation Program for Associative Indexing' in *Statistical Association Methods for Mechanised Indexing* (Ed. Stevens *et al.*), Washington D.C. (1965)

SALTON, G. and LESK, M. E., 'Computer Evaluation of Indexing and Text Processing', *J. Ass. Comput. Mach.*, **15**, 8 (1968)

SALTON, G., *Automatic Information Organisation and Retrieval*, New York, McGraw-Hill (1968)

SALTON, G., 'Automated Language Processing' in *Annual Review of Information Science and Technology* (Ed. Cuadra), Vol. 3, Chicago, Encyclopedia Britannica (1969)

SHARP, J. R., 'Content Analysis, Specification and Control' in *Annual Review of Information Science and Technology* (Ed. Cuadra), Vol. 2, New York, Interscience (1967)

SOERGEL, D., 'Mathematical Analysis of Documentation Systems. An Attempt at a Theory of Classification and Search Request Formulation', *Inf. Storage & Retriev.*, **3**, 129 (1967)

SOKAL, R. R. and SNEATH, P. H. A., *Principles of Numerical Taxonomy*, London, Freeman & Co. (1963)

SPARCK JONES, K. and JACKSON, D., 'Current Approaches to Classification and Clump-finding at the Cambridge Language Research Unit', *Comput. J.*, **10**, 29 (1967)

SPARCK JONES, K. and NEEDHAM, R. M., 'Automatic Term Classification and Retrieval', *Inf. Storage & Retriev.*, **4**, 91 (1968)

SPARCK JONES, K., 'Automatic Term Classification and Information Retrieval', *Information Processing 68. Proceedings of IFIP Congress 1968* (Ed. Morrell), Amsterdam, North-Holland (1970)

SPARCK JONES, K. and JACKSON, D. M., 'The Use of Automatically-obtained Keyword Classifications for Information Retrieval', *Inf. Storage & Retriev.*, **5**, 175 (1970)

SPARCK JONES, K., 'The Theory of Clumps', *Encyclopedia of Library and Information Science* (1969) (Ed. Kent and Lancour), Vol. 3, New York, Marcel Dekker

SPIEGEL, J. *et al.*, *Statistical Association Procedures for Message Content Analysis*, The Mitre Corporation, Bedford, Mass. (1962)

SPIEGEL, J. and BENNETT, E. M., 'A Modified Statistical Association Procedure for Automatic Document Content Analysis and Retrieval' in *Statistical Association Methods for Mechanised Documentation* (Ed. Stevens *et al.*), National Bureau of Standards, Washington D.C. (1965)

STEVENS, M. E., *Automatic Indexing: A State-of-the-Art Report*, Monograph 91, National Bureau of Standards, Washington D.C. (1965)

STEVENS, M. E., GIULIANO, V. E. and HEILPRIN, D. (Eds), *Statistical Association Methods for Mechanised Documentation, Symposium Proceedings* (1964), Miscellaneous Publication 269, National Bureau of Standards, Washington, D.C. (1965)

STILES, H. E., 'The Association Factor in Information Retrieval', *J. Ass. Comput. Mach.*, **8**, 271 (1961)

STILES, H. E., 'Machine Retrieval using the Association Factor' in *Machine Indexing: Progress and Problems*, American University, Washington D.C. (1962)

STILES, H. E., 'Automatic Indexing and the Association Factor' in *Information Systems Compatibility* (Ed. Newman), Washington D.C. (1965)

STONE, D. C. and RUBINOFF, M., 'Statistical Generation of a Technical Vocabulary', *Am. Docum.*, **19**, 411 (1968)

BIBLIOGRAPHY

SWANSON, D. R., 'Research Procedures for Automatic Indexing' in *Machine Indexing; Progress and Problems*, American University, Washington D.C. (1962)

SWANSON, D. R., 'On Indexing Depth and Retrieval Effectiveness' in *Information System Sciences: Proceedings of the Second Congress* (Ed. Spiegel and Walker), Washington D.C., Spartan Books (1965)

SWETS, J. A., 'Effectiveness of Information Retrieval Methods', *Am. Docum.*, **20**, 72 (1969)

SWITZER, P., 'Vector Images in Document Retrieval' in *Statistical Association Methods for Mechanised Documentation* (Ed. Stevens *et al.*), National Bureau of Standards, Washington D.C. (1965)

TAGUE, J., 'An Evaluation of Statistical Association Measures', *Progress in Information Science and Technology, Proc. A.D.I.*, **3**, 391 (1966)

TAGUE, J. M., *Statistical Measures of Term Association in Information Retrieval*, Thesis, Western Reserve University (1967)

TANIMOTO, T. T., 'An Elementary Mathematical Theory of Classification and Prediction', I.B.M. Corporation, New York (1958)

TAULBEE, O. R., 'Content Analysis, Specification and Control' in *Annual Review of Information Science and Technology* (Ed. Cuadra), Vol. 3, Chicago, Encyclopedia Britannica (1968)

TREU, S., 'Testing and Evaluation—Literature Review' in Kent *et al.* (Eds.), *Electronic Handling of Information; Testing and Evaluation*, Washington D.C., Thompson (1967)

VASWANI, P. T. K., 'A Technique for Cluster Emphasis and its Application to Automatic Indexing', *Information Processing 68, Proceedings of IFIP Congress 1968* (Ed. Morrell), Amsterdam, North-Holland (1969)

WALL, E., 'Further Implications of the Distribution of Index Term Usage', *Parameters of Information Science, Proc. A.D.I.*, **1**, 457 (1964)

WARD, J. H., 'Hierarchical Grouping to Optimise an Objective Function', *J. Am. Statist. Ass.*, **58**, 236 (1963)

WESTERN RESERVE UNIVERSITY (Comparative Systems Laboratory), *An Inquiry into Testing of Information Retrieval Systems*, 3 vols, Western Reserve University (1968)

WILLIAMS, J. H., 'A Discriminant Method for Automatically Classifying Documents', *Proceedings of the 1963 Fall Joint Computer Conference; AFIPS Conference Proceedings*, Vol. 24, 161 (1963)

WILLIAMS, J. H., 'Results of Classifying Documents with Multiple Discriminant Functions' in *Statistical Association Methods for Mechanised Documentation* (Ed. Stevens *et al.*), National Bureau of Standards, Washington D.C. (1965)

WILLIAMS, J. H., 'Computer Classification of Documents' in *Mechanised Information Storage, Retrieval and Dissemination* (Ed. Samuelson), Amsterdam, North-Holland (1968)

WYLLYS, T. E., 'Extracting and Abstracting by Computer' in *Automated Language Processing* (Ed. Borko), New York, John Wiley (1967)

248

Index